MENTAL RETARDATION
AND
PHYSICAL DISABILITY

A Book of Readings

Publication Number 901

AMERICAN LECTURE SERIES

A Publication in

The BANNERSTONE DIVISION *of*
AMERICAN LECTURES IN SOCIAL AND REHABILITATION PSYCHOLOGY

The American Lecture Series in Social and Rehabilitation Psychology offers books which are concerned with man's role in his milieu. Emphasis is placed on how this role can be made more effective in a time of social conflict and a deteriorating physical environment. The books are oriented toward descriptions of what future roles should be and are not concerned exclusively with the delineation and definition of contemporary behavior. Contributors are concerned to a considerable extent with prediction through the use of a functional view of man as opposed to a descriptive, anatomical point of view.

Books in this series are written mainly for the professional practitioner, however, academicians will find them of considerable value in both undergraduate and graduate courses in the helping services.

MENTAL RETARDATION

AND

PHYSICAL DISABILITY

EDITED BY

RICHARD E. HARDY

JOHN G. CULL

CHARLES C THOMAS • PUBLISHER
Springfield • Illinois • U.S.A.

Published and Distributed Throughout the World by
CHARLES C THOMAS • PUBLISHER
BANNERSTONE HOUSE
301–327 East Lawrence Avenue, Springfield, Illinois, U.S.A.

© 1974, by CHARLES C THOMAS • PUBLISHER
ISBN 0-398-02879-6
Library of Congress Catalog Card Number: 73-5581

Printed in the United States of America

BB-14

Library of Congress Cataloging in Publication Data

Hardy, Richard E   comp.
   Mental retardation and physical disability.

   (American lecture series in social and rehabilitation psychology. Publication no. 901)
     1. Mental deficiency—Addresses, essays, lectures. 2. Physically handicapped—Addresses, essays, lectures. I. Cull, John G., joint comp. II. Title. [DNLM: 1. Counseling—Collected works. 2. Handicapped—Collected works. 3. Mental retardation—Collected works. WM 300 H371m 1973]
   RC570.H37   616.8'588'008   73-5581
   ISBN 0-398-02879-6

CONTRIBUTORS

Adles, John H., M.D.: Director, Ben R. Meyer Rehabilitation Center, Los Angeles, California

Alexander, Camille D.: Chief, Nursing Service, Community Group Health Foundation, Inc., Washington, D.C.

Berger, Bernard, M.S.W., A.R.W.: Division of the Jewish Vocational Service of Metropolitan Toronto, VRC, Ontario

Bradley, Betty Hunt, M.A.: Columbus State Institute, Columbus, Ohio

Brinkhous, Kenneth M., M.D.: The University of North Carolina, School of Medicine, Chapel Hill, North Carolina

Cleland, Charles C., Ph.D.: Professor of Special Education and Educational Psychology, University of Texas, Austin, Texas

Cull, John G., Ph.D.: Director, Regional Counselor Training Program, and Professor, Department of Rehabilitation Counseling, Virginia Commonwealth University, Fishersville, Virginia

Di Sant'Agnese, Paul A., M.D.: Chief, Pediatric Metabolism Branch, N.I.A.M.D., Bethesda, Maryland

Dunn, John H.: Public Information Officer, Wisconsin Division of Vocational Rehabilitation, Madison, Wisconsin

Dybwad, Gunnar, Ph.D.: Professor of Human Development, Heller School, Brandeis University, Waltham, Massachusetts

Eisendrath, Robert M., M.D.: Harvard Medical School, Boston, Massachusetts

Fendell, Norman: Supervisor of Special Education classes for Manchester Public Schools, Manchester, Connecticut

v

Hardy, Richard E., Ed.D.: Chairman, Department of Rehabilitation Counseling, Virginia Commonwealth University, Richmond, Virginia

Hawkins, David, Ph.D.: University of Colorado, Boulder, Colorado

Menolascino, Frank J., M.D.: University of Nebraska, College of Medicine, Omaha, Nebraska

Moore, Mary V.: PMRS, Tuskegee VA Hospital, Tuskegee, Alabama

Petty, Thomas L., M.D.: Associate Professor of Medicine, Head, Division of Pulmonary Disease, University of Colorado, Denver, Colorado

Rogow, Sally, Ed.D.: Department of Special Education, University of British Columbia, Vancouver, Canada

Steinzor, Luciana, V., Ph.D.: Social Psychologist, New York, New York

Swartz, Jon D., Ph.D.: Associate Professor of Educational Psychology, The Hogg Foundation for Mental Health, University of Texas, Austin, Texas

Vine, William G.: Jewish Family & Child Service of Metropolitan Toronto, Canada

Ward, Rex A., M.D.: O&M Specialist, Blind Rehabilitation Center, VA Hospital, Palo Alto, California

Warnick, Lillian, M.D.: Director, Child Health Service, Georgia Department of Public Health, Atlanta, Georgia

Yannet, Herman, M.D.: Southburry Training School, Southburry, Connecticut

This book is dedicated to significant persons in our lives.

Mrs. Charlie F. Hamilton
Pamplin, Virginia

Mr. & Mrs. Clem Crute Hamilton
Alexandria, Virginia

Mr. & Mrs. Leslie W. Hamilton
Pamplin, Virginia

Mr. & Mrs. Woodfin Hughes
Rice, Virginia

Mrs. Floy F. Tarpley
San Angelo, Texas

The following books have appeared thus far in this Series:

SOCIAL AND REHABILITATION SERVICES FOR THE BLIND—Richard E. Hardy and John G. Cull

UNDERSTANDING DISABILITY FOR SOCIAL AND REHABILITATION SERVICES—John G. Cull and Richard E. Hardy

VOLUNTEERISM: AN EMERGING PROFESSION—John G. Cull and Richard E. Hardy

REHABILITATION OF THE URBAN DISADVANTAGED—John G. Cull and Richard E. Hardy

THE NEGLECTED OLDER AMERICAN—SOCIAL AND REHABILITATION SERVICES—John G. Cull and Richard E. Hardy

FUNDAMENTALS OF CRIMINAL BEHAVIOR AND CORRECTIONAL SYSTEMS—John G. Cull and Richard E. Hardy

THE BIG WELFARE MESS—PUBLIC ASSISTANCE AND REHABILITATION APPROACHES—John G. Cull and Richard E. Hardy

ADJUSTMENT TO WORK—John G. Cull and Richard E. Hardy

VOCATIONAL EVALUATION FOR REHABILITATION SERVICES—Richard E. Hardy and John G. Cull

REHABILITATION OF THE DRUG ABUSER WITH DELINQUENT BEHAVIOR—Richard E. Hardy and John G. Cull

APPLIED PSYCHOLOGY IN LAW ENFORCEMENT AND COR-RECTIONS—Richard E. Hardy and John G. Cull

INTRODUCTION TO CORRECTIONAL REHABILITATION—Richard E. Hardy and John G. Cull

DRUG DEPENDENCE AND REHABILITATION APPROACHES—Richard E. Hardy and John G. Cull

CLIMBING GHETTO WALLS—Richard E. Hardy and John G. Cull

APPLIED VOLUNTEERISM IN COMMUNITY DEVELOPMENT—Richard E. Hardy and John G. Cull

CONTEMPORARY FIELD WORK PRACTICES IN REHABILITATION—John G. Cull and Craig R. Colvin

VOCATIONAL REHABILITATION: PROFESSION AND PROCESS—John G. Cull and Richard E. Hardy

MEDICAL AND PSYCHOLOGICAL ASPECTS OF DISABILITY—A. Beatrix Cobb

SPECIAL PROBLEMS IN REHABILITATION—A. Beatrix Cobb

LAW ENFORCEMENT AND CORRECTIONAL REHABILITATION—John G. Cull and Richard E. Hardy

PREFACE

What constitutes a framework of worthy material for a book which is to be practitioner-oriented and of considerable value to professional social service workers in a time of complex social change? The developers of this book carefully studied the professional literature in order to select writings which could offer a great deal of basic information and useful principles in understanding adjustment problems of both children and adults related to mental retardation and physical disability. The contributors to this book are outstanding persons in their respective fields. Their writings offer more than just directional approaches in specific subject areas. The materials chosen for the book are broad based and while they may deal specifically with blindness, cystic fibrosis, diabetes or mental retardation, there is considerable carry-over in terms of useful information for counseling purposes in the broad range of retardation and disability.

The result of our effort has been the delineation of important pieces of work from the recent literature—works which will be of real value to the practicing social scientist concerned with mental retardation and physical disability. There are many other deserving articles which could have been selected, but we feel that the ones presented here best offer the information intended.

We wish to thank each of the contributors for their cooperation and assistance. We also wish to express special thanks to Miss Susan F. Gilliam for her diligent efforts and skillful assistance.

Richard E. Hardy
John G. Cull

Richmond, Virginia

CONTENTS

PART IV
INFORMATION FOR COUNSELING PURPOSES

MENTAL RETARDATION
AND
PHYSICAL DISABILITY

A Book of Readings

PART I

INTRODUCTION

THE MEANING OF DISABILITY

On Understanding the Understanding of Children

The Effect Upon a Family of a Child With a
Handicap

CHAPTER 1

THE MEANING OF DISABILITY

JOHN G. CULL AND RICHARD E. HARDY

IT IS TRUE that our clients are much more like us than unlike us, but they differ in one major respect. They have suffered the psychological impact of disability and have adjusted or are in the process of adjusting to this impact. In this chapter we shall discuss the factors which affect the psychological adjustment to disability and the mechanism by which an individual adjusts to his disability.

During the First and Second World Wars, behavioral scientists noticed an increased incidence in conversion reactions. Conversion reactions are (American Psychiatric Association) a type of psychoneurotic disorder in which the impulse causing anxiety is "converted" into functional symptoms in parts of the body rather than the anxiety being experienced consciously. Examples of conversion reactions include such functional disabilities as anesthesias (blindness, deafness), paralyses (aphonia, monoplegia, or hemiplegia) and dyskineses (tic, tremor, catalepsy).

The study of these conditions along with other studies led to the development of a discipline known as psychosomatic medicine. Psychosomatic medicine is concerned with the study of the effects of the personality and emotional stresses upon the body and its function. This psychological interaction with physiology can be observed in any of the body systems.

After the establishment of psychosomatic medicine, behavioral scientists (psychiatrists, psychologists, social workers, et cetera) began observing the converse of this new field. Instead of studying the effects of emotional stress on bodily functioning, they studied the effects of physical stress on emotional functioning. Their concern was directed toward answering the question, "What are the emotional and personality changes which result from physical stress or a change in body function or physical configuration?"

ROLE OF BODY IMAGE IN
ADJUSTMENT TO DISABILITY

This new area of study became known as somatopsychology. The basis for this study is the body image concept. The body image is a complex conceptualization which we use to describe ourselves. It is one of the basic parts of the total personality and as such determines our reaction to our environment. According to Horace and English (1966) the body image is the mental representation one has of his own body.

There are two aspects of the body image concept—the individual's ideal (desired) body image and the actual body image. The greater the congruity between these two images, the better the psychological adjustment of the individual; and conversely the greater the discrepancy between these two parts of the self-concept, the poorer an individual's psychological adjustment. This is very understandable. If an individual is quite short and views himself as such but has a strong ideal body image of a tall person, he is less well adjusted than he would be if his desired image were that of a short person. This a simplistic example, but it portrays the crux of psychological adjustment to disability.

In order to adjust to the psychological impact of a disability, the body image has to change from the image of a nondisabled person to the body image of a disabled person. Early in the adjustment process the actual body image will change from that of a nondisabled person to the actual body image of a disabled person; however, for adequate psychological adjustment to the disability the ideal body image must make the corresponding adaptation. Therefore, in essence the psychological adjustment to a disability is the acceptance of an altered body image which is more in harmony with reality.

FACTORS ASSOCIATED WITH ADJUSTMENT

There are three groups of factors which determine the speed or facility with which an individual will adjust to his disability. They help an individual understand the degree of psychological impact a particular disability is having on a client and the significance of the adjustment he must undergo.

The first of these three groups of factors are those factors directly associated with the disability. Psychological effects of disabilities may arise from direct insult or damage to the central nervous system. These psychological effects are called brain syndromes and may be either acute or chronic. In this instance there are a variety of behavioral patterns which may result directly from the disability. In disabilities involving no damage to brain tissue, the physical limitations imposed by the disability may cause excessive frustration and in turn result in behavioral disorders. For example, an active outdoorsman and nature lover may experience a greater psychological impact upon becoming disabled than an individual who leads a more restricted and physically limited life, since the restrictions imposed by the disability demand a greater change in the basic life style of the outdoorsman. Therefore, factors directly associated with the disability have an important bearing upon an individual's reaction to disability.

The second group consists of those factors arising from the individual's attitude toward his disability. An individual's adjustment to his disability is dependent upon the attitudes he had prior to his disability. If his attitudes toward the disabled were quite negative and strong, he will naturally have a greater adjustment problem than an individual with a neutral or positive attitude toward disability and the disabled. A part of this attitude formation prior to the onset of his disability is dependent upon the experiences the client had with other disabled individuals and the stereotypes he developed.

The amount of fear a client experiences or emotion he expends during the onset and duration of the illness or accident leading up to the disability will determine the psychological impact of the disability. Generally, the greater the amount of emotion expended during onset, the better the psychological adjustment to the disability. If an individual goes to sleep a sighted person and awakens a blind person, his psychological reaction to the disability is much greater than if a great deal of emotion is expended during a process of becoming blinded.

The more information an individual has relating to his disability, the less impact the disability will have. If the newly disabled individual is told about his disability in a simple, straightforward, mechanistic manner, it is much easier to accept and adjust to the disability than if it remains shrouded in a cloak of ignorance and mystery. Any strangeness or unpredictable aspect of our body associated with its function immediately creates anxiety and if not clarified rapidly can result in totally debilitating anxiety. Therefore, it is important for psychological adjustment to a disability that the individual have communicated to him, in terms he can understand, the medical aspects of his disability as soon after onset of disability as possible.

When we are in strange or uncomfortable surroundings our social perceptiveness becomes keener. Social cues which are below threshold or not noticed in comfortable surroundings become highly significant to us in new, strange or uncomfortable surroundings. Upon the onset of disability the client will develop a heightened perceptiveness relative to how he is being treated by family, friends and professionals. If others start treating him in a condescending fashion and relegate him to a position of less importance, his reaction to the psychological impact of the blindness will be poor. Professionals can react to the client from an anatomical orientation (what is missing) or a functional orientation (what is left). The anatomical orientation is efficient for classification purposes but is completely dehumanizing. The functional orientation is completely individualistic and as such enhances a client's adjustment to his disability.

Perhaps a key concept in the adjustment process is the evaluation of the future and the individual's role in the future. In many physical medicine rehabilitation centers a rehabilitation counselor is one of the first professionals to see the patient after the medical crisis has passed. The purpose of this approach is to facilitate the patient's psychological adjustment. If he feels there is a potential for his regaining his independence and security, the psychological impact of the blindness will be lessened. While the counselor cannot engage in specific vocational counseling with the client, he can discuss the depth of the vocational rehabilitation program and through these preliminary counseling sessions the counselor can help the newly disabled person evaluate the roles he might play in the future.

The last factor which determines the adjustment process is based upon the individual's view of the purpose of his body and the relationship this view has with the type and extent of disability. The views individuals have of their bodies may be characterized as falling somewhere on a continuum. At one end of the continuum is the view that the body is a tool to accomplish work; it is a productive machine. At the other end is the view that the body is an aesthetic stimulus to be enjoyed and provide pleasure for others. This latter concept is much the same as we have for sculpture and harks back to the philosophy of the ancient Greeks. Everyone falls somewhere on this continuum. To adequately predict the impact of a disability upon an individual, one has to locate the placement of the individual upon this continuum; then evaluate the disability in light of the individual's view of the function of his body.

As an example of the above principle, consider the case in which a day laborer and a film actress sustain the same disabling injury—a deep gash across the face. Obviously, when considering the disability in conjunction with the assumed placements of these two upon the functional continuum, the psychological impact will be greater for the actress; since we have assumed the day laborer views his body almost completely as a tool to accomplish work and the disability has not impaired that function, the psychological impact of the disability upon him will be minimal. However, if the disability were changed (they both sustained severe injury to the abdomen resulting in the destruction of the musculature of the abdominal wall), the psychological impact would be reversed. In this case the actress would view her disability as minimal since it did not interfere with the aesthetic value of her body; while the day laborer's disability would be overpowering since it had substantial effects upon the productive capacity of his body.

The most obvious conclusion to be drawn from the above three factors is that the degree of psychological impact is not highly correlated with the degree of disability. This statement is contrary to popular opinion; however, disability and its psychological impact is a highly personalized event. Many counselors fall into the trap of equating degree of disability with degree of psychological impact. If the psychological impact suffered by a client is much greater than that considered "normal," the counselor will oftentimes become impatient with the client. It should be remembered that relatively superficial disabilities may have devastating psychological effects. The psychological impact of quadraplegia is not necessarily greater than the psychological impact of paraplegia or for that matter, more anatomically supervicial physical disabilities.

ROLE OF DEFENSE MECHANISMS IN ADJUSTMENT

While the three groups of factors discussed above determine the length of time required for adjustment to disability, the path to adjustment is best described by defense mechanisms. Defense mechanisms are psychological devices used by all to distort reality. Often reality is so harsh it is unacceptable to us. Therefore, we distort the situation to make it more acceptable. Defense mechanisms are used to satisfy motives which cannot be met in reality, to reduce tensions in personal interactions and to resolve conflicts. To be effective they must be unconscious. They are not acquired consciously or deliberately. If they become conscious they become ineffective as defenses and other mechanisms must replace them. For the major part of the remainder of this chapter we will look at the defenses most often employed by the disabled in the general order of their use.

Denial

Denial is an unconscious rejection of an obvious fact which is too disruptive of the personality or too emotionally painful to accept. Therefore, in order to soften reality the obvious fact is denied. Immediately upon onset of disability the individual denies it happened. He denies his disability. Then, as the fact of the disability becomes so overwhelming to him that its existence can no longer be denied, there is a denial of the permanency of the disability. The newly disabled individual, while utilizing the defense of denial, will adamantly maintain that he shall be whole again. There will be a miraculous cure or a new surgical technique will be discovered.

While there are few steadfast rules in human behavior, one is that rehabilitation at best can be only marginally successful at this point. Rehabilitation cannot proceed adequately until the client accepts the permanency of the disability and is ready to cope with the condition. This is what is meant by many professionals when they say a client must "accept" his blindness or his deafness. Most clients will never accept their disability, but they should and will accept the permanence of the disability. Denial is the front line of psychological defense, but it may outlast all other defenses. It is most persistently used by persons with deafness, blindness and the plegias.

Withdrawal

Withdrawal is a mechanism which is used to reduce tension by reducing the requirements for interaction with others within the individual's environment. There are two dynamics which result from withdrawal. In order to keep from being forced to face the acceptance of the newly acquired disability, the individual withdraws. As a result of the client's changed physical condition, his social interaction is quite naturally reduced. His circle of interests as determined by friends, business, social responsibilities, church, civic responsibilities and family is drastically reduced. Thus, the client becomes egocentrically oriented until finally his entire world revolves around himself.

Rather than functioning interdependently with his environment to mutually fulfill needs as our culture demands, he is concerned exclusively with his environment's fulfilling his needs. As his world becomes more narrowed, his thoughts and preoccupations become more somatic. Physiological processes heretofore unconscious now become conscious. At this point he begins using another defense mechanism—regression.

Regression

Regression is the defense mechanism which reduces stress by avoiding it. The individual psychologically returns to an earlier chronological age that was more satisfying to him. He adopts the type of behavior that was effective at that age but now has been outgrown and has been substituted for more mature behavior—behavior which is more effective in coping with stressful situations.

As the newly disabled individual withdraws, becomes egocentric and hypochondriacal, he will regress to an earlier age which was more satisfactory. This regression may be manifested in two manners. First he may, in his regression, adopt the dress, mannerisms, speech, et cetera, of contemporaries at the age level to which he is regressing. Secondly, he may adopt the outmoded dress, mannerisms, speech, et cetra, of the earlier time in his life to which he regressed. This second manifestation of regression is considerably more maladaptive since it holds the individual out to more ridicule which, at this point in his adjustment to his disability, quite possibly will result in more emphasis on the defense mechanism of withdrawal. This would be regressive as far as the adjustment process is concerned.

If reality is harshly pushed on him and his defenses are not working, while utilizing the first three defense mechanisms he may as a last resort become highly negative of those around him and negative in general. This negativism is demonstrated as an active refusal, stubbornness, contradictory attitudes and rebellion against external demands. He may become abusive of those around him and may become destructive in an effort to act out the thwarting he is experiencing. This negativistic behavior is an indication the defense mechanisms he is employing are not distorting reality enough to allow him to adjust to his newly acquired disabled status. If, however, he is able to adjust and the defense mechanisms are effective to this point, he will employ the next defense.

Repression

Repression is selective forgetting. It is contrasted with suppression which is a conscious, voluntary forgetting. Repression is unconscious. Events are repressed because they are psychologically traumatic. As mentioned above, the attitudes the client had relative to disability and the disabled has a major bearing upon his adjustment. If these attitudes are highly negative, the client will have to repress them at this point if his adjustment is to progress. Until he represses them he will be unable to accept the required new body image.

Reaction Formation

When an individual has an attitude which creates a great deal of guilt, tension or anxiety and he unconsciously adopts behavior typical of the opposite attitude, he has developed a reaction formation. In order to inhibit a tendency to flee in terror, a boy will express his nonchalance by whistling in the dark. Some timid persons, who feel anxious in relating with others, hide behind a facade of gruffness and assume an attitude of hostility to protect themselves from fear. A third and last example is that of a mother who feels guilty about her rejection of a newborn child and may adopt an attitude of extreme overprotectiveness to reduce the anxiety produced by her feeling of guilt. This example is seen more often in cases of parents with handicapped children.

In this new dependent role the disabled individual will feel a varying degree of hostility and resentment toward those upon whom he is so dependent—wife, children, relatives and so forth. Since these feelings are unacceptable he will develop a reaction formation. The manifest behavior will be marked by concern, love, affection, closeness, et cetera; all to an excessive degree.

Fantasy

Fantasy is daydreaming. It is the imaginary representative of satisfactions that are not attained in real experience. This defense mechanism quite often accompanies withdrawal. As the client starts to adjust to a new body image and a new role in life, he will develop a rich, overactive fantasy life. In this dream world he will place himself into many different situations to see how well he fits.

Rationalization

Rationalization is giving socially acceptable reasons for behavior and decisions. There are four generally accepted types of rationalization. The first is called blaming an incidental cause—the child who stumbles blames the stool by kicking it; the poor or sloppy workman blames his tools. "Sour grapes" rationalization is called into play when an individual is thwarted. A goal to which the individual aspires is blocked to him; therefore, he devalues the goal by saying he did not really want to reach this goal so much anyway. The opposite type of rationalization is called "sweet lemons." When something the individual does not want is forced upon him, he will modify his attitude by saying it was really a very desirable goal and he feels quite positive about the new condition. The fourth and last type of rationalization is called the doctrine of balances. In this type of rationalization we balance positive attributes in others with perceived negative qualities. Conversely, we balance negative attributes with positive qualities. For example, beautiful women are assumed to be dumb; bright young boys are assumed to be weak and asthenic; and the poor are happier than the rich.

The disabled individual will have to rationalize his disability to assist him in accepting the permanence of the disability. One rationalization may be that he had nothing to do with his current condition; something over which he had no control caused the disability. Another dynamic which might be observed is the adherence to the belief on the part of the client that as a result of the disability there will be compensating factors. For example, many newly blinded persons feel they will develop special competencies in other areas such as music, etc.

I once had a paraplegic client whose rationalization for his disability ran something like this: All of the men in his family had been highly active outdoors types. They all had died prematurely with coronaries. The client was a highly active outdoors type; however, now that he was severely disabled he would be considerably restricted in his activities. Therefore, he would not die prematurely. This logic resulted in the conclusion that the disability was positive and he was pleased he had become disabled. Granted, rationalization is seldom carried to this extreme in the adjustment process, but this case is illustrative of a type of thinking which must occur for good adjustment.

Projection

A person who perceives traits or qualities in himself which are unacceptable may deny these traits and project them to others. In doing so he is using the defense mechanism of projection. A person who is quite stingy sees others as being essentially more stingy. A person who is basically dishonest sees others as trying to steal from him. A person who feels inferior rejects this idea and instead projects it to others—that is, he is capable but others will not give him a chance because they doubt his ability. These are examples of projection. With the disabled person many of the feelings he has of himself are unacceptable. Therefore, in order to adjust adequately he projects these feelings to society in general. "They" feel he is inadequate. "They" feel he is not capable. "They" feel he is inferior and is to be devalued. This type of thinking, normally, leads directly into identification and compensation which are in reality the natural exits from this maze in which he has been wandering around.

Identification

The defense mechanism of identification is used to reduce an individual's conflicts through the achievement of another person or group of people. Identification can be with material possessions as well as with people. A person may derive feelings of social and psychological adequacy through his clothes ("The clothes make the man"), his sports car, his hi-fi stereo paraphenalia and so forth. People identify with larger groups in order to take on the power, prestige and respect attributed to that organization ("our team won"). This larger group may be a social club, lodge, garden club, college or professional group.

In adjustment to his disability, the client will identify with a larger group. It may be a group of persons with his particular disability, an occupational group, a men's lodge, a veteran's group, et cetera. But at this point in the adjustment process, he will identify with some group in order to offset some of the feelings he has as a result of the projection in which he is engaging. If successful, the identification obviates the need to employ the mechanisms of denial, withdrawal and regression.

Compensation

If an individual's path to a set of goals is blocked and he finds other routes to achieve that set of goals, he is using the defense mechanism of compensation. A teenager is seeking recognition and acceptance from his peers. He decides to gain this recognition through sports. However, when he fails to make the team he decides to become a scholar. This is an example of compensation. Compensation brings success; therefore, it diverts attention from shortcomings and defects, thereby eliminating expressed or implied criticism. This defense mechanism is most often used to reduce self-criticism rather than external criticism. As the individual experiences successes, he will become less preoccupied with anxieties relating to his disability and his lack of productivity.

Identification and compensation usually go together in the adjustment process. When the client starts using these two defenses, he is at a point at which he may adequately adjust to the new body image and his new role in life.

IMPLICATIONS FOR PROFESSIONALS WORKING WITH THE DISABLED

Almost everyone in our society views handicapping and disabling conditions from an anatomical point of view rather than functional. It is imperative that the counselor help the newly disabled view their disability functionally rather than anatomically. The client should gain an appreciation for the abilities he has left rather than classifying himself with a group based solely upon an anatomical loss.

The rehabilitation counselor should make sure the information which the client has is factual, concise and clear. He should be sure the client's perception of his disability is correct and the cause is completely understood. This understanding greatly enhances the adjustment of the client to his disability.

The client should be helped in exploring his feelings regarding the manner in which he is currently being treated by family and friends. Help him to understand the natural emotional reactions he will have resulting from his newly acquired disability; and help him to understand that the feelings of family and friends are going to be different for a period of time while they themselves adjust to his disability. You should help him to understand that negative feelings which result from his dependent role now that he has become disabled are quite natural. As such he should not repress them but should try to deal with them and look at them very objectively.

Do not fall into the trap of thinking that the degree of disability is correlated with the degree of psychological impact. Realize that each individual's disability is unique unto that individual and his reaction to his disability will be unique.

If you as a counselor are able to observe that the client is employing the defense mechanisms of denial and withdrawal, be sure to make efforts to keep him in complete touch with his environment. Allow his environment to be present for him to call upon as much as he would like without it becoming stifling and demanding in areas in which he can not meet the demands. As he becomes ego-oriented, bring in outside stimulation from news and the world at large, family, comments about family, friends, et cetera, so that he can be reminded that he should function interdependently with his environment rather than independently of his environment.

If aberrant behavior is observed which will hold him up to ridicule as a result of regression, the counselor should point out the manner in which he is regressing. Help him to understand what he is doing; help him to understand some of the mechanics that are going on in his adjustment to disability. However, this counseling should be done in such a manner that will preserve the integrity of the defense mechanism.

Assist him in his fantasy world. If you are fortunate enough to be called in and become part of his fantasy life, be aware of the fact that he is trying on new roles to see how well he fits in these new roles and as such he is asking you to function as a mirror for him to see how he is adjusting to the various new roles in life.

With the defense mechanism of projection, it is very difficult for him to realize that he is projecting even though it may be patently clear and obvious to you or to any other objective person that he is projecting his feelings onto these other people. Perhaps the only real role you can play here is one which is highly supportive of him and his abilities; but at the same time, he should be required to identify the people to whom he is projecting his feelings of inadequacy and inferiority. In other words, encourage the client to identify the "they" to which he refers so negatively so often.

Lastly, in summary, the most important role anyone can play in assisting a client in his adjustment to disability is to be a warm, empathic, accepting individual who is positive in his regard toward the client and one who is pragmatic in counseling and planning efforts with the client.

REFERENCES

American Psychiatric Association: Diagnostic and Statistical Manual of Mental Disorders. Washington, D.C., American Psychiatric Association, 1965.

Horace, H.B., and English, A.C.: *A Comprehensive Dictionary of Psychological and Psychoanalytical Terms.* New York, David McKay Company, Inc., 1966.

CHAPTER 2

ON UNDERSTANDING THE
UNDERSTANDING OF CHILDREN*

DAVID HAWKINS

~~~~~~

IN WHAT I have to say here I shall be both reporting and theorizing; reporting on some recent innovative work in education, and theorizing to explicate the presuppositions of the work and the implications of its findings. The scientific study of childhood intellectual development is, of course, a very complicated and many-sided affair which I cannot even summarize, characterized as it is by many different and even disparate approaches, as well as by large areas where there has been no approach at all.

The study of infancy and childhood belongs, in one very important phase, to that puzzling class of topics for which empirical information is an embarassment rather than an asset. Probably most of the essential behavioral phenomena in this field have long been known to adults, and some of them passed on in disguise without benefit of texts and treatises in the common culture. Mothers often, teachers sometimes, and sometimes perhaps pediatricians, have seen and recorded phenomena that would, if suitably trimmed and ordered, lead far beyond the present state of learned understanding. What matter are the criteria of selection and ordering, and that is why the need for theory is so pressing.

I should like to begin by alluding to the old and sterile

* Used with permission from the *Amer J Dis Child*, Vol 114, Nov 1967.

heredity-environment controversy, which in the present context takes the form of a contrast between the developmental and the experiential. This sterility derives from an assumption shared by straw man developmentalists and straw man environmentalists which is almost certainly false—namely, that the relationship between the two sets of variables is linear. But without this assumption no significance can be attached to the notion that one of these variables is more important than the other except in very extreme or in very carefully limited cases. The true relation between the variables is one of complementarity or covariance, in which a change in one set of variables can be defined in its effects only for specific values of the other variables.

What we should recognize, instead, is that the viewpoints in question are literally just that; they are viewpoints, corresponding to the demands of specific methodologies. The developmentalist has typically been an observer who, with notebook and calipers in hand, has sampled infant and child behavior at periodic intervals and recorded vast amounts of data. The data are then reduced to statistical norms, to ideal types; thus, for example, Gesell or, with quite different intent, Piaget. The environmentalist, on the other hand, has typically been one with the interests and working viewpoint of a teacher, who hopes to record differential changes in development in response to changes in environment. A classic example of this controversy was waged in the thirties, when Stoddard and others at Iowa found themselves in a position to induce radical changes in the environments of young children, and accumulated evidence of large changes in what was then the academically sacred intelligence quotient, the interindividual variance of which had been dogmatically set forth as genetic (Whipple).

The theory of childhood intellectual evolution should not depend, obviously, upon a prior choice of methodology; it ought, as far as possible, to relate usefully to any method of study, even to suggest new ones. But I believe there is one very important feature of the developmentalist view that we ought to take seriously. We know enough about biological development to reject some versions of environmental influence as implausible, except in special cases when substantiated by very powerful evidence. One example of such a claim is the Freudian hypothesis of the unique trauma, as contrasted with those more constant and furrowing environmental influences within which traumata are likely points of consolidation. Another example is the prevalent belief that a thin stream of verbal flow directed at a child, and identified as instruction, will significantly alter his intellectual evolution.

I want to make a careful and plausible argument here, and not overstate it; for even an understatement, I think, will accomplish my purpose. Let me look at the role of experience from two different viewpoints; one is the neurophysiological view, the other the more humane view of a child's characteristic styles of learning. I shall try to show that these two accounts mesh together in certain important respects to give a plausible, coherent picture, a picture which suggests the gross inadequacy of certain highly simplified representations of the learning process, for example, those of classical or operant conditioning. I do not want to say that these are incorrect as representations of the particular phenomena studied, but that their use as representations of the major phenomena of human intellectual development touches only one generic aspect of the process which, although essential, gives us no key to understanding the rest. No theory of brain function in learning can escape critical scrutiny without *some* hypothesis of reinforcement: pathways, or sets of pathways, are affected by use in such a way as to be more available for future use. The nervous system is inherently and essentially "memorious." As far as one can see there is no reason to believe in any one unique mechanism of reinforcement, applicable to all parts of the system, or to the same parts at different times.

There is one general characteristic of brain function, summarized by Lashley in his so-called laws of equipotentiality and mass action, which implies that any function of the brain is widely distributed among its structures (Spencer). Another way of stating this implication, supported by familiar facts of anatomy, is that the brain organization has the style of an elaborate network of essentially complex neuron modules, with hundreds of end-feet of other neurons impinging on a given neuron. I mention this because it fits in a very interesting way with certain theorems in the mathematical theory of computation, namely, that any very big network capable of functioning reliably as a computer must *of necessity* distribute each functional unit of computation among many physical modules of the network. Such theorems assume that in a very large computing network the probability of failure of components, even though small per component, is nevertheless large for the system as a whole. Thus the system will fail if its successful operation depends on error-free functioning of all components. Moreover, there are almost certainly random effects in the organization of the network. A "wiring diagram" of the human brain must specify some 10^{13} connections, and any but a statistical specification of these in genetic terms seems impossible. The theorems in question state that efficient computation in such a system is possible *only* for networks which provide complexity interconnected modules functioning collectively in such a way that each computation is spread among many modules, and each module is doing parts of many computations at the same time (Winograd). Such mathematical models give, in fact, a very clear meaning to the old idea of organic wholeness. Nets of this wholistic type have been called "anastomotic," a word first used to describe the interconnectedness of veins in a leaf, and later the pattern of neuron organization itself.

In this report I want to avoid the technical language of neural nets, physiological or mathematical, partly because a simpler language is possible, and partly because of the application I want to make. For a first move in this direction, let me equate the verb "compute" with the verb "classify." When we compute a function Y of some variable X, we are in general dealing with a situation in which several sets of values of the variable X correspond to a single value of Y. Thus, if we compute a sum of two variables and find it is 12, there are several pairs of natural numbers which could give us that sum. The output of a computation characteristi-′ cally gives us only incomplete information about the input, or again, the computation maps input into output in a many-to-one mapping. Still another way of talking, and this is the one I prefer, is that we may group together all those inputs, which have the same output, as belonging to the same class; they are indistinguishable or equivalent with respect to the computed output. In this sense six and six are indistinguishable, with respect to addition, from five and seven or three and nine. Now just as any computation may be regarded as a classification, so any classification may be regarded as a computation (Hawkins, D.: Taxonomy and Information, to be published in the Boston studies in the Philosophy of Science).

This equivalence of computation and classification is illustrated in matters of organization, as well as in the end-result. In a formal computing network the modules are organized by *ranks*, that is, there are modules of the first rank which compute certain intermediate functions of the input variables. The output of these modules then go as input to modules of the second rank, the output of which is input to those of the third rank, and so on. Nets may, of course, be cyclic, so that output is fed back from later ranks to earlier ones. A characteristic feature is that the number of computing modules tends to decrease in later ranks, since each computational step tends to simplify, to have less variety in its output than its input.

If you think now of any familiar classification system, it operates in the same manner. To begin, we have something given for classification with many properties, i.e., many input variables. These are divided into two or more genera, each with a smaller internal variance than the universe from which the sample was taken. In the next step we find directions for subdivision appropriate to each genus, and thus arrive at lower genera, and this process continues until some stop-rule or decision terminates it. The terminal species thus defined carves up the original universe in the same way that the set of possible outputs of a computation carves up, into equivalent subsets, the set of possible inputs.

There is an interesting point of apparent dissimilarity between these two ways of talking. I have said that in general there will be many computational modules in the first rank of a computing network, the number progressively decreasing in later ranks. Thus a diagram with input at the top and output at the bottom will look like an inverted pyramid. A classification system, on the other hand, looks like a normal pyramid, with undifferentiated input at the top, a few genera in the next rank, more in the next, etc. But notice that the *variety* within the successive categories is greatest at the top and decreases steadily along any pathway of classification. This means that the *first* division of the universe into genera must find the differentiating characteristic of a sample against a very wide background variety. If we think of classification in terms of the *extension* of classes rather then *intension*, its representation is the same as for computation. The most fundamental differentiations we make are often the most complexly mediated, even though we may think of them subjectively as the easiest. A child working with a compound pendulum, apparently finding that it was not working the way he wanted it to, was observed holding the bob in his hand and moving it repeatedly in a desired path. When the teacher made some polite inquiry, he said, "I'm trying to train it." Now a pendulum is at the very opposite pole from an animal, it is totally *un*memorous. But this was a new situation, and the child was very clearly *not* making this "obvious" computation or discrimination. Why not?

A good theory points, sometimes, toward the nonobvious. The theory of computation requires that the distinction between the two wide genera of mechanical vs vital phenomena be computationally a very complex one, even though it may be partially and incompletely acquired at a relatively early age. If you try to design an automation that will discriminate such categories across the wide range of individual instances, you will find that you are, in fact, committed to a very complex computational design; so complex that the meaning of the distinction is still being argued, after 2,000 years! Yet very much of our educational system is based on the assumption that broad divisions of this kind are obvious and need only be properly verbalized. Aristotle said that what comes first in the order of understanding often comes last in the order of experience, and in this he is at one with present-day analysis.

The example of training the pendulum, which can be multiplied many times over, brings up another point. The ways of classifying things and situations, so indispensable to any intellectual grasp, are products of experiential evolution, interacting no doubt with postnatal embryological development; this means that our patterns of discrimination and classifications are inherently adaptive. If we now go back to the language of computation and computational networks, this means that we have a new criterion to impose.

This mathematical model of the anastomotic net has been elaborated in relation to the postulate that any module, any computing element, is inherently unreliable, inherently subject to failure with some small but not negligible probability. In engineering language, its signals must be processed in the presence of noise which may corrupt those signals. But this is an unstable distinction between signal and noise, because we can give it a *sharp* meaning only with reference to a functional definition of the module, to an implied knowledge of a fixed and reproducible operation. If, on the contrary, we demand that such modules and the system composed of them be inherently *adaptive,* then their description as nonconstant and spontaneously variable in operation is as essential to their nature as spontaneous variation, or mutation, to the efficacy of Darwinian evolution. The concept of reinforcement essential to any theory of learning *requires* noise and spontaneous variation just as surely as natural selection does. If there were no noise in such a system and no cushion of redundancy, or anastomosis, in its design, then we would be dealing, I claim, with a nonadaptive system. I cannot prove this statement, but I think I can make it plausible (Block).

In the first place, let us examine the inductive behavior of young children. The other day we had a visit in our laboratory from a group of 3- and 4-year-old children, who immediately spread out among the variety of manipulatable goodies which it provides. One child found a scoop, a large tray of peas and beans, and a sizable equal-arm balance composed of two paper pie plates hung from a cross-arm. She put a scoopful in one pan, and it went down. She put a scoopful in the other pan, which slightly overbalanced it the other way. This process was then repeated some 18 times, with the child being completely engrossed. Of course the amounts were never quite equal, but the balance was insensitive enough to give a sort of tippy equilibrium two or three times. It was interesting that she obviously seemed to adopt a rule early in the game, ie, to put the next scoopful in the upper pan; but what was more interesting was that she *later* mixed her strategy and put the next scoopful in the *lower* pan, whether it had gone down the time before or failed to rise. Each time she watched to see the result of her manipulation. Now anyone familiar with modern psychology would be likely to look at such a phenomenon in terms of operant conditioning, and think of producing a learning curve. But this is entirely inappropriate, for the following reasons. First, the circumstances are such that no well-defined task is involved; from the adults there were no "kindly, but firm" instructions, and the child adopted this collection of equipment on her own. Second, the circumstances were such that the phenomena were essentially multivariate and nonreproducible. The standard learning curve, if you were misdirected enough to draw one, would be rather flat, negative-sloping, or erratic, and would represent the gap between a research stereotype guaranteed to teach nothing, and a more interesting analysis. Substitute a set of carefully defined weights, a clinical ambient in which the child has no significant choices, and an adult who instructs the child to add weights to change the balance. Then, if the child adopted, or was pushed into, an obedient attitude, the standard curve would certainly eventuate. Of course, with a sturdier ego the child might still think of several other things to do, and thus frustrate the curve-fitting.

For my first example I have deliberately chosen a rather highly constrained situation, that of the equal-arm balance. If you substitute for this an unequal-arm balance, with a variety of sizes and densities of things to place or hang on it, the above result is guaranteed: you will not be likely soon to see a child discovering the textbook properies summarized in the law of moments. But what you *can* see is even greater absorption, an attention-span many times longer than what some psychometricians have said is characteristic of children of that age, and much more invention, evidently connected with other sorts of experience already laid down or mapped: of levers, for example, or catapults, or the school-yard seesaw; of weights and densities and volumes. One is tempted to say that any one conceptual topic is touched on in many episodes, and that each episode involves many conceptual topics; and that, in its own way, it is a kind of anastomosis characteristics of the child's native style of learning. The child in my example was not studying the equal-arm balance, or the principle of symmetry, or the additivity of mass, or the uniformity of the gravitational field, or any one of a dozen other conditions which are, in fact, relevant to the operation of the equal-arm balance. A learning curve which assumed that any *one* of these was her goal would be flat or fluctuating, except accidentally. If we can impute any purpose to her, it is one which she would or could not synthesize or verbalize; it is that of exploring connections between a newly-encountered situation and her own partially organized schemes for classifying and sorting experience, in this case inanimate environment. If we had the wit to define this goal in terms specific enough to match the particularities of her preoccupation, we could, I am sure, emerge with a standard learning curve, and be none the wiser for it. Lacking that definition, which even a skillful and watchful teacher keeping track of her development over months might only crudely approximate, we note instead the intensity of her involvement and the watchful style of her operations, and conclude that she has found what is, for the moment, a satisfying match for her insight and capacity.

Let me generalize the description, asking you to imagine a hundred mornings, densely marked with attentive encounters over significant areas of experience as they might be made accessible to this child in a good school. Include in your account, as you well might, the return engagements with any one aspect, for example, the one of balance I have singled out for the sake of vividness. Notice the change in her style of work amid the shifts and recurrences of interest; notice the way in which this pattern of work is coupled to an evolving pattern of peer- and teacher-association both stabilized and enriched by the common bonds that develop among fellow-enquirers. But especially, notice two pervasive characteristics of the entire environment which the particular child has contributed to only slightly and indirectly. One is the physical organization of space and materials which permits this pattern of work to develop quickly within a new group, to proceed harmoniously over time, and to provide attentive encounters between children and things—samples of the wild environment or man-made artifacts—which embody what we know to be potent ideas in such a way as to be useful in many situations and for many purposes. The other thing to notice is the style of organization in the hands of a skillful teacher after a day, a month, and a year of school. What you see here is an evolution from early and excited sampling—what Frances Hawkins calls the Christmas Morning Syndrome—to more quite and steady work. On the average, the variance among activities will remain high and stability will remain relative. A power shovel across the street, a spider found in the corner, a collection of rocks and seed pods, and a rusted horseshoe brought back from a field trip— all these will generate new involvements, new investigations, and create new opportunities for teachers' diagnoses and interventions. Watch for the unusual associations that develop, the cross-category analogies and associations that lead from the study of the pine tree to the geometry of tessellations, from the pendulum to the planets, from a study of seeds and cuttings to new experiments with color in optics and painting.

I give these examples rather breathlessly, but it is no longer Christmas morning; each transition is the cumulative expression of much work by one or a few children. Watch also for the more reflective and synoptic phases: a class-wide discussion, a short lecture by the teacher, a growing commitment to communication in all its forms, including writing and reading, but also talk—endless talk—painting, and clay. Notice how the three R's are woven into all the work, with occasional but not obtrusive formality. The study of figurate numbers leads back to the geometry of tessellations, and on to the construction of a pegboard graph which embodies the algorithms of computational arithmetic.

I will not try to carry the description further in depth, nor beyond the first years of preschool and school, from 4 to 12 in terms of age. I have not often seen such practice in secondary school or college, though I have seen it occasionally in graduate school, and more often in the secret lives of some college students who have learned how to get by the formalities with minimum effort. I see no block to an interpolation across the whole range. And, of course, nothing in my description cuts out the formalities, the tight, nonredundant organization of the physics text, the term-long concentration on the Iliad, or the structure of "p-adic" fields. It demotes them, though, because usually they are seen, somehow, as the whole end and aim of education.

I have said that the pattern of the anastomotic net, anatomically present in the brain, is required by the theory of efficient computation or classification in the presence of noise. I have suggested that an adaptive net must eo ipso function in the presence of noise, as a condition of its adaptability. I have tried to illustrate the native style of such a process by examples from the work of children coping in essentially multivariate situations, where each episode implicitly involves many conceptual topics and each such topic is returned to many times. I have then tried to suggest the evolution, usually gradual, by which children can begin to sort out the multiplicities of variables, begin to develop the abstractions, and later accept the formalities, the tightly constrained, nonredundant organization which is essential to adult understanding, visible above the surface of public discourse as codified knowledge, and often mistaken for understanding. What is under the surface is the far richer preanalytic network of associative connections, for which the human brain is especially apt, established through the adaptive filtering of many megabits of motor-sensory information.

I have also, I hope, made some hints of propaganda against the overwhelmingly dominant style of our schools, which mimics the child who tried to train the pendulum, but with the opposite error; I have suggested, at least, one way of understanding the fact that the schools are filled with bored and disoriented children.

But my main intent is really to suggest a theoretical framework for the comprehension of human learning, to coax psychology into a frame of thought consonant with what skillful teachers, in their often more "anastomotic" intuitive fashion, already know.

I fear, of course, that I have in the process offended all the puritans among you, who I trust are an empty subclass of this audience: both the moral puritans, who want to prepare children for a hard life by making it hard for them to learn, and the scientific puritans, who cannot imagine that a do-it-yourself curriculum, woven together by the art of advisers and teachers and children, can possibly be efficient in comparison with the handy-package approach that has been the principal product of our recent efforts at curriculum reform. The handy packages we need, of course, those that can be used for many purposes, include many not intended by the designers. (In fact, it would be a nice figure of merit to use the ratio of unintended to intended uses, not those that follow the neat postanalytic structures which minimize the large redundancy unnecessary in the formal product, but essential to its evolution; which is mostly absent in the textbook, but present in every educated mind.) From this point of view, indeed, an educated mind could be defined as one that can make its way around in the network of its own resources. It no longer needs to be in school, it has become its own teacher.

If we defined the term "dropout" as the negative of this, what then would the statistics be?

REFERENCES

Block, H.D.: *Adaptive Neural Networks as Brain Models: Proceedings of Symposia in Applied Mathematics.* New York, American Mathematics Society, 1963.

Spencer, K.L.: *Brain Mechanisms and Intelligence: A Quantitative Study of Injuries to the Brain.* Chicago, University of Chicago Press, 1929.

Whipple, G.M. (ed.): *Intelligence–Its Nature and Nurture: Part I: Comparative and Critical Exposition, 39th Yearbook of the National Society for the Study of Education.* Bloomington, Ill, Public School Publishing Company, 1940.

Winograd, S., and Cown, J.D.: *Reliable Computation in the Presence of Noise.* Cambridge, Mass, Massachusetts Institute of Technology Press, 1963.

CHAPTER 3

THE EFFECT UPON A FAMILY OF A CHILD WITH A HANDICAP*

LILLIAN WARNICK

~~~~~~

Family Reaction to Early Identification
Periods of Stress for the Family
Parental Counseling

~~~~~~

ALMOST EVERYONE agrees that the family with a handicapped child is a family with special problems. Most of the available studies about the psycho-social dynamics of families with handicapped children have been the result of the great emphasis placed on mental retardation, beginning in the early 1950's and continuing to the present. One issue occasionally encountered is whether the dynamics of parents of handicapped children are very similar or alike, or whether there are dynamics specific to a particular handicap. Coughlin implies that parental attitudes toward handicapped children are basically the same as those toward all children, except that the disability elicits feelings that otherwise would be less prominent or suppressed. Cohen also sees little differentiation between handicaps. It is also significant that the Wishik study reveals that on an average, a child, if handicapped, will have 2.2 handicaps. Two-thirds of the children in this

*Used with permission from *The New Outlook*.

33

study were multi-handicapped. We must recognize that there are a large number of these children.

The areas studied by various professionals have included: effect on siblings, parental reaction, acceptance, education for family and community, effect of placement, role of counseling and various types of counseling, severity of handicaps, physical versus mental handicaps, and others. As I review some of the studies, it seems to me the *one* significant lesson we learn is that *families,* like individuals, differ greatly. What destroys one home may well serve to strengthen, in some measure, another. Terms such as chronic sorrow, living in a shadow, enduring day by day with anxiety, etc. are terms perhaps true but over-used. During this decade, I believe we have begun to have a more healthy, outgoing approach, that is, one in which professionals and others are discussing freely the *positive aspects* of the child's potential, emphasizing the need for handicapped children to *learn independence* to whatever measure they can, and encouraging the development of *action programs* to provide more services in home communities. Levy, taking a more environmental view, thinks that many of the emotional problems encountered within families may be caused by a lack of services with subsequent feelings of hopelessness. For the family, the expansion of services has brought some degree of hope and assurance that realistic planning for the future is possible. This feeling of hope may even replace the chronic sorrow mentioned in the literature.

Three aspects of family involvement are of special interest to me, mainly because of my experience and closeness to them.

1. Family interaction and reaction when the handicapped child is identified early and some service is made available as compared to reaction when no service is available.

2. Periods of stress for the family.

3. Role of parental counseling.

FAMILY REACTION TO EARLY IDENTIFICATION

For well over a decade, professionals have stressed diagnosis and treatment for the child who had a physical handicap, i.e., vision or hearing loss. The cardinal rule that the earlier such handicaps are identified and treatment started, the *better* the prognosis is accepted. In recent years another facet has been added to this rule; early identification is needed because of the benefit to the family. Fear of the unknown is almost always worse than knowing the facts. Parents who realize that the child has difficulty but are unable to obtain a diagnosis for several years, have many confused, hostile feelings. Often these feelings are much more difficult to *work through* once the facts are made known. Recently, a nine-year-old girl in a center for the mentally retarded was discovered to be deaf. This is a real tragedy. Precious years had been lost which could have been used for appropriate treatment and management. Feelings of hostility, grief (regret), frustration, uncertainty of future, remorse, cannot help but make for difficult family adjustment.

Only rarely can delayed diagnosis of handicap be of any benefit to the family. Olshansky 1962 and Hastings suggest that in some rare instances the retarded child's welfare may be better served if the parents do not know early about the retardation. Thus, the child may be able to create a place for himself in the family which otherwise would have been impossible.

It is important to mention here the thinking of many educators in the area of early childhood education. Today efforts are made to get handicapped children, even those with multiple handicaps, into nursery schools at an early age, often by three years of age. Repeated reports show that the handicapped child in such a facility often will become more independent and learn to adjust and to socialize better. Thus, parents often get a better impression of the child and his ability.

When few services are available to the parents, the family reaction and interaction to an early diagnosis can be very different. Such parents tend to remain in a state of hopelessness, despair, and confusion. Not infrequently, these are the families that isolate themselves from the community and withdraw from social contact. This, then, can become a vicious cycle which increases the anxiety and despair of the family and accentuates the child's difference from other children. It is impossible to measure in any accurate way just *how* valuable service for the child and family are in the early years of the child's life.

The following example will make clear the feelings of two mothers in similar situations: Soon after birth, a mother of a mongoloid baby was told, "This is the worse I have seen—the baby cannot live." The child is now two years old. Family adjustment has been very difficult. In contrast, another mother of a mongoloid child was told, "You take the baby and love her. We will help you along." Imagine the difference in family acceptance and adjustment! This mother did not feel so alone and helpless. It cannot be over-emphasized that if a family can be offered help, in the form of service, there will be less feeling of rejection and despair.

PERIODS OF STRESS FOR THE FAMILY

In any family, even those considered well-adjusted and healthy, stress periods occur. In the family with a handicapped child, certain stress periods have been identified and discussed in the literature. Murray was among the first to indicate the need for lifelong counseling, recognizing that crises will continue to occur. Several good lists of crisis periods have been documented. Hastings' list of seven is important and is frequently cited: 1) birth; 2) developmental delay; 3) school entrance; 4) adolescence; 5) vocational planning; 6) death of a parent; and 7) institutional placement.

Many of us can recall specific examples of families going through these crises. Indeed, some may have personal experience of such times of stress. Regardless of what episodes come to mind and how the particular experience was handled, it is agreed that the supporting role of an understanding professional, with related training and experience, did or could have helped greatly. The American Medical Association has a similar list. I mention it mainly because so much adverse feeling has been directed to the physician and his poor handling of such problems with families. I am convinced that the medical world will be better prepared in the future and hopefully will also understand and appreciate the role of other professional people in dealing with such families. Here are the 12 stress periods listed by the AMA: 1) the family's first suspicion that the child is handicapped; 2) final diagnosis; 3) school entrance; 4) rejection by peers; 5) sibling relationships; 6) acute illness; 7) general family crises, including moving, succeeding pregnancies, etc.; 8) sexual problems at puberty; 9) vocational adjustment; 10) marriage; 11) decision on placement; and 12) separation following placement.

It is important to note that the definition of a crisis depends on its being so defined by the affected family regardless of whether the events meet social and clinical criteria. What may be a marked crisis for one family may be only a minor incident for another family.

In the course of normal development, certain stress periods occur. For years, people involved with human growth and development have struggled to help parents understand and prepare for these periods, e.g., the "terrible" two year-old. Handicapped or not, the basic needs of all children are the same. They are, first and foremost, children.

Wolfensberger makes an interesting classification of three types of crises: 1) the novelty shock, when unsuspecting parents are first told; 2) the value crisis, when parents become aware of child limitation and have emotional rejection because the child cannot live up to expectations; and 3) the reality crisis, when external forces only partially controlled by parents result in an almost impossible situation, e.g., death of a spouse or physical demand made by the child which cannot be met by the family.

Parents in *novelty shock* need information and support. It must be understood that in such a state of shock, only a limited amount of information will be grasped by parents; therefore several meetings will be necessary for the parents to understand. Those in *value crisis* need prolonged counseling or personal therapy. Parents almost always plan for and expect their children to be healthy, normal, and capable. Again, time is required to adjust to any limitation which the child may have. Those in *reality crisis* require practical, down-to-earth help, such as home management, special schooling in community or institution, workshops, etc. And, of

course, a wido range of services to meet the needs of handicapped children at all age levels is needed.

PARENTAL COUNSELING

Much has been written regarding the role of counseling.
Only during the past two decades have professionals really
given much thought to this service as a necessity for parents.
A trickle of reports relating to parent counseling came in
the mid-1940's. These were, for the most part, biased by
including mainly mothers (little to do with fathers) and then
primarily the middle-upper, white class who were main con-
sumers of available clinic services. Often these were also
mothers of the more severely handicapped; therefore, most
of the results report concerning parent-counseling are more
specifically relevant to this group of parents.

An extensive survey conducted in 1961 (Olshansky, 1964,
1963, 1962) indicated that physicians viewed the counseling
of parents as their main role. However, when compared with
answers to a questionnaire to parents, results showed that
perhaps the physician would do well to leave this aspect
of management to other professionals! An interesting survey
by McIntire and Kickhaeker, of parents who received services
in clinics for the handicappped, revealed that parental satisfaction was much higher when a clinic *team* gave service.
Parents also expressed greater satisfaction with diagnostic
evaluation than with guidance and counseling help. Perhaps
the clinic with a team, or the multi-discipline approach, is
more satisfying to parents than the private practitioner.

The good counselor listens; shares information; is well-
informed about available services and referral procedure;
does not make decisions for the family but lets the family
work through their own feelings to possible solution. He sees
the parent as a parent and not primarily as a patient. Furthermore, he has worked through his deep-seated attitudes toward
various handicaps. He, of course, has had training and
experience.

The one-session, one-shot approach which was once widely
used is now being replaced by many sessions. Some parents

who have seen many specialists may still be ill-informed because of inadequate interpretation and counseling.

Murray defines the following six areas listed by parents as important in counseling: 1) acceptance of the fact; 2) financial burden and reality implications; 3) emotional tension in parents; 4) theological conflict; 5) need to distinguish between long-term versus short-term decision-making; and 6) inept, inaccurate, and ill-timed professional advice. Added to this should also be the importance for *both* parents to be seen and informed as well as *good* communication between the involved parties—honest, down-to-earth language with sincerity and empathy, but not pity and sympathy. Repeated adequate counseling is not, however, the whole answer.

Kelman, in 1957, was among the first to emphasize that repeated interpretation and supportive and reassuring counseling are insufficient if practical help in *home management* and daily care of the child is not also available. Counseling must also include more information on *prognosis* and *planning*. In the past, etiology, diagnosis, and parental feelings have been foremost in parental counseling. Counseling should not be based just on today's services but also services likely to be developed in the future. This is especially true with parents of a very young handicapped child. Perhaps nothing changes parental attitudes more than to see the child progress in some of the basic home skills as, for example, toilet training and feeding. Genetic counseling will also be more important in the future and professionals will need to be well informed about it.

Few studies of the group counseling process are controlled and statistically adequate. Harris and Schechtman[4] assigned parents of children in a day-care center randomly to three different types of groups: 1) lecture; 2) group discussion with group leader; 3) informal interaction with day-care director for a total of 10 sessions over a 20-week period. All expressed satisfaction. Those in lecture groups, however, were very satisfied, those in informal contact groups slightly less satisfied, and those in discussion groups least satisfied.

Parents' groups such as the associations for retarded children have served several purposes. When first organized, they were accused of passing on misinformation, becoming preoccupied with pathology, creating disturbances in other parents, etc. Now, however, there is good agreement that such parent groups meet needs no professional or clinic group can or is meeting.

It cannot be denied that the handicapped child does have a profound effect on the family. It is my belief, however, that our society will continue to increase its *understanding* and *concern* for the handicapped to the extent that we will learn to overcome many of the difficulties we have today. The future must provide more *services* and more adequate *acceptance* of the handicapped as worth-while members of our society. As this becomes increasingly real, we shall see families become stronger and have more healthy reactions to each other as well as to the community.

REFERENCES

American Medical Association:Mental Retardation: A Handbook for the Primary Physician. *Journal of the American Medical Association, 191:*183–232, 1965.

Cohen, Pauline C.: The Impact of the Handicapped Child on the Family. *Social Casework, 43:*137–42, 1962.

Coughlin, Ellen W.: Parental Attitudes Toward Handicapped Children. *Children, 6:*41–45, 1941.

Harris, D.B. and Schechtman, Audrey: *A Study of the Modification of Parental Attitudes Toward an Understanding of Mentally Retarded Children.* Duluth: Institution of Child Development and Welfare, University of Minnesota, 1959.

Hastings, Marguerite: The Social Worker's Role in Helping Families of Mentally Retarded Children Meet Crisis Points. In a Multidisciplinary Approach to the Diagnosis and Treatment of Mental Retardation. *Johnstone Bulletin, 2:*58–63, 1960.

Kelman, H.R.: Parent Guidance in a Clinic for Mentally Retarded Children. *Journal of Social Work, 34:*441–47, 1953.

Levy, J.H.: A Study of Parent Groups for Handicapped Children. *Exceptional Children, 19:*19–26, 1952.

McIntire, Matilda S. and Kiekhaeker, T.C.: Parental Reaction to a Clinic for the Evaluation of the Mentally Retarded. *Nebraska Medical Journal, 48:*69–73, 1963.

Murray, M.A.: Needs of Parents of Mentally Retarded Children. *American Journal of Mental Deficiency, 63:*1078–88, 1959.

Olshansky, S.: Chronic Sorrow: A Response to Having a Mentally Defective Child. *Social Casework, 43:*191–94, 1962.

Olshansky, S., Johnson, Gertrude C., and Sternfeld, L.: Attitudes of Some GP's Toward Institutionalizing Mentally Retarded Children. In *Institutionalizing Mentally Retarded Children: Attitudes of Some Physicians.* Washington, D.C.: U.S. Government Printing Office, 1964.

Olshansky, S. and Kettell, Marjorie: Attitudes of Some Interns and First-Year Residents Toward the Institutionalization of Mentally Retarded Children. *Training School Bulletin, 59:*116–20, 1963.

Olshansky, S., Schonfield, E., and Sternfeld, L.: Attitudes of Some Obstetricians Toward Mental Retardation. *Obstetrics & Gynecology, 19:*133–36, 1962.

Olshansky, S. and Sternfeld, L.: Attitudes of Some Pediatricians Toward the Institutionalization of Mentally Retarded Children. *Training School Bulletin, 59:*67–73, 1962.

Patterson, Letha L.: Some Pointers for Professionals. *Children, 3:*13–17, 1956.

Wishik, Samuel M.: *Georgia Study of Handicapped Children.* Atlanta: Georgia Department of Public Health, 1964.

Wolfensberger, Wolf: Counseling Parents of the Retarded. In *Mental Retardation,* ed. Alfred A. Baumeister. Chicago, Aldine Publishing Co., 1967, pp. 329–86.

PART II

┌──────MENTAL RETARDATION──────┐

CHAPTER 4

WHO ARE THE
MENTALLY RETARDED?*

Gunnar Dybwad

~~~~~~

Prevalence and Degrees
Areas of Confusion
Confusions about Prognosis
An Illustration
An Eye to the Individual
References

~~~~~~

NOT ONLY IN THE United States but in many countries around the world, there is today an unprecedented interest in the welfare of mentally retarded children and adults. Whole new systems of services to aid them and their families are being developed, supported by extensive governmental and private efforts. A vast literature has appeared during the past 10 years. Millions are being spent on research and demonstration projects.

Yet, one encounters with increasing frequency the questions: Who exactly are the mentally retarded? Where are they? How many are there? The suggestion has even been seriously made that there is no such thing as mental retardation. Those who make it point out that as the term *mental retardation*

* Used with permission from *Children*, Vol. 15, No. 2, March-April, p. 43-48, 1968.

covers a multitude of widely divergent conditions, resulting from separate biological or cultural origins and manifesting themselves in different, unrelated forms, there is no logical basis for a collective designation.

For a good many years, similar arguments have been raised against the term *mental illness,* which also covers a large conglomeration of conditions of diverse origin.

I cannot subscribe to such a view. It seems to me that for the daily practice of persons engaged in rehabilitation, health, and welfare services both these terms are useful. I am willing to concede that there may be some validity for speaking of mental illnesses rather than mental illness and also for using some plural forms for the collective terms *epilepsy, cerebral palsy,* and *mental retardation.* Yet we have traditionally used the singular in a plural sense without any real problems in communication.

A different position would have to be taken by physicians, biochemists, and other biological scientists concerned with specific diagnostic and therapeutic considerations. But when a discussion is focused on the social manifestations of retardation and the social measures needing consideration. I think we can find a sufficiently firm point of departure in the concept of mental retardation defined as *significantly subaverage intellectual functioning, manifested during the development period, and associated with distinct impairment in adaptive behaviors.*

This is the definition of the American Association on Mental Deficiency with the addition of two qualifying adjectives. I have modified "subaverage" with the word *significantly,* as suggested by John Kidd (1964) and "impairment in adaptive behaviors" with the word *distinct.* This modification conveys disagreement with the view of those who are inclined to extend the concept of mental retardation to cover relatively minor deviation from the norm. Both from the point of view of the persons so characterized and from the point of view of effective administration and practice, a more circumscribed concept is preferable, one that would exclude the broad and confusing area termed "borderline."

In 1953, an expert committee of the World Health Organization suggested for international usage the term *mental subnormality*, subdivided into two categories: *mental deficiency* for cases of biological origin, and *mental retardation* for cases of sociocultural origin. Even though this proposal was a focal point of a widely distributed pamphlet published in 1954 and entitled "The Mentally Subnormal Child" (World Health Organization), this terminology has not been accepted, and the World Health Organization today is using the general term *mental retardation* in its official documents.

Where does this leave us as far as the boundaries of mental retardation is concerned? In the past, the likely answer to this question would have been that an IQ rating of 70 or 75 on a standard intelligence test would constitute the upper boundary. But today one would have to answer the question differently, saying that in general the term *mentally retarded* does not usually apply to anyone with an intelligence score above 70 or 75 but by no means includes all with lower scores, and in exceptional cases may apply to persons who score higher. Whether or not a person should be designated as mentally retarded depends not just on measured intelligence but also on the second criterion in our definition of mental retardation: *a distinct impairment of adaptive behavior of the social performance in day-to-day living normally expected from a person of a particular age by the community (or culture) of which he is a part.*

Thus a man who scores 65 on an intelligence test and who at the same time shows himself well able to adapt to the social demands of his particular environment at home, at work, and in the community should not be considered retarded. Indeed, we now know that he is not generally so considered. This is why large-scale attempts to identify the mentally retarded in a given community always end up with a far smaller number of persons than had been predicted from the expected distribution of intelligence.

However, in spite of growing acceptance of this second criterion, "social adaptation," attempts at quantifying it through measures similar to the various intelligence tests have thus far failed. This is why at this time it is impossible to give a clear answer to the question, "Who are the mentally retarded and how many are there?" It seems clear, nevertheless, that the still widely made statement that 3 percent of the population are mentally retarded is no longer tenable.

PREVALENCE AND DEGREES

But what *do* we know about the prevalence of mental retardation? We know that in the so-called developed countries between .1 and .2 percent of the population—in other words one to two persons per thousand—are so retarded as to require residential care under present circumstances.

With a somewhat lesser degree of certainty, it can be said that in the developed countries between 3.5 and 4.5 persons per thousand would score below 50 on an intelligence test.

In looking at these two figures, it is important to recognize that the first, of one to two persons per thousand in need of residential care, includes a large number of persons who could score above 50 on intelligence tests but are markedly impaired in social adaptation.

Attempts to get a true estimate of how many mentally retarded persons there are outside these two categories have thus far resulted in widely varying figures—the lowest ones coming from the Scandinavian countries. Cultural factors and educational policies seem to play a major role in this regard. We must today admit that we know far less than we *thought* we knew 5 or 10 years ago!

But what about the qualitative aspect of mental retardation? What can be said about different degrees of retardation among the mentally retarded? Here, too, we find that our knowledge is far less definitive than we once thought. Twenty years ago, anybody who had taken a course in psychology "knew" that the mentally retarded consisted of morons, imbeciles, and idiots and that these terms were defined by IQ scores from 50 to 70 or 75 in the first instance, from 25 to 49 in the second, and from 0 to 24 in the third. Later, as increasing opposition was expressed in regard to these particular terms, "mild," "moderate," and "severe" were substituted as more appropriate and were adopted by the WHO in its 1954 report (World Health Organization).

It was a happy state of affairs for those of us involved in decisions about mentally retarded persons. All we needed was a psychometrician to provide an IQ score for our subject and, presto, we not only knew to which of the three levels of mental retardation to assign him, we also could find out from charts in textbooks just what could be expected of him. And since IQ's were believed to be fixed, that was that.

But then came disturbing new discoveries. First, IQ's as an expression of a person's intellectual functioning were found to be subject to distinct changes if conditions in his life changed to a sufficient degree. And second, social adaptation was found to be a crucial factor, along with measured intelligence, in judging the degree of a person's mental retardation.

And how has practice in health, welfare, and rehabilitation agencies responded to these discoveries? Quite remarkably, it seems to me, by ignoring them and continuing to use the old convenient terms and basing judgments almost entirely on the measured IQ.

AREAS OF CONFUSION

Educational practice has unfortunately confused the situation even more.

In the 1950's educators in our country commendably sought to widen school programs for the mentally retarded beyond the classes existing for the mildly retarded. They believed that persons of less intellectual endowment than those admitted to these special classes required quite different methods of teaching. They therefore made a distinction between the kind of programs to be provided for mildly retarded persons whom they regarded as capable of profiting from an "educational" process and for the moderately retarded whom they regarded as capable of being "trained" only to do the simplest tasks, incapable of rational thinking, and unable to acquire any kind of academic skill. Hence the terms "educable" and "trainable" came into use.

Unfortunately, shoddy thinking brought about a perversion in the use of these terms. Originally they described two types of schooling, but nobody had suggested that *all* children with

IQ's between 25 and 49 would be capable of profitably attending classes at the "trainable" level. Yet, by and by, more and more workers and writers in the field of mental retardation simply referred to *all* children with IQ's between 25 and 49 as "trainable." The result, of course, was that some "trainable" children have been found by the schools to be untrainable, that is, inadmissible to the classes. Still worse, some workers refer to postschool young people and adults as "educable" or "trainable" even though no sheltered workshop has ever found performance in an "educable" or a "trainable" class to be a reliable predictor of performance in the workshop, where quite different kinds of skill are demanded under quite different circumstances.

Another remnant from the period when a person's intelligence was regarded as static is an unfortunate misunderstanding of the psychological concept "mental age." Intelligence tests consist of a succession of subtests corresponding to the performance that can be expected from the average child of a specific age. It is all right to say that a certain 20-year-old person scored on a certain part of an intelligence test only as high as could be expected of a 3-year-old child. It is a questionable practice, however, to combine this 20-year-old person's rating on various parts of the test and say that he scored the same as would be expected of a 3½-year-old child when what actually happened is that on some parts of the test he scored as low as a 2-year-old and on others as high as a 6-year-old.

Most people do not keep in mind that the term "mental age" refers to the result of a mathematical averaging of a large number of scores on test items. This leads to the further misconception that a 20-year-old man with a "mental age" of 3½ is *like* a child of 3½ and therefore should be treated like such a child.

This is, of course, disastrous nonsense. There are no 3½-year-old children who are 5 feet 7 inches tall and weigh 160 pounds, who have had 20 years of some kind of social experience, who have mature sexual organs, and who have the strength to stand for several hours lifting heavy logs onto a truck. Mentally retarded persons are *not* "eternal children," and this sentimental way of referring to them is an insult to their dignity as human beings.

CONFUSIONS ABOUT PROGNOSIS

Another point needs to be emphasized. Mental retardation is not infrequently associated with physical handicaps, particularly with sensory disturbance, crippling orthopedic conditions, cardiac and respiratory irregularities, neurological defects, and deficiencies in motor coordination and muscle tone. Any or all of these defects may substantially impair a retarded child's social adaptation and also deprive him of opportunities for intellectual stimulation. Yet often we judge the rehabilitation potential of retarded persons without first making a determined effort to alleviate such physical handicaps through medical intervention and thereby bring about improvement in the person's general ability to function.

Too frequently a diagnosis of a child's condition is automatically read as a prognosis instead of merely as an assessment at a given time under given circumstances that is subject to change with time or under changed conditions such as increased stimulation or therapeutic or educational intervention. The confusion between diagnosis and prognosis leads to a vicious cycle: when a mentally retarded person is regarded as unable to learn a certain task, he is excluded from training programs and thus deprived of an opportunity to prove himself, and his subsequent very poor performance is then regarded as bearing out the initial low estimation of his capacity.

Nevertheless, retarded persons have made remarkable progress in general functioning in spite of initial low test performance when vigorous steps have been undertaken to ameliorate adverse conditions in their lives and to subject them to appropriate schooling or vocational and social training.

While in isolated instances some excellent work has been done in this country, the major work in demonstrating the rehabilitative potential of seriously retarded persons has been done in England. Since 1955, Alan and Ann Clarke, Beate

Hermilin, Neil O'Connor, Jack Tizard, and Herbert Gunzburg have been reporting in the professional literature the result of studies that clearly show how badly the capacity of persons with IQ's under 50 have been underestimated (Clarke, 1965; Clarke, 1955; O'Connor; Gunzburg).

Again, with outstanding exceptions, we in this country have been rather slow to emulate the pattern set in England in developing work training for the seriously retarded or even to recognize adequately in our professional literature the significance of the findings of research done there. In fact, professional workers often seem to react with hostile resentment when confronted with information regarding the vocational and social achievements of severely retarded persons.

AN ILLUSTRATION

At this point, it seems pertinent to summarize the case of a young worker in an industrial training unit that is part of the mental retardation facilities in the city of Oxford, England. The case is presented in more detail in an article by Paul Williams in the *Journal of Mental Subnormality* (Williams).

This young man, John, is today 18 years of age. He is an only child, whose mother, a teacher, was 44 years old when he was born.

John's early childhood was uneventful. At age 2, he started to talk and could say a number of words distinctly. However, by the time he was 5, he was clearly severely retarded, and so he was placed in a local training center similar to our classes on the "trainable" level. At that time, he scored a social age of about 18 months on the Vineland Scale. In the following year, at age 6, he failed to score on the revised Stanford-Binet intelligence test and, again, scored a social age of less than 2 years on the Vineland Scale. He was away from school a great deal because of illness, and while he was ill he stopped talking altogether. He has had no recognizable speech since.

During the ensuing years until he was 15 years old, John remained in the lowest class at the training center, a class that caters to the "babies"—preschool aged children—as well as to older children who are very severely handicapped with both physical and mental deficiencies.

This is a good example of a practice (common in this country as well as in England) that is purely for the convenience of the staff and administration and does not take into account the major needs of the children involved. Severely physically handicapped retarded children are a particular "bother" and therefore all too often are left with the lowest ability group even when they have a greater degree of intellectual ability and could profit from stimulation of more intelligent children.

When John was 15, he was admitted for a temporary stay to a newly opened junior hostel for retarded children and adolescents in Oxford so that his mother could have a brief vacation. This type of institution represents an important new kind of service in England that is rarely found here. To the great surprise of everybody, John adjusted well to the hostel and made definite improvement in his ability for self-help. When the time came for him to return home, the staff suggested that it might be well if he could stay at the hostel for 5 days each week and spend his weekends in his mother's home.

This arrangement was made, and as a consequence John improved a great deal in his general functioning. Nevertheless, 6 months after his admission to the hostel, his rating on the Vineland Scale was only 2 years 2 months. On the Minnesota Preschool Scale, form A, he passed only one item, showing a nonverbal mental age of approximately 2 years and a verbal mental age of less than 18 months. He still had no speech.

Here, then was a young man with mental retardation about as severe as one is likely to see in the community, who had had the benefit of a "training center" for 10 years, and whose advance during all those years was so minute as to suggest a dour prognosis. Nevertheless, when a new industrial training unit for the mentally handicapped was started in Oxford, the director of the hostel strongly urged that John be admitted to it. Naturally, the training unit received this suggestion with much skepticism, but, nevertheless admitted John for a trial period.

For the first 2 days the manager of the industrial training

unit spent a great deal of time working directly with John. In the beginning he had to hold John's hands and force the action required for the simple task he was to do—stripping some plastic material from the product. After a while John began to dislike being held, and he began to work independently. After 3 weeks he had fully mastered the task and could be placed at a work table with other trainees. He thus became a member of the working group.

I cannot go into all the details of John's growing adjustment, but I will describe briefly his subsequent work performance. During a typical morning's work, he sorted pieces of plastic of two shapes but of the same color and of about the same size. He worked slowly but steadily. During one half-hour period he sorted 700 items without making a single mistake. He also demonstrated that he remembered and could take up again without error a working procedure that had been taught to him 2 to 3 months earlier but that he had not been engaged in for some time. He also showed an ability to identify and correct mistakes that he made in his work and to react appropriately when two boxes in which he was placing parts were switched—he would switch his hand movements in order to continue to put the right part into the right box.

John still scores a nonverbal mental age of between 2 and 2½ years on tests. He still has no recognizable speech but can understand simple commands, and he recognizes his own name. However, his placement in the hostel has made it possible to involve him not only in a work program but also in a program of recreation and social activities, an opportunity he never had before.

It is often said that we should not push persons of such extremely low intellectual capacity into work—that this is a cruel and unethical procedure. Yet all the evidence seems to point to work performance as the factor that stimulates such persons sufficiently to enable them to participate in and enjoy group recreation programs and other pursuits.

I have purposely chosen an illustration from the lower levels of mental retardation because it seems to me that we have, at this time, more to learn from the lower levels that we can apply to the upper levels than the other way around. But, certainly, I am aware that quantitatively the bulk of our work must be directed toward the less severely retarded, a vastly larger group of persons.

AN EYE TO THE INDIVIDUAL

It seems obvious that we have been far too much influenced by prejudicial generalizations about the expected learning capacity of mentally retarded persons as a whole and have let these generalizations stand in the way of efforts to help each retarded child and adult reach toward his highest possible level of life fulfillment at home, at work, and at play.

One of the most significant areas of recent exploration in the field of mental retardation deals with the development of the self-concept in mentally retarded children, regardless of the degree of their handicap (Cobb, Edgerton). Further studies are needed to find out how the retarded person sees himself among his classmates or his colleagues in a workshop, whether less or more severely handicapped or nonhandicapped; how he sees persons who teach him or work with him; and how this relates to how the workers sees him. For example, what does it mean to a retarded adolescent to be treated in school like a little child, singing nursery rhymes and playing "silly" games although after school hors he hoins the rough life of the city streets?

Studies are needed to show the problems arising from the different kinds of worlds confronting the retarded—the world of home, the world of school, the world of the street and community, the world of work—and their often so different levels of language, feeling tone, and expectations.

Research is also needed to develop criteria for making an adequate quantitative assessment of capacity for and performance in adaptive behavior. And such scales must be tested in day-to-day practice to provide an operational basis for the presently accepted definition of mental retardation.

Above all, developmentally appropriate activities need to be provided for the mentally retarded for all aspects of life at every stage of life.

REFERENCES

Clarke, A.D.B.; Hermilin, B.F.: Adult imbeciles: their abilities and trainability. *Lancet*, August 13, 1955.

Clarke, Ann M.; Clarke, A.D.B.: Mental deficiency—the changing outlook. London, England, Methuen & Co., Ltd., 1958. (Second edition, 1965.)

Cobb, Henry: Self-concept of the mentally retarded. *Rehabilitation Record,* May–June 1961.

Edgerton, Robert B.: The cloak of competence: stigma in the lives of the mentally retarded. Berkeley, University of California Press, 1967.

Gunzburg, H.: Social rehabilitation of the subnormal. London, England, Bailliere, Tindall & Cox, 1960.

Kidd, J.W.: Toward a more precise definition of mental retardation. *Mental Retardation,* August 1964.

O'Connor, N.; Tizard, J.: The social problem of mental deficiency. New York, Pergamon Press, 1956.

Williams, Paul: Industrial training and remunerative employment of the profoundly retarded. *Journal of Mental Subnormality,* June 1967.

World Health Organization: The mentally subnormal child: report of a joint expert committee convened by WHO, with the participation of United Nations, ILO, and UNESCO. WHO Technical Report Series No. 75, Geneva. April 1954.

CHAPTER 5

REFLECTIONS ON MENTAL RETARDATION AND CEREBRAL PALSY*

HERMAN YANNET

~~~~~~

IDEALLY, the aim of our therapeutic and management programs for those with cerebral palsy should be as close
an approximation as possible of an independent social and
industrial integration at maturity into the community. Unfortunately, an acceptable level of success regarding this goal
is frequently not achieved, even in the presence of professional interests and skills and the availability of necessary
facilities. Most often it is the presence of a severe degree
of motor disability that makes it impossible. However, too
often, even when the motor handicap is not a crucial factor,
the presence of associated handicaps secondary to the basic
cerebral abnormality militates against successful integration.
These include sensory disorders, especially hearing and
vision, perceptive defects, convulsive disorders, language disabilities, personality defects, and mental retardation. It is to
the latter that I will confine this discussion.

Mental retardation, like cerebral palsy, is a graded handicap. It varies from the most profound degrees, where the
maximum mental age achieved will be significantly less than
6 to 12 months, to minor defects that merge with the lower
end of the normal distribution curve for intelligence. For
the most profound defects, our management goals can hardly

* Used with permission from *Am J Dis Child*, Vol. 112, Oct. 1966.

be higher than the simplest of custodial care. The health and comfort of the patient, an acceptable solution of the family problems which are invariably present, and a satisfactory parental adjustment is, at the present time, all that can be achieved. For those with minimal retardation the principles of management are not strikingly different from what they would be for those with equal motor handicaps but of average intelligence, as long as one is aware of the mild degree of retardation in planning and supplying the educational and industrial training facilities.

It is with the group between these extremes that our problems of management may become difficult. The reason depends on the dual nature of the handicap that the moderately retarded present. In addition to its effect in impairing the learning processes necessary for the education, industrial training, and social integration programs, moderate degrees of mental retardation may interfere with and impede the cooperation required for adequate and satisfactory rehabilitation procedures as they apply to the patient with motor handicap. While new techniques resulting from educational research in learning mechanisms have greatly improved the public schools' approach to the nonmotor handicapped in the so-called "trainable classes" and in our sheltered workshops, the translation of these programs into the field of the rehabilitation of the motor-handicapped moderately retarded child has much room for progress. This aspect of management, at present, is probably in the same stages of development that faced the educators who were attempting to apply educational techniques designed for the mildly retarded or even the intellectually average, to the rapidly expanding needs of the more severely retarded children. The results were not encouraging at first, but, fortunately, have been rapidly improving. Rehabilitation of the cerebral palsied is essentially a learning process and requires active participation of the subject. As has been demonstrated in the academic, self-help, and socializing fields, progress by the moderately retarded individual should be greatly enhanced by the newer specialized teaching techniques developed for this type of child and based on a broader and deeper understanding of fundamental educational principles that may be involved. The special teachers, industrial trainers, rehabilitationists, and physiotherapists dealing with such children can expect greater and more effective results as these newer teaching methods become more widely disseminated.

While the diagnosis and severity of cerebral palsy can often be made fairly early in infancy, the estimation of the severity and nature of the intellectual deficit in a cerebral palsied child is not so readily apparent or ascertainable. In early childhood comprehensive psychological evaluations primarily supply a quantitation of the child's present achievement levels only, and not necessarily his capacity. While their accuracy in this respect of reproducibility of the results by different examiners is high, their interpretation regarding prognosis presents a real difficulty. Allowances for the effects of deprivation of developmental opportunities, a factor almost invariably present in the cerebral palsied child, are notoriously unreliable. Moreover, certain aspects of development which may be described by such terms as "motivation" and which are so vital in the cooperation necessary for satisfactory rehabilitation cannot be adequately measured or even evaluated in the presently available intellectual testing procedures. While testing programs and resulting labeling may be required for preliminary screening and administrative purposes, for most of these children exposure for a reasonable period to initial therapeutic management programs will still be necessary. The response to these programs must remain the crucial deciding factor in the determination of the therapeutic goals to be sought and the types of subsequent programs to be developed.

Regardless of the intellectual status, the young child with cerebral palsy who is going through the exploratory and subsequent therapeutic programs is best handled in his own home. The extreme importance of the early mother-child relationship to the satisfactory development of emotional and personality structure, as far as possible, is unquestioned not only for the normal child, but especially so for the handicapped. Moreover, the type and constancy of the all-day care demanded during these early periods of training and physiotherapy can rarely be met as well in any other type of residential facility as they can in the home. For the older, moderately retarded cerebral palsied child the problems and needs are quite different, and for a small number some type of residential care other than that of the home may be required. This is a decision that will eventually face parents of these relatively few children, and it should be our responsibility to so orient them that the decision reached will be for the best interest of the child and the family.

Another aspect that should be mentioned is the inadvisability of prolonged segregation of the mentally retarded, with or without cerebral palsy, during the developmental period if future community integration is a possibility. This has two serious handicaps. For the involved child, it greatly limits the necessary learning opportunities inherent in living in a normal environment with normal children who are themselves in the period of growth. Of equal importance, it deprives the normal child of the opportunities to learn to live with the handicapped so that better future community acceptance is achieved. There are, of course, other techniques for improving community acceptance, including public education and demonstration programs, but none are as effective as early integration of the handicapped with normal children in their day to day activities wherever possible. Our experience with the problem of epilepsy demonstrates this well. Twenty-five years ago, in spite of intensive publicity campaigns, little progress along this line was apparent until the bars against allowing the epileptic child to attend the public schools were lowered and eventually removed. The situation now, although not completely resolved, is certainly vastly improved over what it was. Similar results could be expected regarding the cerebral palsied and other handicapped children.

In summary, mental retardation is a serious handicap to the satisfactory rehabilitation of the cerebral palsied child. However, except for the most profoundly involved, suitable programs can be devised and significant progress can be expected in a reasonable proportion of these children. In fact, there are very few who cannot be helped to some degree.

CHAPTER 6

EMOTIONAL DISTURBANCES IN MENTALLY RETARDED CHILDREN*
DIAGNOSTIC AND TREATMENT ASPECTS

FRANK J. MENOLASCINO

Sample
Chronic Brain Syndromes
Functional Psychoses and Mental Retardation
Adjustment Reactions of Childhood
Psychiatric Disturbance: Not Further Specified
Comment
Summary
References

THERE is increasing concern for the emotional plight of mentally retarded children. Emphasis has changed from attempts at differentiation between emotional disturbance and mental retardation in young children, to exploring the interaction of both of these disorders in any given child. In this presentation I shall review our experiences with 256 children who had been evaluated by a multidisciplinary team as part of a larger total referral sample, and who had been judged to be *both* emotionally disturbed and mentally retarded.

* Used with permission from *Arch Gen Psychiat*, Vol 19, Oct. 1968.

SAMPLE

Since 1958 there has been an active multidisciplinary mental retardation clinic at the University of Nebraska College of Medicine. Primary attention has been given to the evaluation of young children who had been suspected as manifesting the symptom of mental retardation by a variety of referral sources. From 1958 to mid-1966 a total of 1,025 young children were thoroughly evaluated (including individual psychiatric examinations). The presence and type of emotional disturbance in any given child were formally arrived at during a case conference wherein the psychiatric findings were considered part of the overall clinical findings. A previous report on this clinic reviewed our diagnostic methods, social-cultural population characteristics and associated findings (Menolascino, 1965b).

The sample of 256 emotionally disturbed and mentally retarded youngsters contained 153 boys and 103 girls. The age range was from 1.6 years to 14.2 years with the mean being 8.2 years for boys and 7.8 years for girls.

(All of the children in this study were noted [on full multidisciplinary team initial evaluation(s) and follow-up evaluation(s)] to be mentally retarded. Accordingly, *not* included in this sample are the children who had primary emotional disturbances that had presented with the "facade" of mental retardation [Menolascino, 1966].)

The frequency and types of emotional disturbances noted in this sample of children are presented in the Table. The diagnosis of an emotional disturbance was based on an individual psychiatric examination of each child (Haworth), psychological evaluation(s), family assessment, and within the context of the remaining findings on each child when discussed at case conference.

These 256 children presented a perplexing number of type(s) of clinical findings. This group tested both the diagnostic acumen of our clinical team and the ability of the team members to freely communicate and interdigitate their respective clinical impressions and treatment recommendation.

Our team has come to refer to this group of children with

PSYCHIATRIC ASPECTS: EMOTIONALLY DISTURBED
AND MENTALLY RETARDED CHILDREN

AAMD Category*	CBS† With Behavioral Reactions	CBS With Psychotic Reactions	Functional Psychoses	Personality Disorders	Adjustment Reaction	Psychiatric Disorder NES
I Infection	11	0	0	0	3	1
II Intoxication	6	0	0	0	0	0
III Trauma or physical agents	20	3	0	0	4	2
IV Disorder of metabolism, growth, or nutrition	0	0	0	0	0	0
V New Growth	2	0	0	0	0	0
VI Unknown prenatal influence	28	3	1	1	7	3
VII Unknown or uncertain cause with structural reactions manifest	64	17	4	1	19	8
VIII Unknown or uncertain cause with functional reaction manifest	3	20	3	2	25	1
Subtotals	134	43	8	4	58	15
N = 256			Total 262‡			

* The etiological classification and definition of mental retardation employed were those of the American Association on Mental Deficiency (1961).

† The psychiatric diagnostic entities are consistent with the nomenclature of the American Psychiatric Association (1952).

‡ The "mixed" clinical pictures (eg, a child with a chronic brain syndrome, with associated behavioral reaction and an adjustment reaction) resulted in more final diagnosis (262) than the number of children (256).

distinct clinical indices of both mental retardation and emotional disorder as "mixed cases" since they do present signs and symptoms of multiple disorders. For example, in the children who manifested chronic brain syndromes with associated behavioral reactions, we frequently noted combined clinical findings of an underlying cerebral dysfunction process with associated physical, neurological, intellectual, and emotional symptoms. We view these particular complex disturbances as representing a chronic brain syndrome with associated adaptive emotional problems secondary to the underlying cerebral disorder and/or reactive to the interpersonal environment. These children have forcibly focused our attention on such problems as: reformulation of the behavioral aspects of a chronic brain syndrome in early childhood; the ever widening spectrum of causative factors noted in the autistic reactions of childhood (Menolascino, 1965a) and relative interpretations of the interactive role(s) played by family psychopathology in both the evolution and maintenance of a given child's emotional problems.

The *four* most frequently noted behavioral reactions in this sample of emotionally disturbed mentally retarded children will be reviewed; treatment and management considerations will be stressed.

CHRONIC BRAIN SYNDROMES

DESCRIPTIVE ASPECTS. The 177 children in these two categories (chronic brain syndrome with behavioral reaction and chronic brain syndrome with psychotic reaction) displayed *similar* types of emotional disturbances which were differentiated primarily on the basis of the *degree* of the emotional disturbance noted and the associated family interactional dynamics. Here we have noted descriptive behavioral symptom clusters ranging from hyperkinesis, impulsiveness, and other signs of labile emotional control, to stereotyped hand movements, frequent panic reactions (to minimal environmental stimuli), autism, withdrawal. Frequently occurring personality features in both of these groups were: inability to respond adequately and smoothly to changing environmental influences (reflecting both inadequate personality organization and limited adaptability); relative inability to delay gratification(s) in concrete situations with resultant proneness to diffuse anxiety manifestations; and frequent instances wherein the limited intellectual abilities had apparently hampered the children's ability to learn from ongoing psychosocial experience(s) (perhaps because of the associated decreased capacity for conceptualization and transmission of intrapersonal and interpersonal needs). Such personality features seemingly limited their effective ability to form close and consistent interpersonal relationships of a nature which could help buffer and augment their developmental needs.

A wide range of associated handicaps such as motor dysfunction, conclusive disorders and delayed speech development have been noted in these two groups of children (83% of these two groups of children had one or more of these associated handicaps). The majority of these children had displayed delayed or borderline developmental milestones which had been of concern to the parents. However, this development delay apparently did not seem cause for further evaluation until the onset and persistence of overt behavioral manifestations. We would like to stress this point because we have often noted that there had been an escalation of the child's behavioral disturbance during a time of family perplexity about his rate of development. Considerations such as these have made us more cautious as to viewing the behavioral components of these two groups of children as being, "Just due to brain damage." These interpersonal aspects were consistently intermingled with behavioral and developmental delays which became clinically more understandable if the child was viewed as being adaptively at a much younger developmental age than his current chronological age.

MANAGEMENT CONSIDERATIONS. These children initially demanded a treatment ledger sheet of their specific assets and deficits. Such an overview avoids the common error of a singular diagnosis and subsequent singular treatment approach. This ledger was shared with the child's parents at the time of interpretation of our findings. Clarification of the parents' understanding of the child's multiple needs and their level of past expectations from him consistently led to mutual augmentation of treatment recommendations. It is my opinion that the most important aspect of a successful treatment approach to these children and their parents is the use of multiple treatment modalities such as: (1) supportive play therapy, (2) psychotropic medications, (3) family counseling, (4) correction or amelioration of any associated somatic handicaps, (5) aid in seeking community resources, and (6) sequential follow-through visits to assure the continuity of needed services.

The family interpretation interview considerations are particularly helpful for the parents of the preschooler with mild mental retardation, since these parents had been frequently told, "he is just slow—he will catch up—." The associated emotional problems had been doubly interpreted as an "emotional block to his learning," and as being secondary to "toxic" child care practices. Though some of these family constellations were in need of individual psychotherapy for themselves (30% of these two groups), we have been impressed by the therapeutic effect of a series of structured interviews which initially focused on a tactful review of our findings and then provided an opportunity for ventilation and clarification of parental responses and/or attitudes. This approach focused on the mutual engagement of both parents in the augmentation and follow-through the recommendations for their child.

Needless to say, this management approach is not new. However, I am continually impressed by the negative results of the frequent singular diagnostic-treatment approaches to these children in the past. It appears that these children with chronic multiple handicaps and a propensity to emotional disorganization are too commonly treated in a symptom-to-symptom temporal time sequence, rather than with a total approach which flexibly focuses on multi-level physical, emotional, educational, social, and family needs over a long-range basis.

In contrast to the group of children with chronic brain syndromes and associated behavioral reactions, *all* of the children who had chronic brain syndromes with associated psychotic reactions necessitated periods of brief hospitalization. The clinical features of marked personality disorganization with associated depleted family resources (emotional and physical) tended to preclude treatment and management attempts on an outpatient basis. Therapeutic focus during hospitalization was on increased interpersonal stimulation, play therapy aimed at the child's current developmental level, collateral family counseling, psychotropic medication, and ongoing experiences in a therapeutic preschool program. In this regard, I have been impressed by the rapid diminution of the acute aspects of these psychotic pictures shortly after admission to an inpatient setting (without major residuals suggestive of personality scarring). Since many workers list childhood schizophrenia as the only psychosis noted in mentally retarded children, I would stress again the need for diagnostic clarity in this clinical area. As discussed elsewhere our experience(s) suggest that there are distinct and major differences in the historical, clinical examination, and family dimensions of this particular group of psychotic children.

The degree of emotional disorganization and the physical pathology noted should not detract from treatment considerations or prognosis in these two groups of children. From a treatment standpoint, the presence of organic pathology simply means that we are talking about the problems of learning or relearning certain ego functions never acquired, or lost due to affliction of the organic substratum. The collaborative employment of a psychiatrically oriented nursery school program for these children with retarded functioning (utilizing the structure of an educational setting and its behavioral shaping attributes) can facilitate both the emotional and educational therapeutic needs.

FUNCTIONAL PSYCHOSES AND MENTAL RETARDATION

Descriptive Aspects. The presence of a functional psychosis in a child who is functioning at a subnormal intellectual level has long been problematical as to etiological, diagnostic, and associated treatment considerations (Menolascino, 1965a; Eaton, 1966; Despert; Robinson; Rutter) (Children from our total sample who had indices of a primary childhood psychosis are not included in this paper. We have discussed the diagnostic and treatment-prognosis dimensions of our experiences with such children elsewhere [Eaton, 1966; Eaton, 1967]). To some clinicians the presence of clinical signs of neurological or physical impairment(s) tends to rule out the possible coexistence of a major "functional" psychiatric disturbance. This view is not compatible with our experiences wherein we have noted distinct differences between the coexistence of a functional psychosis (eg, schizophrenic reaction of childhood) with an underlying chronic brain syndrome, versus the essentially different type of psychotic reactions noted in other children who also have chronic brain syndromes (eg, chronic brain syndrome with psychotic reaction). The occurrence of schizophrenic reactions in children with Down's syndrome (Menolascino, 1965c) clearly illustrates the development and presence of a functional psychosis in a child with distinct neuropathological determinants (the tissue pathology referent of a "chronic brain syndrome" in Down's syndrome refers to the underdeveloped frontal and cerebellar areas of the brain (Hilliard), whereas the behavioral descriptive referents [ie, schizophrenic reaction of childhood] are noted in the quality-quantity of the interpersonal transactions present).

The writer is aware of the contradictions and problems inherent in the *concurrent* utilization of the American Psychiatric Association and American Association on Mental Deficiency nomenclatural systems in the assignment of patients in this particular category. The APA nomenclatural system rather clearly divides ". . . mental disorders associated with organic brain disturbances," from ". . . those occurring without such primary disturbance of brain function." (American Psychiatric Association) Accordingly, the children listed in the bottom horizontal column of the Table would be formally listed in the APA nomenclature system as "chronic brain syndrome of unknown cause" (plus the addition of qualifying phrases concerning the presence of mental retardation *and* the superimposed emotional disturbance). Admittedly, the frequent absence of clear-cut physical and/or neurological signs of a chronic brain syndrome in childhood (Ingram) tends to make this a rather arbitrary clinical categorization. In our sample, the impressions of a chronic brain syndrome were gleaned from the retrospective review of the personal and clinical histories, the findings by other members of our multi-disciplinary team, *and* our past experiences in following up similar subsamples of such children. These diagnostic difficulties are compounded when one concurrently utilizes the AAMD nomenclatural system (American Association on Mental Deficiency), since category VIII stresses both ". . . due to uncertain (or *presumed* psychologic) cause with the functional reaction alone manifest" (p. 39). The clinician is cautioned, "No case is to be classified in this division except after exhaustive medical evaluation" (p. 39). However, *if* such precautions are taken and the child is noted to be mentally retarded with the above noted clinical-historical indices but of uncertain cause, *with* a superimposed emotional disturbance—then what? Lastly, it has been our most consistent experience(s) that young children who display mental retardation due to presumed psychological cause (eg, the facade of mental retardation [Menolascino, 1966]) present quite different initial diagnostic findings and follow-up (posttreatment) results.

This diagnostic issue became even more difficult when dealing with a child who had indices of mental retardation which "exhaustive medical examination" suggests is of uncertain cause (as to etiology), *and* has a superimposed functional psychosis (eg, propf-schizophrenia). Creak (1963) splendidly reviews this diagnostic quandry—replete with eight cases who underwent postmortem study. Though such postmortem findings (and the associated general impression that AAMD category VII "should" have been utilized) are helpful after-the-fact guidelines, they hardly comfort the clinician in the current clinical encounter. These diagnostic issues suggest the need for further refinement in both the clinical-diagnostic and etiological-nomenclatural approaches to this topic.

The eight children noted in this group presented very challenging differential diagnostic problems. Five of these children were noted to have clinical signs (on pediatric and neurological examination) of diffuse neurological impairment; the other three did not display such findings but were moderately retarded and had seizure disturbances with electroencephalogram (EEG) findings of generalized brain dysrhythmia. The early developmental histories on all eight of these children revealed distinct developmental delays but with fairly intact psychosocial development except for personality immaturity. Between 2½ and 4 years of age the quality of the early personality adjustment in each of these children was noted to insidiously undergo change towards withdrawal, bizarre motor posturing (or ritualistic mannerisms), marked preoccupation with certain inanimate objects, echolalic speech, and regression of previously acquired social-adaptive skills. When initially examined they displayed many of these noted features, and severe signs of autism (averted eye contact, preserve and highly personalized hand movements, and brief periods of apparent loss of contact with the environment without any known precipitating environmental reasons or associated convulsive phenomena). Further, on initial examination the levels of adaptive functioning noted in these children was far below their previously described levels of delayed functioning. Thus, we felt that they represented instances of a schizophrenic adaptation with associated regressive phenomena occurring against the backdrop of delayed early developmental milestones. The family aspects revealed frequent instances of sudden family disruption (eg, the death of a father in two instances was closely related with the onset of the child's disturbance). Major and chronic psychopathology was noted in the remaining six family constellations. We are aware that other workers may list these children as primary psychiatric disturbances, or as "atypical children." (Rank). A crucial point to differentiate here is whether we are dealing with a "primary" case of childhood schizophrenia, or a schizophrenic reaction in a mentally retarded child. Since we noted in the personal and clinical histories a coexistence of specific factors from both the intrinsic and extrinsic parameters, and well validated periods of personality regression and disintegration, we viewed them as a schizophrenic reaction (propf-schizophrenia) that was literally engrafted upon the previously displayed indices of mental retardation (Menolascino, 1965; Rutter; Lanzkron).

MANAGEMENT CONSIDERATIONS. Our management approach to this group of children with primary mental retardation and an associated functional psychosis was accomplished in an inpatient setting. The global quality of the child's multiple deficits in ego functioning was further studied, and an attempt was made to conceptualize the ego functions which were particularly disturbed in each patient, in conjunction with the possible etiological reasons for such impairments. Close attention was given to the mixed etiological factors that are so commonly present in groups of such psychotic children. Once the pattern of ego disturbances had been delineated, it was time to plan specific treatment strategies and tactics (eg, support of intact ego functions, personal incorporation of therapist, testing of reality determinants in a sequential fashion, etc) for improving the child's overall pattern of personality functioning. Since similar treatment approaches have been described in the literature (Alpert), we shall only stress the corollary need for special educational dimensions in such comprehensive treatment approaches.

ADJUSTMENT REACTIONS OF CHILDHOOD

DESCRIPTIVE ASPECTS. The 58 children noted in this group were very complex from a diagnostic-descriptive viewpoint since all of them presented with multidimensional problems in adaptation. The symptomatic cluster of obstinacy, temper tantrums, enuresis, disobedience, stealing, and masturbation were commonly noted against a background of much free-flowing anxiety, cognitive developmental delays, mild language retardation, and frequently associated physical and/or sensory handicaps. Further, the impact of each parent's emotional health status on their child, the effects of the interactional family factors, and possible situational crisis features were frequently noted in these complex child-family interactional patterns. In many instances, the child had seemingly sensed the parental perplexity and dissatisfaction with his slow developmental abilities, and had entered into an interpersonal vendetta with their mixed feelings being his target. Unfortunately these very parental mixed feelings became the vehicle for further confusion and acting out on the child's part.

A frequent form of adverse child-parent(s) interactional problem noted in this group occurred when chronic parental dissension (especially with rejection overtures) had produced anxiety and confusion in the child with subsequent feelings of massive insecurity. Thus the parental psychopathology seemed most frequently to be based on two major factors: their reaction to the child's atypical or abnormal developmental attainments, and the communication patterns and personality characteristics of the parents themselves.

Interestingly, other children in our *total* sample had been noted to have similar historical information of such interpersonal impasses in their past history, but they had apparently been helped by therapeutic interventions earlier (eg, family doctors, ministers, nursery school placement, etc).

MANAGEMENT CONSIDERATIONS. Management considerations in this group of children necessitated a modified psychotherapeutic relationship(s) for the child and his parents. These modifications had to be inserted because of the child's intellectual handicap, the frequent accompaniment of concretistic thinking, and associated limitations in how he actually perceived his environment as to perceptual-psychological considerations. In this particular group of children, family counseling was of extreme importance. Alterations in family attitudes (with encouragement toward more healthy, constructive, and consistent expectations for/from their child), and decreases in the anxiety levels in mother and/or father, tended to provide sufficient support to allow the child to improve in his adjustment. Where there was major family psychopathology and poor motivation to involve themselves in collateral treatment, we have noted that nursery school placement can provide the child at least with a partially corrective emotional-educational experience.

The psychotherapeutic approach to these children also differs from traditional approaches since the total picture is not self-limiting after treatment. The child remains with a chronic adaptive handicap (lower social-adaptive and intellectual ability) and parental treatment considerations have to include guidance as to available special educational facilities, and realistic future developmental expectations from the child. The clinician must be fully appreciative of the mixed etiologies that are frequently present since mixed prognoses are also in order in these instances. We would like to underscore this point since in the past we had commonly had the treatment experience (and expectations) that psychotherapeutic procedures would eventuate in the "evaporation" of the associated finding of mental retardation in these children. Reevaluation of some of our former viewpoints has made us more appreciative of parental problems in relation to their child's normal strivings for growth toward independence. Many of these parents, especially those with other children, had sensed the child's actual need for extra involvement and supervision, although many of them overreacted this area.

PSYCHIATRIC DISTURBANCE: NOT
FURTHER SPECIFIED

DESCRIPTIVE ASPECTS. This group of 11 children commonly displayed frequent periods of general irritability against a personality backdrop of passivity, inflexibility, and personality immaturity. All of this group of children were in the moderate range of mental retardation. These particular behavioral referents seemed most closely associated with the child's delayed intellectual development, and contained many of the personality characteristics of young mentally retarded children described by Webster (1963).

This was our "wastebasket category," since the behavioral repertoire of these children was only mildly atypical for their given mental age and negative family interactional factors were only questionably operative when closely examined. Here we noted the behavioral ingredients of possibly more structured behavioral reactions in the future. For example, they represented behavioral reactions from which a future possible adjustment reaction of childhood might possibly arise if the currently tenuous family interactional pattern became less cognizant and/or empathetic about the child's developmental handicaps and associated emotional needs.

MANAGEMENT CONSIDERATIONS. Management considerations in this last group of children tended to hinge on adequate transmission of diagnostic findings to the parents and subsequent help in altering their previous expectations from the child. Since realignment of parental expectations from their child tended to lead to more realistic parental demands upon the child (in keeping with his developmental level), these treatment considerations have embodied principles of secondary prevention in psychiatry (Caplan).

COMMENT

As in other areas of medicine, diagnosis and treatment must be individualized in terms of the child, his presenting symptomatology, and the psychosocial family milieu. Concerning the psychiatric aspects of mental retardation, this medical maxim becomes clinically more difficult to apply because of the wide etiological umbrella of mental retardation, the frequently associated multiple handicaps, the rapidly changing psychosocial needs of the developing child, and the complexity of family interactional patterns. The experiential factors may also mask, modify, or exaggerate the underlying patho-physiological processes in some of these children. For example, the quality and quantity of early mothering, the parental handling of developmental crisis situations, social-cultural factors, the family's initial and long-range reaction and adjustment to the child's chronic disabilities, the effect of overt distortions of bodily appearance on the child's self-image, and the timing of the etiological insult in relation to the stage of physical growth and psychosexual adjustment —any or all of these factors may determine the child's future quality of adjustment *more* than the intrinsic factors that are present. These considerations again caution one against singular hypotheses as to etiology and/or treatment.

In the previously presented descriptive and treatment overview of the four most common emotional disturbances which we have noted in a relatively large sample of young mentally retarded children, we have attempted to delineate some of the behavioral reaction patterns secondary to cerebral insults, the role of superimposed interpersonal conflicts and their residuals, and those instances wherein these and a variety of other factors were noted to be operative. We have stressed that treatment approaches must address themselves first to the global nature of the child's personal-social interaction problems, and only secondarily focus on specific handicaps such as a seizure disorder, motor dysfunction, or speech and language delay.

Many of these behavioral disorders can be helped by widely differing treatment methods and approaches. This is not surprising when we consider that they are the outcome of a multifactorial complex of forces which suggests that the equilibrium is likely to be positively altered by modifying any of a number of factors. Selective inattention to the multiple diagnostic-treatment challenges that these children commonly present can lead to faulty diagnosis and incomplete treatment. These considerations were particularly pertinent to our previously reviewed group of mentally retarded children with concomitant adjustment reactions of childhood, since this particular emotional disturbance is, by definition, a transitory disorder. Delineation of the child's multiple assets and deficits (emotional, physical, social, sensory, etc) and close attention to realignment of the family support system led to combined treatment-preventative approaches to these child-parent(s) units. For example, helping these family units to effectively deal with the conflicts that led to the presenting clinical symptoms, and then develop new ways of mutual problem solving (so that similar conflicts in the future would not have to be dealt with by past psychopathological mechanisms), provided effective treatment intervention with preventative considerations in the foreground.

No treatment approach is successful unless a long-range working relationship with the family has been established. Initial tactful interpretation interviews can provide the "foothold" for the establishment of such a relationship. Within the context of such a mutual contract of help with the family, these multidimensional treatment needs can be delineated, augmented, and followed through. Here the psychiatrist must open his vistas to the special contributions of the allied professions in his efforts to arrange a life plan for the child which will be both therapeutically positive and eventuate in self-realization for the child. In such treatment planning we have noted that it is helpful to focus not on what the child presently *is*, but on what he can *become*.

Future clinical research in the evaluation and treatment of young children who display both emotional disturbance and mental retardation must attempt to elucidate further guidelines as to the types and modifications of personality development in these young children with multiple handicaps (Webster). We also need more basic information of possible impairments in their usual mechanisms for handling conflicts (eg, Are they able to fantasize adequately? Are the psychosexual stages of personality also atypical because of the associated cognitive defects? Do their chronic brain syndrome aspects impair their ability to delay gratification with resultant proneness to diffuse anxiety?, etc). These and similar considerations suggest that mental retardation may provide limitations for emotional maturation above and beyond the emotional consequences of social nonacceptance or decreased adaptive abilities because of the retarded cognitive functions.

These diagnostic issues are extremely important from the viewpoint of the current treatment models that are based on such issues. For example, the overall similarity of the indicated treatment approaches for each of the subgroups in this report suggests that the current nomenclatural considerations may be misleading in their overriding concern with correlating treatment to underlying causes (etiology). This similarity of treatment approaches utilized strongly suggests that we may be viewing these disorders at a descriptive level—rather than at an etiological level of explanation and/or current knowledge. The term "autism" is an excellent example of this particular quandry since it is variously employed to imply etiological and/or descriptive dimensions. When utilized as an etiological "label," it tends to elicit rather specific theoretical-clinical approaches to treatment. However, its use as a descriptive term applied to ongoing behavioral vignettes does not elicit any specific theoretical-clinical approach(s) to treatment. Indeed, as Gardner (1967) has succinctly pointed out, the description approach to the treatment of emotional disturbance in the mentally retarded may well call for a basic reexamination of both the current models of treatment and the orientations of those who can most effectively provide such treatment services.

Some of these challenges for wider utilization of psychiatric principles concerning personality functioning and child care in the field of mental retardation are currently being explored. For example, nursing and associated child care disciplines which embody current psychiatric concepts have been noted to be effective in providing positive therapeutic intervention for rumination syndromes in young mentally retarded children (Wright). Similarly, the continuing professional posture toward children with Down's syndrome as being the "Prince Charming" of the mentally retarded, may indeed *be* a contemporary fairy tale (Menolascino, 1956c)! Lastly, the larger community issue of the need for training the future psychiatrist to provide comprehensive services for the mentally retarded may be the supreme challenge to the attitudinal changes that must continue to evolve if we are to truly embrace the current dynamic tempo in the field of mental retardation (Menolascino, 1967).

SUMMARY

In summary, the foregoing considerations imply that psychiatric disorders in young mentally retarded children are relatively frequent occurrences, and differ qualitatively from what is noted in nonmentally retarded children. We would underscore the urgent need to evolve more specific methods of treatment for large groups of multiply handicapped young children. The psychiatric treatment and management aspects of emotional disturbances in mentally retarded children has been largely neglected. Yet it is apparent that the need for these services does not vanish as the IQ drops below 70. The increasing realization that the mentally retarded child has a personality as well as an intelligence quotient is likely to be accompanied by further positive developments in this clinical area.

REFERENCES

Alpert, A.A.: Special Therapeutic Technique for Certain Developmental Disorders in Pre-Latency Children. *Amer J Orthopsychiat, 27*:256–270 (April) 1957.

American Association on Mental Deficiency: A Manual on Terminology and Classification in Mental Retardation. *Amer J Ment Defic*, 1961.

American Psychiatric Association: *Diagnostic and Statistical Manual of Mental Disorders*, Washington, D.C.: the Association, 1952.

Caplan, G.: *Principles of Preventative Psychiatry*, New York: Basic Books Inc., 1964, pp. 89–112.

Creak, E.M.: Childhood Psychosis. *Brit J Psychiat, 109*:84–89 (Jan) 1963.

Despert, J.L., and Sherwin, A.C.: Further Examination of Diagnostic Criteria in Schizophrenia Illness Psychoses of Infancy and Early Childhood. *Amer J Psychiat, 114*:784–790 (March) 1958.

Eaton, L., and Menolascino, F.J.: Psychotic Reactions of Childhood: Experiences of a Mental Retardation Pilot Project. *J Nerv Ment Dis, 143*:55–67 (July) 1966.

Eaton, L., and Menolascino, F.J.: Psychotic Reactions of Childhood: Experiences of a wmental Retardation Clinic; Follow-up Study. *Amer J Orthopsychiat, 37*:521–529 (April) 1967.

Gardner, W.L.: What Should Be the Psychologist's Role? *Ment Retard,* 5:29–31 (Aug) 1967.

Haworth, M., and Menolascino, F.J.: Video-Tape Observations of Disturbed Young Children, *J Clin Psychol, 23:*135–140 (April) 1967.

Hilliard, L.T., and Kirman, B.H.: "Mental Deficiency." In *The Pathology of Certain Syndromes,* Boston: Little, Brown & Co., 1965, pp. 225–273, chap. 6.

Ingram, T.: "Chronic Brain Syndromes in Childhood Other Than Cerebral Palsy, Epilepsy, and Mental Defect." In MacKeith, R. and Bax, M. (eds.): *Minimal Cerebral Dysfunction.* London, Heinemann Medical Books, Ltd., 1963, pp. 10–17.

Lanzkron, J.: The Concept of Propf-Schizophrenia and Its Prognosis. *Amer J Ment Defic, 61:*547–554 (Jan) 1957.

Menolascino, F.J.: Autistic Reactions in Early Childhood: Differential Diagnostic Considerations, *J Child Psychol Psychiat, 6:*203–218 (Dec) 1965a.

Menolascino, F.J.: Emotional Disturbance and Mental Retardation, *Amer J Ment Defic, 70:*248–256 (Sept.) 1965b.

Menolascino, F.J.: Psychiatric Aspects of Mongolism. *Amer J Ment Defic, 69:*653–660 (March) 1965c.

Menolascino, F.J.: The Facade of Mental Retardation: Its Challenge to Child Psychiatry. *Amer J. Psychiat, 122:*1227–1235 (May) 1966.

Menolascino, F.J.: Mental Retardation and Comprehensive Training in Psychiatry. *Amer J Psychiat, 124:*459–466 (Oct) 1967.

Rank, B.: Adaptation of the Psychoanalytic Technique for the Treatment of Young Children With Atypical Development. *Amer J Orthopsychiat, 19:*130–139 (Jan) 1949.

Robinson, J.F.: The Psychoses of Early Childhood. *Amer J. Orthopsychiat, 31:*536–550 (July) 1961.

Rutter, M.: The Influence of Organic and Emotional Factors on the Origins, Nature, and Outocome of Childhood Psychosis. *Develop Med Child Neurol, 7:*518–528 (Oct) 1965.

Webster, T.E.: Problems of Emotional Development in Young Retarded Children. *Amer J Psychiat, 12:*34–41 (July) 1963.

Wright, M., and Menolascino, F.J.: Nurturant Nursing of Mentally Retarded Ruminators. *Amer J Ment Defic, 71:*451–459 (Nov) 1966.

Chapter 7

THE USE OF THE PLAYROOM IN EDUCATION OF MENTALLY RETARDED CHILDREN*

Betty Hunt Bradley

~~~~~~

THIS PAPER attempts to describe the use of the playroom in education of mentally retarded children. These observations are a result of 10 years' work with children at the Columbus State Institute. Most of these children had been classified as brain-injured and ranged in intelligence from below 30 through 60. Their chronological ages extended from 6 to 14 years with mental ages ranging from 18 months to 6 years. The playroom has been used for a variety of purposes, as it has served as a source for reduction of tantrum behavior, a modified exercise room, and as a setting for individualized training. Sometimes children require a change of environment from their classroom to a less structured setting. For a hyperactive child, restriction to one position for an extensive time may be very disturbing. As one of our older boys expressed it, "The teacher on the outside made me so nervous I couldn't stand it. I almost climbed the walls. She wanted me to sit still." Educational training was based primarily on techniques described by Gellner in this particular unit but employment of playroom activities could be related to any type of educational curriculum.

Despite the paucity of research with play therapy for the moderately retarded child, there have been some extensive

* Used with permission from *Rehabilitation Literature*, 31, 1970.

investigations by Leland (1965) and his associates at the Passons State Hospital and Training Center, Parsons, Kansas. They concluded that a firmer theoretical basis should be applied in therapeutic work with this population. General overviews and discussions relating to play technics are presented by Cowen (1955), Axline (1949), Allen (1942), Stacey and DeMartino (1957), and Sarason (1959). Axline (1947, 1948), Maisner (1950), Mehlman (1953), Mundy (1957), Fisher and Wolfson (1953), Thorne (1948), Heiser (1954), Tilton and Ottinger (1964), Leland and Smith (1965), and Subotnick and Callahan (1959) have all supplied additional data relating to play therapy with retardates. There has been some use of video tape observations of play behavior (1967). Robinson and Robinson (1965) conclude from a review of studies on this topic that under favorable conditions play therapy may be beneficial but not a requisite in establishing contact with retarded children.

One of our more successful playroom procedures is related to those suggested by Leland and Smith (1965), although at the time of application it was not as clearly defined. It was felt by the staff that certain specific problems were blocking the progress of children within both the classroom and the institution. Usually these involved aggressive outbursts, lapse in social behaviors, withdrawal, or some specific behavior that was creating a problem.

A large, sturdy 12-year-old boy was making marked progress in school except for his temper tantrums, which occurred when he was not the winner or the first in any group activity. This resulted in his dismissal from his recreational program within the cottage and also caused numerous playground fights with his peers. Individual attention was directed toward making Richard feel important while at the same time giving him experiences in losing gracefully. This involved an individual program in which the psychologist, office secretary, and other staff members played table games with him which he both won and lost. Prescribed rules were established for appropriate behavior for both winners and losers. Richard was taught how to lose without a display of temper. This involved modifying his aggressive behavior, which had formerly consisted of picking up the heavy game tables and hurling them at the unfortunate victors.

The problem, although minor in comparison with some displayed in the classroom, was preventing Richard from making progress within the institution. He certainly would not be accepted within the institutional regular school program if he picked up the furniture and threw it at the teacher every time he failed to be the most important person in the group. In a new environment with children functioning at a higher level in many areas, Richard would be certain of not being the most important person within the classroom. This approach did allow him to make a transition to a more advanced department in the school and his classroom adjustment was reported to be fairly satisfactory although his desire for recognition continued to be strong.

Our attention to specific problems of children within the classroom seems to aid the teachers in their attitudes as well as the children. There was a reduction of pressure on the child when the teacher felt that someone was concerned with and focusing on a problem she considered to be important. There is a danger in using this procedure in that the playroom may become the dumping ground for all the management difficulties in the classroom. The psychologist and teacher should carefully evaluate the behavior to determine if there is a need for individual work or whether the behavior can be dealt with more appropriately through other procedures.

The following observations and reports summarized from our records illustrate some of the individualized programs that have been used in Project #50.

Diane was placed in the playroom to reduce physical movements, hyperactivity, and to increase her attention span in the classroom. She made considerable progress in these areas with decrease in attempts to run through the halls and fewer instances of knocking down the light fixtures with balls. She also approached the table for individual work on her own initiative.

Her favorite activity in playroom work consisted of looking at picture books and naming the pictures. Diane had much difficulty in completing any task requiring eye-hand coordination and destroyed most of the paper-pencil work given to classmates by eating it. She was given her own papers but no pressure was placed on her finished products since she displayed a great dislike for such activity. Diane was able to establish fairly good peer relationships with the exception of occasions when she agitated children to create tantrum behavior. In a group she was an exciting influence due to her pleasure and energy in all situations, but she responded to isolation when the excitement became extreme. Her playroom program continued for a period of 6 months (30 minutes daily) and was dropped at the conclusion of the school term because her behavior had improved.

Jacob was a small, active boy who entered the group with no speech but some word comprehension. He had playroom work twice a week in addition to regular classroom activities. Reports from the psychologist indicated that Jacob continued to improve in his ability to speak. After a period of 3 to 4 years, he was able to repeat at least 75 words. These words were not perfectly formed but he attempted to form letters and sounds in imitation of the psychologist. He used a few of these words to communicate his desires. However, most of the psychologist's attention was directed toward getting him to try to copy sounds and words and encouraging him to make noises and word sounds. Jacob would work for only 10 to 15 minutes on these activities and the majority of his time in his playroom session was spent playing with a tub of water. This enjoyment of water play was one of the few means of motivating any type of performance from Jacob. He refused to do any activity unless allowed to have this water play. He preferred to play alone with his cups, dishes, pitchers, pails, sand, and bottles of water. Jacob became very excited if anyone approached his apparatus and would tip all his water onto the floor if a child or adult moved toward him. Sometimes he displayed tantrum behavior when forced to leave this activity.

Jacob could relate to adults and enjoyed teasing them. He could be very affectonate. However, most of his responses were directed toward adults rather than children. Jacob was placed in the playroom with another child on the premise that this stimulation might encourage some positive relationships. This did not occur. The other child was ignored except when he moved toward the water play area, whereupon Jacob threw a chair at him.

Danny continued to have much difficulty in controlling his behavior and in adjusting to any group situation. He began to run away from the situation and reported these escapes in terms of an exciting "Cops and Robbers" activity in which he played the part of the hero. According to cottage reports he was usually found quickly as a tag-along with the more adequate runners. Danny's ability to reason and apply any conclusion to everyday behavior was extremely limited. He verbalized acceptable behavior but could not tranfer or remember his own resolutions long enough to be of any assistance in regulation of behavior. He was unable to make use of his rather high academic ability in reading (3rd to 4th grade level) because he could not withstand any pressure within the classroom. He had tantrums if he was given any academic work that he felt was too difficult for him.

One of Danny's problems was that, while he was aware of his specific difficulties, he did not seem to be able to find any suitable method of coping with them. His 45-minute playroom session was only partially effective, as his primary problem was group participation. Another boy was added to his session and this proved to be helpful to him in providing practice in establishing a social relationship. Danny decreased his continuous beating up of the smaller children in Project #50 and did try to build a friendship with this one boy in his therapy session.

Another procedure that has been used with our low children has involved teaching them how to play. Children with visual-motor handicaps, classified according to Gellner (1959), often have to be taken through the actual operations involved in a task rather than having it demonstrated. Usually this involves individual attention until the child responds to some toys and activities, and then another child may be introduced for the purpose of encouraging parallel play. Selection of children becomes a critical factor, especially in initial contacts. If an aggressive child is paired with a quiet child the aggression is likely to increase, with the result that the psychologist spends too much time attempting to re-establish limits to prevent bodily injury. Each child should be made aware and learn the restrictions upon his behavior before he is placed with another child. Some limits regarding physical attacks must be firmly established.

The equipment in the playroom varies in accordance with the population and purpose of the session. Sometimes the psychologist has used a small adjacent room for painting or craft work. The playroom equipment used includes sand-boxes, balls, drums, dolls, dishes, items for water play, pull toys, and many miscellaneous preschool toys. Finger paint has been used successfully, especially for children who do not mind being messy. Some completely reject this activity and insist on using brushes or paint-with-water books. Sand is only partially successful, again depending upon the individual child. Closely packed sand in an old stocking can provide a child with a dangerous weapon and sand battles are a frequent occurrence. However, this can be controlled by the imposition of limits. Difficulties involving the use of sand and water have frequently occurred.

It is much more satisfactory to have a variety of settings for different types of therapy, as described by Leland and Smith (1962). Some of the very retarded children may start their play therapy in a setting they describe as unstructured with employment of an unstructured approach. This allows use of sand, water, clay, and paper in a room that can withstand these consequences. However, if it is necessary to use the same room for a variety of needs, some modifications may be necessary. For example, one child enjoyed dumping his buckets of water into the sand making a very soupy mess. This seemed to be working nicely for him but created difficulty for other children who wanted drier sand for their projects.

Storage boxes and cabinets are necessary to preserve materials and reduce cleaning efforts. If the same room is used for many sessions the therapist must schedule sufficient time for clean-up and change of materials. This may become a problem if more than one therapist is using the room.

Hemphill (1954) in her work in Project #50 conducted several pilot investigations of playroom behavior. In establishing her playroom environment she selected a large, bare room (18 by 18 feet) with high ceilings painted a quiet blue-green. Materials were introduced very gradually to her group of moderately retarded children, since it had been observed that these children did not respond appropriately to a roomful of toys. Hemphill's notes indicated that in a free situation the children with mental ages of 2, 3, and 4 years did not really use the material but relied on activities such as sifting sand through their fingers. During the extensive observation period of the play behavior of small groups of these moderately retarded children she stated that there was little fantasy play or little constructive play with blocks or manipulative material. Block play tended to involve piling or sorting of blocks rather than projects of building bridges, houses, or train tracks. There was little identification with small objects such as small doll figures. In order to encourage the children to play with dolls, a large 48-inch doll was used and most of the play with this doll involved manipulation such as dressing and undressing. Rarely was the doll considered to be a playmate or an imaginary figure. There was a lack of constructive activities such as building as one observes in nursery school. The rocking boat was used more as a rocking chair with children sucking fingers and thumbs as they rocked back and forth rather than having any connection with boats or transportation functions. Hemphill also reported that her group seldom brought past experiences into the playroom. Trips, cottage experiences, and family outings were infrequently discussed.

A pilot study by Hemphill that was not completed due to her move to another location indicated some promising results. One purpose of this investigation was to determine if there was a differential response to playroom materials in accordance with their Gellner (1959) disabilities. Hemphill suggested that children would tend to avoid their disability area in a choice situation, and behavior in a disability area forced on them would consist of means of escape, hyperactiveness, and inappropriate use of materials. She also felt that the children might attempt to convert material. If visual motor materials are difficult for a child he might avoid it in preference to other material that is less demanding.

The design of this study consisted of three play environments: visual-motor, auditory, and a combination of both. The visual-motor environment contained 34 toys in which eye-hand coordination and manipulation of material were required. The auditory environment, also 34 toys, involved sounds, puppets, and drums. Success with auditory materials could be gained easily through minimal manipulative effort. A combined environment of 68 toys was also presented. These toys were arranged on low tables in the playroom and two children came for 20-minute sessions daily. Only partial analysis of this experiment is available due to the move of the investigator. However, recorded observations give some support to her original hypotheses.

The playroom becomes an effecting bridge in establishing a working relationship with the child and allows the teacher and psychologist to direct their attention to the whole child rather than just focusing on fragmental problem areas. Our experiences in a combination of classroom work and individual playroom work with a psychologist have helped improve staff communication and adult-child communication and provided some means of solving specific behavioral difficulties interfering with educational progress.

REFERENCES

Allen, Frederick H.: *Psychotherapy with Children.* New York, W. W. Norton & Co., 1942.

Axline, Virginia M.: Mental Deficiency—Symptom or Disease? *J Consult Psychol,* Oct., 1949. *13';5:*313–327.

Axline, Virginia Mae: *Play Therapy: The Inner Dynamics of Childhood.* Boston, Houghton Mifflin Co., 1947.

Axline, Virginia M.: Some Observations on Play Therapy. *J Consult Psychol,* July-Aug., 1948. *12:4:*209–216.

Cowen, Emory L.: Psychotherapy and Play Techniques with the Exceptional Child and Youth, p. 520–575. In Cruickshank, William M. (Ed.): *Psychology of Exceptional Children and Youth.* Englewood Cliffs, N.J., Prentice-Hall, 1955.

Fisher, Louise A., and Wolfson, Isaac N.: Group Therapy of Mental Defectives. *Am J Mental Deficiency,* Jan., 1953, *57:3:*463–476.

Gellner, Lisa: *A Neurophysiological Concept of Mental Retardation and Its Educational Implications*, a series of five lectures given under the auspices of, and published by, the Dr. Julian D. Levinson Research Foundation for Mentally Retarded Children, Cook County Hospital, Chicago, 1959.

Haworth, Mary R., and Menolascino, Frank J.: Video-Tape Observations of Disturbed Young Children. *J Clin Psychol*, Apr., 1967. *23:2:*135–140.

Heiser, Karl F.: Psychotherapy in a Residential School for Mentally Retarded Children. *Training School Bul*, Feb., 1954. *50:10:*211–218.

Hemphill, Stella: *Play Behavior of Brain-Injured Children.* (Staff document) Project #50. Columbus, Ohio, Columbus State Institute, 1954.

Leland, Henry, and Smith, Dan: Unstructured Material in Play Therapy for Emotionally Disturbed, Brain Damaged, Mentally Retarded Children. *Am J Mental Deficiency*. Jan., 1962. *66:4:*621–628.

Leland, Henry, and Smith, Daniel E.: *Play Therapy with Mentally Subnormal Children.* New York, Grune and Stratton, 1965.

Maisner, Edna A.: Contributions of Play Therapy Techniques to Total Rehabilitative Design in an Institution for High-Grade Mentally Deficient and Borderline Children. *Am J Mental Deficiency*, Oct., 1950. *55:2:*235–250.

Mehlman, Benjamin: Group Play Therapy with Mentally Retarded Children. *J Abnormal & Soc Psychol*, Jan., 1953. *48:1:*53–60.

Mundy, Lydia: Therapy with Physically and Mentally Handicapped Children in a Mental Deficiency Hospital. *J Clin Psychol*, Jan., 1957. *13:1:*3–9.

Robinson, Halbert B., and Robinson, Nancy M.: *The Mentally Retarded Child: A Psychological approach.* New York, McGraw-Hill Co., 1965.

Sarason, Seymour B.: *Psychological Problems in Mental Deficiency, 3rd ed.* New York, Harper & Bros., 1959.

Stacey, Chalmers L., and DeMartino, Manfred F., comps. and eds.: *Counseling and Psychotherapy with the Mentally Retarded: A Book of Readings.* Glencoe, Ill., Free Pr., 1957.

Subotnik, Leo, and Callahan, Roger J.: A Pilot Study in Short-Term Play Therapy with Institutionalized Educable Mentally Retarded Boys. *Am J Mental Deficiency*, Jan., 1959. *63:4:*730–735.

Thorne, Frederick C.: Counseling and Psychotherapy with Mental Defectives. *Am J Mental Deficiency*, Jan., 1948. *52:3:*263–271.

Tilton, James R., and Ottinger, Donald R.: Comparison of the Toy Behavior of Autistic, Retarded, and Normal Children. *Psychological Reports*, Dec., 1964. *15:3:*967–975.

CHAPTER 8

TEAM WORK EXPERIENCE FOR THE MENTALLY RETARDED

NORMAN FENDELL

~~~~~~

ONE OF THE MOST significant developments in rehabilitation and special education during the past decade is the growth of the work study programs for retardates in high schools throughout the nation. Educational curriculum has been designed to facilitate the student's transition from school to employment by providing actual work experience directly related to the academic offerings. What is to be done with the trainables (IQ below 50) and a substantial segment of the educables (IQ between 50 and 80) not qualified to participate in these community work stations? Joseph Weingold (1963), executive director of the New York Association for Retarded Children, has a theory that can be applied to this situation: "Each new service demonstrates a new need and opens up additional areas of exploration. This is what I call the Pandora Box Theory of social service."

It is essential that we specifically identify that segment of our retarded population unable to function independently in a work study program. Accepting the incidence of mental retardation as 30 in 1,000, one of these 30 is "dependent," requiring hour-by-hour supervision in an institutional setting. The second group, 4 out of every 1,000 population, is the "semi-dependent" group, who may have the capacity to perform useful work and live at home in the community. Special

* Used with permission from, *Rehabilitation Literature, 31,* 1971.

educators refer to this group as trainables. The third is the "marginally independent" group, who represent 25 per 1,000 of the general population. These are the educables, by far the largest group, many of whom eventually become either completely or partially self-supporting.

Special educators and rehabilitation specialists who have been working with these groups recognize certain factors that can be determined with reasonable certainty. As a general rule, the trainable retardate does not vocationally survive in competitive employment. There are a few exceptions, such as working for a relative. A substantial portion of the educable retarded school population exhibiting such characteristics as social immaturity, emotional maladjustment, limited attention span, or poor coordination are not eligible for community job stations due to inability to perform at a sufficient level.

In short, there are segments of our retarded school population who need vocational training that is not being provided within the structure of present work-study programs on the secondary level. Many states have mandatory legislation requiring local school boards to provide a program for these students until they reach 21 years of age. Only if special education is to be equated with a professional form of babysitting, would the teacher be justified in presenting a "watered-down" curriculum, meaning an elementary curriculum at a reduced level; such a curriculum is guided by unrealistic goals and implemented with knowledge the retardate will never use.

With the recognition that direct experience preceding the recorded history and providing the foundation for basic education is the most effective path to learning for these students, curriculum must be revised to provide these students with the opportunity for vocational training, namely, *team work experience*.

In team work experience, which has furnished groups of mentally retarded students with supervised work in a variety of community settings, a vocational instructor is responsible for the supervision and training of the work crews at the job stations. Students spend half the day with the special education teacher following a vocationally oriented curriculum and are assigned to groups of five for supervised work experience. It is not expected that the vocational instructor should be certified in special education; common sense and the ability to communicate with the retarded are sufficient.

In January, 1970, the Manchester (Connecticut) Board of Education received an allocation, under the 1968 Amendments to the Vocational Education Act of 1963, designated to provide vocational education to the handicapped. An occupational instructor, who is a graduate student in rehabilitation, has been hired on a part-time basis. Students are learning to wash cars at a local service station, shovel snow for private homeowners, wash windows at a local convalescent home, and care for lawns. The vocational instructor, special education teachers, and supervisor hold periodic meetings to discuss the progress of the participating students and determine how the school curriculum can be enriched to meet the vocational needs of this group.

A community work station has also been established at the Manchester Senior Citizen Center, where an instructor has been hired two days a week to provide a food service training program. The students have been learning about the care and maintainence of equipment, safety, preparation of sandwiches, and the correct way of serving. An outcome of this project is a low-cost luncheon every Monday for the Senior Citizens. A typical menu includes an egg salad sandwich, beverage, and fruit cup for 40 cents. There has been a very enthusiastic response and the Senior Citizens are petitioning for daily service.

The instructor has established a training program with three major objectives: 1) development of marketable skills in food service, 2) encouragement of proper attitudes toward work, and 3) growth of desirable social skills within a realistic work setting. If a student sets a table incorrectly, there is sufficient time for the supervisor to again explain the correct way and require that he do it right. One of the basic failures of many apprentice programs is the lack of supervisory time given to teaching a skill to a retardate. For example, a trainee might be shown how to operate a dishwasher once and then be on his inadequate resources. In the team work approach, students learn their jobs to the point where their success is almost guaranteed. While no one expects that every student will develop skills to the point of complete competitive employment in the community, all develop a great deal of self-reliance.

An examination of the literature indicates that the crew approach has been successful in a variety of places and settings. While automation and the increasing complexities of industrial society are rapidly eliminating some of the traditional job sources for the retarded, it is encouraging to note the development of new techniques.

For example, the U.S. Department of Health, Education, and Welfare has financed a research and demonstration project utilizing the "team approach" in the Kfar Nachman Institution near Tel Aviv, Israel (Chigier, Fendell). This project has hopeful implications for thousands of severely retarded adolescents institutionalized throughout the world. The Israeli retardates, ranging in chronological age from 17 to 22 years and with mental ages of 6 years or less, would probably spend their lives in closed residential facilities. Dr. E. Chigier, pediatrician and project director, asks the following question:
Is the institution to be a place of custody for them? At worst, a prison, at best a convalescent home—or can the institution provide a meaningful existence? (Chigier)
A group of the Israeli adults, hitherto considered "hopeless cases," have been trained in weeding, hoeing, pruning, and fruit-picking. They work as a supervised group in citrus groves and are paid for their production. For such human beings on the fringe of society, for generations condemned to months and years of idleness, an opportunity to enrich their lives physically and mentally by being productive is a beacon of light.

The San Juan Unified School District in Sacramento, California, is using groups of trainable students as a cleanup crew at a public recreation area, cleaning ditches, pulling weeds, and doing brush removal, and also for numerous gardening jobs (Hansen). In Chicago, two teachers and a group of retardates operate a pet shop.

In our society, money is the basic incentive for motivating

productivity. In regular high school work-study programs for the retarded and in sheltered workshops, this same incentive has been used successfully. While the primary emphasis of team work experience has been on training in occupational skills, it is recognized that the moderately retarded are entitled to a monetary reward for their economic product. This represents an adult role that they can attain. It is improbable that they will ever assume other adult roles, such as father, homebuilder, or automobile owner.

The vocational instructors have made some interesting observations in relation to remuneration as an incentive. Receiving money for washing cars, shoveling snow, and working in food service was important for members of the team; the actual amounts did not make too much difference. Piece rates help the students to see the relationship of effort, production, and pay. While candy, free meals, and trading stamps have been used as rewards, the financial incentive, without doubt, was the most effective.

Can a complex industrialized society in which inefficiency, waste, and marginal productivity are negative factors make provision for team work experience? Supervised work in the community is similar to the sheltered workshop for "terminal clients"; both projects invariably operate at a financial loss. Dr. Max Dubrow (1961), director of the New York ARC Workshop, justifies the habilitation philosophy of helping the retardate in our economy to achieve his highest level of functioning in the following terms:

If there are values of dignity, worth, and self-respect inherent in work per se, these values should apply to sheltered as well as to competitive employment. The absolute amounts of productivity or earnings are not necessarily the only or even the major criterion which determine these values. A client whose best efforts yield only a modest wage can be as proud of his achievements as another client who earns considerably more but operates at much less than his optimum potential. We have to guard against a tendency to equate meaning of work with wages earned.

The U.S. Department of Labor has given official status to the marginal productivity of the moderately and severely mentally retarded. Rehabilitation facilities can receive Work Activity Center Permits, requiring no minimum wage, because of the "inconsequential product and therapeutic nature" of the programs for these clients. Traditionally, vocational rehabilitation services have concentrated on the more able mentally retarded, who have the potential for gainful employment. In order to be realistic, services for the less able should focus on the rehabilitation goal of living more independently in the community, rather than vocational placement.

Legislation was proposed in Congress in 1957, 1959, and 1961 to amend the federal Vocational Rehabilitation Act of 1954, providing seriously handicapped adults with appropriate rehabilitation services that would enable them to "achieve such ability of independent living as to eliminate or substantially reduce the burden of their care." In spite of the fact that this proposed independent-living rehabilitation legislation has been rejected by Congress, there are indications that similar proposals will eventually be passed in the forthcoming decade. The moderately and severely retarded deserve a share of the Great Society.

There are six distinct advantages of the team work experience.

1. The instructor works with a group of five retardates on a job and is able to provide individual instruction for each member.

2. Team members have the opportunity to compete with persons in their own ability range, which encourages each member to work his hardest. They do not become discouraged by the necessity of competing with so-called normals.

3. Team work provides social experiences in a community setting, allowing the participating members to work together in harmony.

4. The team approach provides some of the members with the work skills that might eventually lead to competitive employment. The less able retardate, who can make a very limited contribution to the total effort of the team, can still be included.

5. Teams can become proficient by constant repetition of

the same job, as in washing cars. They can do more work and earn more money.

There will be many possibilities for the team work experience concept during the coming decade. A great deal will depend on the initiative and creativity of the program administrators. Teams could be used to do the domestic work for homeowners, clean up parks and public recreation areas, and operate a "pet-walking" service.

The primary goal of team work experience will always be to help the mentally retarded adjust to independent living. There appears to be general agreement among the specialists that this is best carried out in a work-oriented program, giving the individual a feeling of productivity and values conforming to the cultural norms. Since Americans have always admired the "team spirit" of the athletic field, there is reason to believe that team work experience will be accepted with equal enthusiasm.

REFERENCES

Chigier, E.: The Use of Group Dynamics in the Rehabilitation of Severely Retarded Adolescents in an Institution in Israel. *Annual, Israel National Soc for Rehab of the Disabled*, Oct. 1968. 5:53–58.

Dubrow, Max: Patterns of Programming. Paper presented at conference at Manns Choice, Pa., May 25, 1961.

Fendell, Norman: Israel's Eternal Children. *Digest of the Mentally Retarded*, Fall, 1969. 6:1:19–22.

Hansen, Carl E.: The Work Crew Approach to Job Placement for the Severely Retarded. *J Rehab*, May-June, 1969. 35:3:26–27.

Weingold, Joseph T.: The Place of the Community in the Vocational Rehabilitation of the Mentally Retarded Secondary Student. Lecture at Syracuse University. May 15, 1963.

CHAPTER 9

THE RANCH*

JOHN H. DUNN

~~~~~~

V IC HELLMAN'S 60-ACRE WORKSHOP just northwest of Milwaukee represents one of the really imaginative and
more effective approaches to the rehabilitation of the mentally retarded.

Naturally enough, it's labeled The Ranch.

Though classified as a rehabilitation facility in Wisconsin
DVR parlance, it bears little resemblance to the sheltered
workshop usually thought of in this reference. In fact, Vic
would resent the comparison, so sold is he on this unique,
open-air attack on retardation. He is fully aware of the value
of sheltered workshops by virtue of his long experience as
a training supervisor in Jewish Vocational Services. On the
other hand, he feels that The Ranch represents a giant step
forward in the training of the retarded, and results thus far
give him good grounds for enthusiasm.

The Ranch has no walls to close in on and stifle the young
retardates. Let Vic explain what this means in his own words.

"What The Ranch has done for these kids is to let them
have the opportunity to spread their wings. One boy is a
perfect example. He was in classes for the retarded in a Milwaukee high school, and he was sent here as a classroom
disrupter. When he came I spoke to him about his difficulties
in school."

His explanation to Vic suggested that the problem was not

* Used with permission from, *Rehabilitation Record,* July-August, 1971.

in the boy but rather in the system and its lack of anything meaningful for him in the classroom.

"Did you ever sit in a room where the walls kept pushing you down?" the boy asked.

"I told him I knew he had capabilities and asked him if he thought he could make some rabbit hutches from plans I had. He said he'd sure like to try, and so I told him to grab a partner and the necessary tools and make one for me. He did a great job. I told him we needed 48 more, and this was no make-believe job. We had to have them because we were breeding rabbits.

"The boy did real well. We had him here about a year and then placed him down in Milwaukee in metal processing. He went in as a laborer and ended up as an inspector within a few months."

Later, the boy asked Vic if he thought the army would accept him.

"I knew he could make it, but when I asked him if he wanted some help enlisting, he said he wanted to try it alone. He enlisted, and last December 13 he came and knocked on the door here, fresh from Vietnam. His only comment was 'Who said a damn retarded can't make it? Here I am!'

"He took pride in himself. He took pride in the fact that he could make good. And he proved the whole theory that the teacher would not believe, that the classroom walls came in on him. One of the supervisors from the Milwaukee school system made the same point, when he told me 'I like The Ranch and The Ranch concept because the classroom has no walls.' "

Vic admitted that the no-walls idea sometimes encourages the kids to run off into the isolation of the 60 acres.

"And do you know where they run to? Up in the woods. This is wrong, and we'll reprimand the kid, but how many of us so-called normals would like to have a chance to run up into the woods and sit? So you can't really call it wrong. We're now planning to build a chapel in those woods."

Plans for the chapel are moving ahead, thanks to community support in nearby Menomonee Falls and elsewhere. The Jaycees' and Jaycettes' "Pennies for The Ranch Chapel" campaign is nearing the $7,000 mark. A Catholic parish at Winneconne, 125 miles north, is building a new church and offered its old one to The Ranch.

"We couldn't take the building itself, but we have all the pews, altars, stained glass windows, and light fixtures. The people up there feel so proud that parts of their church will come down to our God's Corner Chapel," Mr. Hellman said.

The Ranch is on a state highway only minutes away from fire and police protection and from the community hospital in the Milwaukee suburb of Menomonee Falls. Although it now has strictly a day program, future plans call for a residential facility.

Vic Hellman's ideas for The Ranch came as an aftermath of a heart attack 7 years ago. Following the death of his retarded 6-year-old son in the 1950's, Vic took the money from memorials and set it aside, hoping someday to help the retarded. While recuperating from the cardiac seizure, he got the idea for The Ranch, and it seemed like a fitting tribute to his son. Memorials for his 15-year-old daughter, killed in a car accident 4 years ago, helped expand the facility.

"And so in The Ranch, I have more than my own desires. I have my family," Vic said.

Animals are basic to any ranch, and this one is no different. They breed sheep and sell the lambs; breed cows and raise the calves for market.

"This means dollars and cents to The Ranch. We took five calves to market the other day and averaged $108 each. This allows us to do more building, more developing. But the calves play another important role in our program. When the calf is really young, the kids have the responsibility first to bottle feed it; then they do the regular feeding. And they must make sure the calves go down three times a day for water. Now we could eliminate this by putting a water station right down there in the pen, but we would be eliminating the responsibility they are assuming," Vic noted.

Not everyone can see the value in having the retarded work with animals, he admitted. A skeptic from one agency insisted that a kid isn't going to make a living petting a cow all his life.

"Such critics don't recognize that for the first time in his life, the retarded boy has someone who is dependent on him, even though it might just be an animal. But, by golly, they've got something to relate to, and they've got something that will relate to them.

"Here's a perfect example. One boy we had here had no form of communication. He wouldn't talk. Then one of my supervisors said he thought he had the answer. He gave him a pig and showed him how to train it. Soon the boy was communicating with the pig, had him jumping over logs, walking up steps, and, on cue, sitting down on his back end to get something to eat. The boy could walk away while we held the pig on a leash, and the pig would cry like mad. Unleashed, the animal would run over to the boy and reach up to be petted.

"We got the boy talking one day when we said to the pig, 'Piggy, you don't look as though you've had anything to eat. Maybe we should get somebody who could take care of you.'"

"I did too feed piggy," the boy quickly replied.

"It was a rebellious remark, but it cracked the ice! And now no matter who he sees, the boy goes up to him and says hello and tries to talk and tries to communicate what he's been doing. And this has been great. It took over a year and could not have been achieved in a simple workshop job.

"When you can get the retarded or some other handicapped person who needs our service to first accept us, then you can start your training. And that might take 6 hours, 6 days, 6 months or 6 years. And it's such a variable that no one can come up with a statistic that would be an honest one," Mr. Hellman stressed.

In addition to its domestic livestock, The Ranch also has a full-fledged zoo, particularly important from a public relations standpoint. People come from miles around to see the animals and birds, and while there they learn something about mental retardation.

Vic is no shrinking violet, either in size or personality. He knows he has something worthwhile in The Ranch, and he is eager for others to know about it. His regular newsletter keeps a large audience informed as to developments at The

Ranch. In addition he appears as Farmer Vic on Milwaukee's TV channel 4. He brings an animal to the program, discusses it, and urges viewers to visit The Ranch.

"After they are out here to see the animals, we can show them the things the kids have done. I can't ask people to come out just to look at the kids. . . ."

What does the visitor see? First, the neatly maintained grounds.

"All the landscaping is the boys'. And the rock garden. We brought those large rocks out of our own field and used mule power and a stone boat; the old fashioned way of doing it. The kids harnessed and drove the mules. Now I know they are not going to get a mule job in Milwaukee, but the job helps them learn responsibility. This is much different from 9 months of packing checkers in a box under a sub-contract."

And the boys have done much more to build up The Ranch.

"They put in the basement for the school building. When you walk through the barn at the start of the tour, you go through a cave-like entrance. The kids made it out of field stone with beams overhead. The kids took straight beams and made them look like rustic old beams."

And they put up fences on the property.

"What does a kid accomplish doing this? Obviously, he won't make a living putting up fences, but in making it he'll have to learn how to plan, and that's important for anything he is going to do. What tools will he need? How far apart do the poles go? That question makes numbers a reality. And when he is through, he can look at the fence and be proud that he made it or had a big part in making it!"

Emphasis at The Ranch is not on the development of specific job skills but on good work habits.

"All we're trying to do out here is to instill good work habits in our boys," Vic said. "First of all we emphasize being on time. Good grooming, courtesy, and good peer relationships are stressed. And they learn to take an assigned task and complete it.

"If they can develop good work habits of this type, these habits are transferable to any work situation. There are problems with the short attention span of some retarded. Also, boredom sometimes creeps in on the job. To guard against that, we always have about 12 jobs going at all times, and the moment boredom is evident, we transfer that kid to a different situation. If he gets bored, he's going to drop out. And quite frankly, I think we so-called normals react the same way."

Vic is death on the old approach of training a retarded youth for some specific service-type job such as dishwashing.

"It doesn't take much ingenuity to put an MR into a dishwashing job, but to make him a factory worker who can progress to be a machine operator, this takes placement, and most important, it takes followup. We keep in touch with the employers, but the most beautiful thing is that we have the kids calling us all the time with news of their job changes.

"A Negro boy called up to tell me that he could make more per hour by riding down to the Kenosha plant of an automobile manufacturer, and he wondered if it was all right with me. I said it was tremendous. Here was a trainable making $3.45 an hour."

Vic, who doesn't believe in IQ's, indicated that the boy tested at about 45 and had come to The Ranch from a Milwaukee school established for trainable retardates. Environment played a major role in his retardation, coming as he did from a low income, disadvantaged family.

His DVR file revealed good manual dexterity as the only bright spot in testing, and early efforts to establish direction for the boy failed. He showed no aptitude for upholstery, and small engine repair was also out. They tried many things, including horse training, but to little avail.

"He was really a nice kid who would try anything, and he didn't accept the fact that he was retarded," Mr. Hellman said. "We finally got him a job at a Milwaukee factory, but the spent too much time riding the elevator and was let go. His next job was at an automobile plant, and there his dexterity has paid off on an assembly line. By transferring to the Kenosha plant, he indicates he's up to $3.45 an hour."

Vic noted another trainable now making $2.60 an hour at a Milwaukee factory. This boy is retarded and also has epilepsy.

"But he's been working a couple of years with no absences."

Some of his boys do go into food service, as in the case of four Ranch graduates who became a part of the Marquette University food-service setup.

"Then there was a big shift, with the service being taken over by a private group. And though there was a complete reshuffling under the new management, our retardeds stayed on because of their attendance and work records."

Mr. Hellman is proud of the work records of many of his boys, such as those at a chocolate factory in Milwaukee.

"Six of our boys received their 2-year pins at the factory. But before the company president made the award at a formal presentation, he said he would have to stop for an explanation. 'The next six pins I give out are to men who have never missed a minute. I'm sorry I can't say that about all of you.'"

Job placement by The Ranch has been very successful.

"Our placement record is 39 percent of the boys we've worked with as opposed to 23 percent in a large sheltered workshop in the area. And our placements are good ones. They stick. Those that we've placed have averaged about 11 months in training. You can't put a time limit on training."

The staff likes to expose the boys to a variety of work. They keep emphasizing that a boss likes a man who can do many jobs, and a number of employers seem satisfied with Ranch graduates. For instance, one Milwaukee shop employs seven men, five of whom came from The Ranch. Two run spot welding machines, and the others are doing general work, shipping and receiving, and stock handling. Some boys get into Ranch-related work.

"Last summer we had five kids up north doing farm work. We have one boy at a horse training stable in Illinois, and he's assistant trainer. He came from a family of 10, of which three are retarded. We're getting his brother next week."

Occasionally the placement problems have been of a type that can't be anticipated. For instance, The Ranch had 12 graduates in a Milwaukee factory which a union tried to organize. Some of the organizers made threatening remarks to the boys, and before long they were afraid to go to work. Vic knew the union head and knew also that he was concerned with the retarded.

"I asked him what he would do if a union moved in and harassed retarded kids with threats. He said he would take violent action, and then I told him it was his union. He looked into it, and there was no further trouble. Later they lost the election and blamed me."

But out of this came something good.

"Jointly we are holding classes with union organizers on how to handle a situation where the handicapped are involved. They have openly declared this is a new project of theirs, and our kids are going to get a break since they're not going to get fought so hard."

At the time of the interview, 53 boys were at The Ranch, ranging in IQ from 28 upward. But Vic opposes use of IQ measurements, being more concerned with how the boys do in their work assignments than how they score on the standardized tests.

Most of the boys come either from DVR or the Milwaukee School Board. Sixteen is the minimum for DVR; there is no top limit. Some are in their thirties. While retardation is the basic problem, it is sometimes complicated by other conditions, as in the case of the cerebral palsied, epileptic, brain damaged, and emotionally disturbed, among others, being served at The Ranch.

Vic gets some tragic cases. He cited a 21-year-old referred by a county social worker.

"We found him a foster home, and he came to The Ranch during the day. He didn't speak when we got him here, only grunted, and you had to look into his eyes to tell which way he grunted. He was with us about 18 months, and we finally found a job for him in Menomonee Falls. He is still working, going into his third year. He missed only one day with a cold. He still doesn't communicate too well, but he's a taxpayer now, and before we got him he spent 8 years in the basement with his dog.

"It's no wonder that some of them have severe emotional problems and stammer and stutter. Take that boy over there. He's from a broken home, and his mother gave me three phone numbers to try in case of an emergency. All three are taverns."

The Ranch thus works with a highly diverse group as related

to race, age, background, and disabilities. Vic wishes that the world outside those 60 acres could get along as well together as the boys do there.

"If only we normals would listen to what these retarded tell us, such as there is no such thing as prejudice; there is no hate. They love more intensely, and if they do have a problem, they air it, and it's done. We have the usual conflicts, and we let the kids iron them out themselves. We don't step in unless there's a threat of violence."

Vic Hellman believes that in many instances the handicapped's limitations are at least partially parent induced.

"The overprotective parents feel that their handicapped child should not participate in sports or otherwise compete because the child has something wrong with him. But we don't look at what the kid has wrong. We just take his assets, utilize those, and ignore his handicap. And the kid ignores it and will work twice as hard."

Athletic competition is encouraged.

"One of the biggest sports the kids have is wrestling at noon. It's not at all uncommon to see 10 or 12 wrestling matches going on at the same time. And there's a supervisor out there to make sure no one pulls anything that might be harmful. We have one boy with cerebral palsy who has such bad legs it's pitiful, but he beat one of the strongest boys here the other day, and he didn't use his legs at all, just his waist and arms. But he was participating in bodily contact as men and boys know it."

Another thing Vic is proud of is their newly developed agility course.

"There aren't too many such courses around, and this one is creating quite a stir. I designed it to instill competition. And it's working. We first run the kids against a stop watch, and then we take like times and pit them against each other. It's not uncommon to hear at the end of a race, 'You might be able to run faster, but I can work better, because my supervisor told me.' The kids run through a series of mazes, and for motivation there may be a six pack of candy for the winner."

The Ranch staff has six full-time and two part-time members. In addition, the Milwaukee School Board assigns two teachers and a teacher's aide full time. Services of a school social worker and a speech therapist are available part-time. Although separate agencies may be involved, such as DVR and the Milwaukee schools, the programs are developed together, and there is no apparent separation, the boys going from program to program.

In the well-equipped shop of the school section, the boys have industrial arts-type instruction. They learn to handle tools, power and nonpower. Some become quite skillful. Take the case of the young man who showed exceptional talent in stone cutting. A lapidary specialist out of Milwaukee volunteers his services once weekly at The Ranch, and at present he is training the boy as an opal cutter. It is expected that the youth can eventually setup a profitable shop in his home.

The Ranch lacks the rigidity of more formal approaches to training the retarded.

"When our kids have problems, and they have them on the job, that's when we sit down and talk with them. We don't schedule an appointment later, because by that time the problem is forgotten, even though they've never had a solution."

"We have a speech therapist who comes out here from Milwaukee. I think it would warm your heart to see how she does her speech therapy many times right where the boys are working, using the work situation as a tool in speech therapy. Isn't this a lot better than taking a kid out of his environment, over to a building he isn't used to, seating him on a hard chair, locking the door, and then trying to teach him?"

Vic Hellman believes The Ranch demonstrates that his approach to the rehabilitation of the retarded is humane, economically sound, and successful. He proves daily that the retarded don't necessarily have to be trained as robots for simple, routine jobs, but that once given a chance for self-expression, often they reveal hidden talents.

As he continues to improve the services at The Ranch, he is also going ahead with an even greater extension of this concept. On a 500-acre tract near Green Bay, Vic plans to use The Ranch approach to rehabilitate the disadvantaged as well as the retarded.

PART III

PHYSICAL DISABILITY

Chapter 10

CARING FOR CHILDREN WITH SICKLE CELL ANEMIA*

CAMILLE D. ALEXANDER

~~~~~~

The Nurse
Feelings About the Disease
A Child's Problems
Hospital Care
Care Between Crises
Other Workers
Continuous Care
Education and Casefinding
References

~~~~~~

THROUGHOUT HIS LIFE the child with sickle cell anemia faces the possibility of sudden painful crisis episodes that may keep him in the hospital or away from his normal activities for days. In caring for a child in a sickle cell crisis, the focus of the pediatric health team is on the child and his family.

There is as yet no cure and no magic formula for treatment of this wasteful disease of black children. But there are specific approaches to the crises and problems that can be individualized according to the needs of each child, his family, and the setting involved.

* Used with permission from, *Children,* November-December, 1971.

Black families have been largely alone in their struggles against sickle cell anemia, an inherited disease with chronic aspects (Scott, 1971a). Although estimates suggest the disease affects 1 in 500 black Americans, no actual survey has been made to accurately define the incidence of sickle cell anemia in the black population. There has been no mobilization of finances, research, and other resources against sickle cell anemia comparable to the nationwide campaigns against phenylketonuria (PKU) and cystic fibrosis. Yet the latter diseases of whites do not affect as large a segment of the population as sickle cell disease—PKU occurring in 1 of 10,000 live white births and cystic fibrosis in 1 of 1,000 to 2,000 live white births (Marlow).

Fortunately Federal funds have recently been earmarked to support research and to expand the efforts to find a cure. Some support will also go to providing service, which must not be overlooked as part of the sickle cell disease picture.

Furthermore, black health professionals and the black community as a whole must be included from the beginning in all planning, research, administration, and service activities related to the disease, since they are directly affected by such programs.

THE NURSE

As the health professional who is responsible for daily care of the child with sickle cell anemia, the hospital staff nurse has a crucial role to play as a member of the pediatric health team. In examining the nurse's work as it applies to sickle cell anemia, I have drawn on my experience in the Department of Nursing Service and the Department of Pediatrics at Howard University-Freedman's Hospital in Washington, D.C., for a general guide.

I do not intend to imply that the Department of Pediatrics at Freedman's Hospital institutes comprehensive care for every young patient. The work load, environment, and makeup of the comprehensive multidisciplinary team affect the implementation of care for the patient and the interaction of professional and subprofessional health workers.

However, I believe the approaches used at Freedman's Hospital can be as useful to the nurse serving in a physician's office, home, community health agency, and public or parochial school as in the hospital.

The major functions of the hospital staff nurse in relation to sickle cell anemia lie in the following areas:

1. Anticipatory guidance.
2. Coordination and continuity of patient and family care.
3. Health education and casefinding.

Although I see these as major functions in caring for a child with sickle cell anemia, I believe they may also apply to children with other chronic illnesses.

By "anticipatory guidance" I mean the process by which the staff nurse anticipates for parents and interprets to parents the kinds of behavior that can be expected of children with sickle cell anemia at various ages and at various times of stress (Scott, 1971b).

FEELINGS ABOUT THE DISEASE

In trying to reach the child and his family, the nurse must first assess the way parents feel about the child's illness. Her impressions of the child's and the parents' reactions to sickle cell disease may change as she meets the family in different settings—the home, clinic, school, doctor's office, or emergency situations—and according to the age of the child and the severity of his condition.

The nurse also must keep in mind that parents often fear censure or reproach by those in authority and, in their effort to gain approval, may hide their feelings or hold back information regarding the child. By phrasing open end questions and restating the parents' comments, the nurse gives them an opportunity to examine their feelings about themselves and the child. She listens calmly, accepting and encouraging the parents to express their negative feelings in order to help them clarify their own thinking.

Health professionals are better able to help a child if they understand some of the family's fears. It is not unusual for children to sense the parents' apprehension about hospitalization. I have found it helpful to ask the parents about their past hospitalizations and talk about their hangups in an attempt to separate their experiences from the child's experience.

A hospitalized child with sickle cell anemia may ask questions that his parents are unprepared to discuss: "Am I going to get well?" "Am I going to die?" Other questions of this type may appear in a disguised form. By telling the parents how to recognize the child's apprehension and encouraging them to let the older child talk about the unpleasant aspects of the disease when he asks unexpected questions, the nurse provides anticipatory guidance that enables the child and the parents to adjust to reality.

The nurse also tries to relieve the child's anxieties about his illness. One way of doing this is to allow the child to explain what is happening to him, and to listen closely to what he says. Role playing of a doctor or a nurse often encourages a child to voice some of his own apprehensions. The young child often expresses his frustrations best through play activities involving finger paints, clay, singing, drawing, dolls, music and noise, and pounding boards.

A CHILD'S PROBLEMS

The child with sickle cell anemia is faced with many of the following problems that the well child does not face:

He has to visit the doctor and go to the hospital frequently.

He takes special medications.

He needs protection from colds, pneumonia, intestinal upsets, and other infections that may precipitate crises.

He suffers from episodes of crisis lasting approximately 1 week and occurring several times a year.

He is thin and small for his age.

He may exhibit feelings of inferiority because of his inability to compete physically with his friends and classmates.

He is frequently absent from school and is sometimes behind his age group.

The nurse can alleviate some fears of the parents of a school-age child by stressing the following positive factors:

Sickle cell disease does not affect intelligence.

Between the crisis episodes the child may join in the usual activities of his age group, with the exception of strenuous sports that result in fatigue. Physicians hold differing opinions about the sports and activities an affected child may safely engage in.

Parents who know in advance that their child may not always be able to participate in strenuous sports can steer him into school, church, and other activities in which he can excel. Activities that may earn the acceptance of friends in his age group include art, painting, handicrafts, debating, composition, chess, checkers, and monopoly.

Through informal counseling the nurse can do a great deal in helping parents recognize and anticipate the needs of a preschool child entering the hospital for treatment of sickle cell anemia for the first time. A child usually reacts to separation from his family in three phases. The first phase is the period of protest; the second, the period of despair; and the third, the period of comfortable adjustment. Parents who have been advised in advance of what reactions to expect can ease the transition of a child from the home to the hospital. For example, the mother may ask the child to help select and pack the items he will need for his hospital stay. Or she may let the child draw a picture of the hospital, the doctor, and a nurse as she tells him what he will experience.

HOSPITAL CARE

A child admitted repeatedly to the hospital in a sickle cell crisis or other emergency situations requires understanding and emotional support from nurses and parents alike, particularly in terms of previous traumatizing experiences that may have occurred in the hospital. He needs to be reassured that his parents have not rejected him. Parents should be encouraged to visit him regularly and, when possible, participate in his care so he does not feel that they have "given him up" to the hospital.

A child hospitalized in a sickle cell crisis requires the following kinds of medical and nursing care:

1. Administration of medication to relieve pain and antibiotics to control respiratory infections and pneumonia.

2. Administration of oxygen and blood transfusions as indicated.

3. Adequate fluid intake and output.

4. Proper nutrition through the serving of well-balanced meals.

5. Care of the skin, good hygiene, and precautions to avoid bruises and cuts that may lead to infection.

6. Maintenance of proper elimination.

7. Assurance of proper rest.

8. Encouragement of normal exercises and activity after the crisis state has subsided.

During the hospital stay, the health team provides medical and nursing care and the nurse continues to give anticipatory guidance to the child and his family. Since children often have distorted ideas about illness and what is happening to them in a hospital, a simple explanation of the procedures for treating sickle cell anemia should be given frequently to both the patients and the parents. An older child can be encouraged to write a story about his hospital stay for discussion with parents and hospital staff.

To continue as a normal a pattern of daily living as possible for a hospitalized child, numerous hospitals around the Nation have set up special programs to provide diversional activities. Aimed at meeting both the child's psychological and physical needs, the program at Freedman's Hospital is operated by a Recreational Therapy Department within the Department of Pediatrics.

CARE BETWEEN CRISES

Before a child with sickle cell anemia leaves the hospital, he and his parents need information about how to prevent or minimize crisis episodes. This vital role often falls to the staff nurse, although it may be assumed by any health professional. In counseling parents about the child's activities between the crisis episodes, the nurse may offer the following advice:

Make sure you and the child know how active the doctor wants the child to be. If you do not understand, ask a direct question about what is prohibited.

Do not overindulge the child with toys and gifts.

Treat the child as normally as possible, but set and enforce limits for him.

Answer questions about sickle cell anemia from other children in the family honestly.

Explain the nature of the disease to older children so they will not resent the treatment and special care the child with sickle cell anemia needs. Usually older children welcome an opportunity to be taken into the parents' confidence.

Serve well-balanced meals selected from the basic four food groups. Encourage frequent small meals when the child's appetite is poor and supplement the diet with milkshakes.

OTHER WORKERS

I will not attempt to describe the team process by which professional and subprofessional health workers interrelate with each other, the young patient, and his family. However, I will describe briefly some of the team members at Freedman's Hospital and their roles in caring for the child with sickle cell anemia.

In addition to the physician and the staff nurse, the dietitian, child psychiatrist, social worker, public health nurse, physical therapist, and speech therapist are members of the pediatric health team. The teacher and the school nurse often assist the team.

The dietitian plays a key role in interpreting the dietary needs of the child with sickle cell anemia to his family. In an informal discussion with the mother, she suggests ways of making liver and greens appetizing, but points out that the child should not be forced to eat liver or any other food. After the mother and the dietitian review the basic four food groups and discuss selection of foods to meet the nutritional needs of the child, the dietitian encourages the mother to serve basic foods to the entire family. Frequently mothers ask the dietitian to recommend foods that can be substituted or exchanged for those in a special diet. The dietitian also reports to the health team about nutritional problems.

The child psychiatrist provides individual counseling to

the parents upon request, and explains the effects of sickle cell anemia on child behavior, growth, and development.

The social worker cooperates with the physician, hospital staff nurse, and public health nurse in planning and coordinating activities related to discharge of the young patient. Other major activities of the social worker include evaluating family relationships, assessing the parents' acceptance and understanding of sickle cell anemia, determining the financial impact of the illness on the family, and assessing and interpreting to the health team the behavior of families with psychosocial problems that may effect the adjustment of the patient to his illness. The social worker also coordinates hospital social services with those of community agencies.

The hospital-based public health nurse and the community-based public health nurse complement each other in planning with the parents prior to and following the child's discharge from the hospital. Cooperatively or individually they evaluate the family's ability to meet the needs of the child, assess available nursing care, health information, and provisions for meeting related needs of the child and his family, and assist parents in understanding and accepting the illness. They also report verbally and in writing their observations and assessments of the family to the pediatric team so followup medical and nursing care can be planned after the child returns home. By coordinating and providing liaison activities, these nurses promote continuity of care to the patient and family before and after the child's discharge from the hospital.

The physical therapist serves as a consultant on the pediatric health team. Among other services, she assesses the child's functional ability, strength, and mobility, and plans for the physical therapy. This includes interpreting physical therapy needs to the members of the health team, particularly to the public health nurse, who is available to direct the family in carrying out recommendations.

The speech therapist also serves as a consultant to the health team. He evaluates the child's speech and language disorders and develops a treatment plan. Assessments are made periodically to determine progress and necessary modifications in the plan. In addition, the speech therapist explains the child's speech and language needs to the family.

Although not technically a member of the health care team, the school teacher who understands sickle cell disease obviously is better able to help the child and his family. The school teacher must try to protect the child from drafts in the classroom and exposure to colds and other infections that may precipitate a crisis. She needs to be aware of the signs of an impending crisis. These include complaints of pain in the back, arms, hands, feet, legs, or the abdomen; the appearance of a slightly yellow hue to the whites of the eye; and listlessness.

The child may have prolonged periods of absenteeism from school due to a sickle cell crisis. Therefore, the school teacher must be supportive to the child and family in regard to his school work and the chronic nature of his illness.

The school nurse, the hospital-based public health nurse, and the community public health nurse work cooperatively with the child and his family. The school nurse helps the teacher recognize symptoms of impending crisis and deviations from normal behavior that may be related to the child's illness. The nurse helps school administrators find ways of meeting the needs of children with sickle cell anemia and uses all her contacts with the child, teacher, and family for teaching about health and providing emotional support. Her activities also include regular reports to the health team about the child's school adjustment.

CONTINUOUS CARE

The health team's second major area of involvement in relation to sickle cell anemia is to ensure that the service to the child and his family is both coordinated and continuous. We are all too aware of the gaps in the health care system and the fragmentation and duplication in care and services.

I cannot help but wonder how often the information in the child's health records is transmitted from the private physician's office to the hospital when hospital admission is contemplated. When the child transfers from one school to another, how soon does his health record follow? How well does the hospital plan with the public health agency for discharge and home followup? When information in health records is not transmitted among the various services in the community or utilized by them, the child is the loser.

EDUCATION AND CASEFINDING

The third area of concern for the health team is health education and casefinding. Surely our nation, with its highly developed communications system, is able to increase the awareness of thousands of black Americans about the disease, its disabling effects and high death rates, and other implications involved in its transmission to children. A nationwide multifaceted program, similar to veneral disease eradication efforts in the 1940s and 1950s, would involve informing the public about the disease itself, screening potential carriers, and counseling families at risk regarding the genetic aspects of sickle cell anemia.

Black mothers should be routinely screened for sickle cell disease in prenatal clinics, and, when the trait is found, given genetic counseling. Every black child admitted to a pediatric unit of a hospital should routinely have the test for sickle cell anemia. In addition, Head Start programs, schools, colleges and health clinics are appropriate sites for screening. Men inducted into the Armed Forces could be screened and given appropriate counseling as part of their physical examinations.

Members of the health team must give parents and young adults up-to-date, valid information regarding the sickle cell trait. In addition to information, health education programs must make available screening for sickle cell disease and genetic counseling so that the affected person is able to act on the facts regarding the inheritance of the disease.

REFERENCES

Marlow, R. Dorothy; Sellers, Gladys: Textbook of pediatric nursing. (Second edition.) Philadelphia, W. B. Saunders Co., 1965.

Scott, Roland B.: A commentary on sickle cell disease. *Journal of the National Medical Association*, January 1971a.

Scott, Roland B.; Kessler, Althea D.: Sickle cell anemia and your child —questions and answers on sickle cell anemia for parents. Department of Pediatrics and Child Health, Howard University College of Medicine, Washington, D.C. Spring 1971b.

CHAPTER 11

SPEECH, HEARING, AND LANGUAGE IN DE LANGE SYNDROME*

MARY VIRGINIA MOORE

Language, Hearing, Speech
Conclusions
Summary
References

THE NECESSITY AND the difficulty of differential diagnosis are heightened when the speech pathologist con-
fronts a multiply-handicapped patient. A patient with de
Lange's syndrome presents many problems. The purpose of
this paper is to summarize the clinical characteristics of de
Lange's syndrome with special reference to speech, hearing,
and language development.

Bruck described a patient in 1889 with symptoms later
associated with de Lange's syndrome (Durham, 1960). After
Cornelia de Lange of Amsterdam reported three cases in the
early 1930s, her name was given to the entity. By 1966, 76
cases had been reported (Salazar, 1966). Later McArthur and
Edwards (1967) described 20 patients seen in a single
institution. The syndrome has been comprehensively
reviewed by Jervis and Stimson (1963), Ptacek and co-workers

* Used with permission from, *Journal of Speech and Hearing Disorders*, 35:66,
1970.

(1963), and Silver (1964). Individual patients have been discussed in the light of the disciplines of psychiatry (McIntyre and Eisen, 1965), dermatology (Schuster and Johnson, 1966), and ophthalmology (Nicholson and Goldberg, 1966).

Children with de Lange's syndrome have a typical facial pattern with small nose, anteverted nostrils, a thin, downturned mouth, eyebrows that meet at the midline, and long curly eyelashes. Their grim, mask-like appearance, devoid of expression, is remarkable. Anomalies of the extremities are frequently reported. Abnormally small limbs, flexion contractures of the elbow, and absence of fingers are typical. The children have growth failure and mental retardation, and the majority have hypotonicity, mottling of the skin, syndactyly of the second and third toes, and increased hair on the body (Silver, 1964). Many of them have low birth weight, although most result from pregnancies of reportedly normal duration. Silver (1964) summarized more than 125 abnormal findings. The mainfestations vary among cases.

Schuster and Johnson (1966) report that the incidence of de Lange's syndrome is one in 10,000 live births. The etiology of the syndrome is not known. The absence of a consistent molecular or chromosomal abnormality, the lack of data concerning concordance in twins, and the sporadic nature of the appearance of the syndrome are against a predominately gene-controlled etiology. However, an increased incidence of consanguinity has been reported and suggests that rare recessive genes may be involved (Silver, 1964). McArthur and Edwards (1967) included chromosome studies on their 20 patients, and all were normal. They consider the possibility of a chromosomal deficiency that is not detectable. Their discussion of genetic implications is thorough.

LANGUAGE, HEARING, SPEECH

The de Lange patient may be referred to a speech, hearing, and language clinic with the complaint of delayed language (Ptacek et al., 1963), hearing defect (Jervis and Stimson, 1963), or unusual vocal quality (Schuster and Johnson, 1966).

Delayed Language

Delayed language is reported consistently in de Lange patients.

Mental retardation is reported in all cases. McIntire and Eisen (1965) document their conclusions with results from the Stanford Binet, the Peabody Picture Vocabulary Test, Figure Drawings and visual motor tests. They describe their patient as mildly retarded. Most cases are severely retarded.

Significant hearing loss is usually noted (Silver, 1964). Low set ears are reported in several cases. Silver's patient had ears that were normally placed but the external canals were very small. Apparent deafness has been observed. McIntire and Eisen (1965) report mildly depressed hearing sensitivity bilaterally in the low frequencies with moderate bilateral sensorineural loss in the high frequencies. Hearing of speech in their patient was mildly depressed.

General language delay commensurate with intellectual delay is, of course, expected. Hearing loss, retarded motor development, a pattern of infantile illnesses (Silver, 1964), and specific disabilities of the speech mechanism (Jervis and Stimson, 1963) contribute to delay. Familial reaction to the birth of this type of child may present less than ideal environmental stimulation for language learning. Any one of these factors can be responsible for profound language delay. Sophisticated language and audiological measurements are needed. Only gross estimates are available for most patients.

Mental retardation overlaid with hearing loss may be the most significant etiological factor in the delay of language skills in de Lange patients.

Speech Development

Little information is available regarding speech development in de Lange patients. McIntyre and Eisen (1965) estimate the expressive and comprehensive vocabulary of their seven-year-old patient as being below a four-year level. Since they chose the Stanford-Binet, which demands speech from the testee, to evaluate the intellect of their patient, it may be inferred that the patient was using speech intelligible to strangers. No specific comment is made regarding the child's articulation, voice quality, or fluency. McArthur and Edwards (1967) summarize 23 cases and conclude that "the major retardation was that of speech. Speech was far more retarded than comprehension and learning."

A characteristic vocal quality is noted in the crying of de Lange patients. Nicholson and Goldberg (1966) describe it as a feeble, low-pitched cry. Schuster and Johnson (1966) report that patients have "low-pitched, growling, gutteral, deep and raucous cry . . . so characteristic that the diagnosis can be made without seeing the patient." Silver's (1964) patient was a small, strong, irritable, retarded child with a weak, low-pitched, growling cry. Ptacek (1963) summarized the findings in 35 cases and found that the unusual cry was noted in 12 of these reports. The vocal characteristic is present at birth and continues. The cry of one patient (Schuster and Johnson, 1966) was spectrographically analyzed and found to be of low frequency and intensity.

Abnormalities of the speech mechanism are reported: micrognathia, upturned nostrils, small nose, profuse rhinorrhea, wide space between mouth and nose, downturned lips, a "beak" at the midline of the upper lip, a narrow palatal arch, palatal clefts, and malspaced teeth. However, these peripheral deviations do not seem significant in explaining the reported voice quality. Resonatory problems associated with cleft palate, poor palatal function, and general inactivity of the articulators may be present, but they do not account for the deviant phonatory characteristics of pitch and loudness. Other reported anomalies may be significant: short, thick necks; webbing of the neck; sucking and swallowing difficulties; poor feeding habits in the first year; episodes of regurgitation; and general muscular hypotonia. Does the marbling of the skin affect the epidermal tissue of the larynx? Abnormal thyroid glands have been found postmortem: Is the low-pitched, growling cry secondary to malfunctioning thyroid glands?

CONCLUSION

Children diagnosed as having de Lange syndrome have problems related to the development of language. Even the children with mild symptoms of de Lange's syndrome are strapped with enough anomalies to significantly interfere with normal language learning. The individual variations in types and degrees of abnormalities should remind the clinician to approach each patient individually.

While the clinical manifestations have been reported comprehensively in medical literature, a paucity of information exists regarding speech, hearing, and general language development in patients with de Lange syndrome. The relative rareness of the condition places a burden of reporting on those speech pathologists who evaluate de Lange patients.

SUMMARY

The clinical features of de Lange syndrome (reported incidence 1/10,000) are described in medical literature. More than 125 abnormal findings have been reported, including delayed language, hearing loss, and a low-pitched, growling vocal cry. This paper discusses the implications for speech, hearing, and language. The need for sophisticated language reports is apparent.

REFERENCES

Durham, R.H.: *Encyclopedia of Medical Syndromes.* New York: Hoebner, Med. Div. Harper (1960), p. 145.

Jervis, G.A., and Stimson, C.W.: De Lange syndrome. *J Pediat*, 63, 634–645 (1963).

McArthur, R.G., and Edwards, J.H.: De Lange syndrome: Report of 20 cases. *Canad med Ass J*, 96, 1185–1198 (1967).

McIntyre, Matilda S., and Eisen, J.D.: The Cornelia de Lange syndrome—a case report with mild mental retardation. *Amer J ment Defic*, 70, 438–442 (1965).

Nicholson, D.H., and Goldberg, M.F.: Ocular abnormalities in the de Lange syndrome. *Arch Ophthal*, 75, 214–220 (1966).

Ptacek, L.J., Opitz, J.M., Smith, D.W., Gerritsen, T., and Waisman, H.A.: Cornelia de Lange syndrome. *J Pediat*, 63, 1000–1020 (1963).

Salazar, F.: Dermatological maifestations of the Cornelia de Lange syndrome. *Arch Derm*, 94, 38–43 (1966).

Schuster, D.S., and Johnson, S.A.M.: Cutaneous manifestations of the Cornelia de Lange syndrome. *Arch Derm*, 93, 702–707 (1966).

Silver, H.K.: The de Lange syndrome. *Amer J Dis Child*, 108, 523–529 (1964).

CHAPTER 12

REHABILITATION OF MULTIPLE
SCLEROSIS PATIENTS*

JOHN H. ALDES

~~~~~~

Treat the Patient as a Whole
Diet, Urologic Disorders
Group Therapy Vitally Important
Organized Exercise Program Debated
References

~~~~~~

SINCE THE ETIOLOGY of multiple sclerosis remains unknown, it necessarily follows that there is yet a cure to be found. In the 130 years since this disease has been called multiple sclerosis (Association for Research in Nervous & Mental Diseases, McAlpine), numerous methods of treatment have been brought forth by the medical profession and the laity. On each occasion high hopes were held by those afflicted, only to be disappointed when the claims were not substantiated by the results obtained (Schumacher; Marks; Putnam; 1947).

It is estimated that in the United States alone there are over a quarter of a million persons afflicted with multiple sclerosis (Limburg, MacLean, Kurland). Multiple sclerosis literally means "many scars." It is a demyelinating disease and usually is slowly progressive. Remissions occur fre-

* Used with permission from, *Journal of Rehabilitation* March-April, 1967.

quently with improvement or partial restoration of impaired function, sometimes for many years, but often with exacerbations of the disability in a more severe form.

Unfortunately the etilogy of multiple sclerosis is still unknown and, consequently, a cure or a preventive measure is yet to be found. Numerous treatments have been advanced by the medical profession and scientific researchers, each with high hopes, but without the hoped-for results (Brickner; Putnam, 1939; Peterson; Harrower; Schlesinger; Kabat, 1943; Aldes, 1956; Horton;). However, intensive research continues, and it is hoped that, with the discovery of the etiology, a cure—or better still a preventive measure—for multiple sclerosis will be found. In the meantime, it is the responsibility of the physician to keep patients afflicted with multiple sclerosis and its residuals in the best possible physical condition for the time when they may benefit by the fruits of this research.

TREAT THE PATIENT AS A WHOLE

In our study and care of patients with multiple sclerosis at Cedars of Lebanon Hospital over a period of 18 years, we have found that total rehabilitation is an important factor in maintaining the patient at his highest functional level and preventing irreversible pathologic changes. The patient must be treated as a *whole*, not just for a specific symptom. Because of the multiplicity of pathologic problems, medical and paramedical, specialists play a vital role in the rehabilitation program; the internist, the neurologist, the urologist, the gynecologist, the orthopedist, the ophthalmologist, the radiologist, and the psychiatrist must join forces with the physiatrist and the rehabilitationist, each contributing his specific knowledge and skill.

It is important that the patient be kept in good physical condition in order to gain maximum benefit from the functional phase of rehabilitation, which is an integrated program of physical therapy, hydrotherapy, corrective therapy, and occupational therapy (including retraining in the activities of daily living), and speech therapy. The psychologist, the vocational rehabilitation counselor, and the medical social service worker all play an integral part in the rehabilitation program, including bringing the patient's family, church, and community into the picture.

Thus, the rehabilitation program is geared to treat the *whole* individual and not just his disability. (See Figure 1.)

In the functional phase of rehabilitation, an all-active-resistive therapy program is of great value, whether the exercise is for neuromuscular reeducation of a patient with paralysis, for physical conditioning in convalescence, or for exercise conditioning of motor skills in the normal individual. The program should be based primarily on the principles of muscle physiology.

The concepts are as follows: (Kabat, 1950; Kabat, 1947; DeLorme)

1. Repeated activation of the nervous pathway from the brain to the muscle causing muscular contraction is the basis of the therapeutic effect of voluntary motion. If this pathway is excited frequently and strongly enough, improvement is characterized by an increase in the power of muscular contraction, increase in endurance, increase in muscle hypertrophy, and greater ease of muscular action in more complex coordinated patterns of voluntary motion.

2. Continued muscle activity is essential to maintain the power, endurance, and coordination of the neuromuscular mechanism. Increased activity improves voluntary motor function; decreased activity drains the efficiency and power of the neuromuscular system, resulting in muscular atrophy.

3. Voluntary motion performed by contraction of the agonist muscle results in reciprocal inhibition and relaxation of the antagonist.

4. Training of new patterns of motion is dependent on formation of new pathways in the central nervous system and a progressive decrease in the resistance at synapses in such pathways by repetitive activity. To be successful, training of a motor skill requires that the essential motions be carried out effectively in the same pattern many times. A major factor is progress, step by step, from simple to more complex motions.

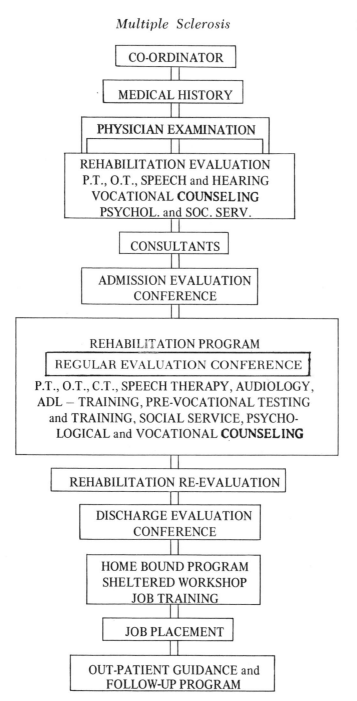

5. Successful repetition of the pattern of motion renders performances progressively less difficult.

It has been our observation that multiple sclerosis patients, while able voluntarily to contract a muscle through only a portion of its range, can produce a strong contracture in the same muscle through another portion of its range. This leads us to conclude that reflex contractions in the multiple sclerosis patient may be normal, producing a contracture impossible to break by resistance; yet the patient is quite unable, voluntarily, to contract the entire muscle.

We feel, therefore, that in order to regain good function, it is essential that the entire pathway from the brain to the muscle be reeducated.

In a total rehabilitation program for the patient with neuromuscular disease—multiple sclerosis category—careful evaluation of his disabilities is most important in order to obtain realistic therapeutic goals. Detailed knowledge of the type and extent of the patient's disabilities is necessary since treatment, although following a general pattern, is individualized for each patient. The extent of the patient's residual capabilities must be determined to outline a well-planned rehabilitation program.

The evaluation of the patient's disability is based on the results obtained from testing his functional organs of motion, amount of spasticity, muscle function, contractures, coordination, ataxia, and activities of daily living (Gordon; Rusk; Aldes, 1957b,c).

Although there has been almost universal recognition of the importance of psychosocial evaluation concerning the attitudes and temperament of each patient in the therapeutic process, there has been and remains a most significant area that is overlooked: the fact that an individual's occupation—where he spends the majority of his waking hours and most of his physical energy, and is required to effect maximal psychological adjustment—more nearly reflects his life experience than any other single aspect of his existence. Yet, in a review of medical records, one sees little more than a general and frequently inexact statement of a job title.

An evaluation, from a physical-medical point of view only.

is inadequate without knowledge and understanding of the physical demands of the patient's occupational history. Without such information, we cannot determine the extent to which disease limits or even modifies the required performance of the patient's usual job duties. Further, without evaluation of the physical demands the patient can meet, we are unable to select potential work in which he may possibly engage. It is quite conceivable that a patient even with a chronic disease may not necessarily be limited in terms of the demands of his own particular job.

In determining the patient's total capacity to engage in work, both physical therapy and occupational therapy evaluations are essential. The physical therapy evaluation includes—in addition to the standard evaluation of manual muscle testing, range of motion, gait evaluation, and activities of daily living—a separate specific physical capacities appraisal. This consists of a series of critical physical factors in job performance. Such factors as pushing, pulling, lifting, carrying, etc. are considered.

The occupational therapy evaluation comprises prevocational testing, activities of daily living, and job sample activity (work simulation) which are valuable in the total occupational assessment. Included is aptitude testing where specific occupational validity has been established, rather than generalized testing with only remote occupational relationship. Each of these disciplines is needed to complete the total assessment of potential occupational goals.

The medical evaluation of the various body systems—i.e., respiratory, cardiac, gastrointestinal, and genitourinary—is necessary for a complete picture of the patient's physical status and a determination of his endurance. Patients with multiple sclerosis are afflicted with the same diseases as are other individuals. Thus, in addition to a functional program of rehabilitation, the patient is on a supportive medical regimen to keep him in the best possible physical condition.

DIET, UROLOGIC DISORDERS

We feel that the multiple sclerosis patient should be placed on a highly fortified multi-vitamin regimen with an increase in Vitamin B-1 (thiamine chloride). Diet is also important for weight control and adequate food intake; a high protein, low fat diet is most beneficial (Aldes, 1957).

One of the paramount problems of the multiple sclerosis patient is the presence of urologic disorders which contribute greatly to repeated exacerbations. The urologist is an essential member of the rehabilitation team, for his frequent evaluation of the patient's genitourinary system is important in maintaining the patient in the best possible physical condition.

In our functional program for the multiple sclerosis patient, we have found that the reflex resistive exercise phase is an important factor. This phase is given both actively and passively, assisted and unassisted. The program is carried out by a therapist under supervision of a physician at a minimum of three times a week.

GROUP THERAPY VITALLY IMPORTANT

We have also found that group therapy is a vital factor, psychologically, in helping the patient to better understand and adjust to his disability and to enter more enthusiastically into the rehabilitation program. It serves to enhance the maximum benefit to be derived within the potential of the patient's handicap. In many cases, loss of confidence is the main barrier to a total rehabilitation.

We have observed that the multiple sclerosis patient who takes part in only the clinic program does not progress as well as the patient who is also on an active home program. The home program should be considered an integral part of the rehabilitation program since it is planned to improve the patient's muscular capacity by repetition.

The patient is taught to perform exercises for his upper and lower extremities by the use of a bilateral system of pulleys; in this manner, he can do exercises for shoulder abduction, adduction, and rotation. He is also taught exercises to strengthen the muscles of the thigh, leg, and foot with the pulley or by improvising a weight onto his shoe. If necessary, a member of the family can assist the patient in the performance of any phase of the exercises.

In the clinical program, if indicated, the patient is taught the activities of daily living such as eating, dressing, and personal hygiene. If necessary, he is instructed in the use of a wheel chair. The patient who is fully ambulatory, without cane or crutch, is trained to improve his gait, adding to his over-all coordination. The program is so planned that no phase is extensive or lengthy enough to cause injury to the musculature by overexertion or fatigue, which should be avoided at all times. The entire rehabilitation program is thus geared toward making him as independent as possible within the limits of his physical capacity.

ORGANIZED EXERCISE PROGRAM DEBATED

There has been considerable controversy about the advisability of placing multiple sclerosis patients on an organized exercise program. It has been claimed by some that the patient suffers greater exacerbations, while others feel that the ordinary daily activities afford enough exercise.

However, in our experience over the past 18 years, we have found that multiple sclerosis patients on a functional exercise program—outlined to meet their specific needs—progress far better than do the patients who remain confined to a wheel chair or in bed. Those patients on a *total* rehabilitation program maintain a high level of well-being, experience fewer exacerbations, and are able to maintain their functional level.

REFERENCES

Aldes, J.H.; Peterson, R.D.; and West, E.S.: The Use of Glycocyamine-Betaine in the Rehabilitation of Neuromuscular Disease Patients. 2nd International Cong. Phys. Med., Proc. Copenhagen, Denmark, 1956.

Aldes, J.H.: Glycocyamine-betaine as an adjunct in the treatment of neuromuscular disease patients. *Jour Ark Med Soc*, (April 24) 1957a.

Aldes, J.H.: Rehabilitation in Multiple Sclerosis. 1st Ann Conf on MS, So. Calif. MS Soc., (February 21) 1957b.

Aldes, J.H.: Rehabilitation of the Multiple Sclerosis Patient. Proc 7th World Congress Int Soc for the Welfare of Cripples. London, England, 1957c.

Assoc. for Research in Nervous & Mental Diseases. *Multiple Sclerosis*, *Vol 2*, Paul B. Hoeber, New York, 1921.

Brickner, R.M.: A critique of therapy in multiple sclerosis. *Bull Neurol Inst New York, 4:*665, 1936.

DeLorme, T.L.: Restoration of muscle power by heavy resistive exercises. *Jour Bone & Joint Surg, 27:*645 (October) 1945.

Gordon, Edward L.: Multiple Sclerosis, Application of Rehabilitation Techniques. National M S Soc, New York, 1951.

Harrower, Molly: Psychological factors in multiple sclerosis. *Ann New York Acad Sc, 58:*715–719 (July 28) 1954.

Horton, B.T.; Wagener, H.P.; Aita, J.A., and Woltman, H.W.: Treatment of multiple sclerosis by the intravenous injection of histamine. *JAMA, 124:*800.

Kabat, H., and Knapp, M.D.: The use of prostigmine in the treatment of poliomyelitis. *JAMA, 122:*989 (August 7) 1943.

Kabat, H.: Studies of neuromuscular dysfunction X: treatment of chronic multiple sclerosis with neostigmine and intensive muscle re-education, *Permanente Med Bull,* Vol 5, No. 1 (March) 1947.

Kabat, H.: Studies of neuromuscular dysfunction XII: rhythmic stabilization; a new and more effective technique for treatment of paralysis through a cerebellar mechanism. *Permanente Med Bull,* Vol 8, No. 1 (January) 1950.

Kurland, Leonard T., and Westland, Knut B.: Epidemiological factors in the etiology and prognosis of multiple sclerosis. *Ann New York Acad Sc, 58:*682–701 (July) 1954.

Limburg, C.: The Georgraphic Distribution of Multiple Sclerosis and Its Estimated Prevalence in the United States. *Assoc Res Nerv & Ment Disc,* Proc. (1948) *28:*15, 1950.

MacLean, A.R.; Berkson, J.; Woltman, H.W. and Schionneman, L.: Multiple Sclerosis in a Rural Community. *ibid 28:*25, 1950.

Marks, M.: Observations on pharmacological agents recently suggested for multiple sclerosis. *Ann New York Acad Sc, 58:*705 (July 28) 1954.

McAlpine, Douglas; Compston, Nigel D.; Lunsden, Charles E.: *Multiple Sclerosis.* Edinburgh & London, E. & S. Livingstone Ltd., 1955.

Peterson, R.D.; Beatty, C.H.; Dixon, H.H.; and West, E.S.: Effects of Glycocyamine on Creatine Phosphate Levels in Rat Muscle. Fed. Amer. Soc. for Exper. Biol. Proc. 339–254 (March) 1953.

Putnam, T.J.: Criteria of effective treatment in multiple sclerosis. *JAMA, 112:*2488 (June) 1939.

Putnam, T.J.; Chiavacci, L.V.; Hoff, H. and Weitzen, H.G.: Results of treatment of multiple sclerosis with dicoumarin. *Arch Neurol & Psychiat, 57:*1 (January) 1947.

Rusk, Howard A.: The Problems of Rehabilitation in Multiple Sclerosis. Assoc Research Nerv & Ment Dis Proc. (1948) *28:*595, 1950.

Schlesinger, E.B.: Use of curare in oil in treatment of spasticity following injury of spinal cord. *Arch Neurol and Psychiat, 55:*530 (May) 1946.

Schumacher, G.A.: Multiple sclerosis, *JAMA, 143:*1059 (July 22); 1146 (July 29) 1950.

Chapter 13

UNMASKING THE GREAT IMPERSONATOR—CYSTIC FIBROSIS*

Paul A. di Sant' Agnese

~~~~~~

IF YOU met Chris on the street, you would never suspect that this good-looking boy of eight was gravely ill. Watching him swing along with his school books—laughing, shouting, pushing, and being pushed by his classmates—you probably would take him for just another bubbling, healthy child.

But Chris is a victim of one of the most serious diseases that attack children—cystic fibrosis. During the night, Chris sleeps under a plastic tent. He is immersed in a dense mist of water and chemicals which he breathes to loosen and liquefy the thick, gluey mucus that, because of his illness, accumulates in his lungs.

During the day, to further dislodge the tenacious, abnormal mucus that interferes with normal lung operation and to combat the lung infection it promotes, Chris at times dons an aerosol mask and inhales a prescribed dosage of antibiotics. This therapeutic procedure is followed by another called postural drainage—getting the patient to cough up the loosened mucus. Tilting the boy in various positions, his parents clap with cupped hands over the affected areas of his lungs, in the manner taught by a physical therapist.

"It's like getting catsup out of a bottle when it's thick," the therapist explained to them.

* Used with permission from *Today's Health*, Vol. 47, No. 2, 1969.

Several times a day, every day, this lengthy, burdensome routine must be repeated. The pressure on the whole family—emotionally, physically, and financially—is great. Cystic fibrosis (CF) is a very demanding and expensive disease.

Some families crack under the strain. Others—some with two, three, even four children who have CF—stand firm. As one mother told a social worker who was studying the impact of the disease on family relationships:

"No one who has a CF child—let alone two or more—can live a normal life. Every phase of living is affected. Savings evaporate; spare time is at a minimum; energy is exhausted. Sleep is broken regularly at night to attend the coughing child. Cooking is restricted. No smoking is allowed in our house. We haven't had any new furniture since a CF child came into our lives 11 years ago. We've had no vacations except visiting relatives. It's just plain *hard* to make a happy life for my family. But somehow you manage to go on meeting your responsibilities."

It is hard. But people do go on, bolstered by hope. This hope is based not just on wishful thinking but on scientific evidence that substantial progress in the battle against CF is being made.

Thirty years ago, before cystic fibrosis was recognized as a separate disease, there was no hope for its victims. Their early deaths, mostly in infancy, were attributed to respiratory, gastrointestinal, and other conditions. In recent years, thanks to greater awareness of this complex "new" disease, improved diagnosis, and the use of effective antibiotics to increase the life span of patients, the disorder has been recognized with increasing frequency throughout the world.

Today CF is probably the most common lethal inherited disease of white children. (Reported incidence among Negroes and Orientals is rare, but this may be due to insufficient knowledge of the disease among these groups.) In the United States, an estimated two to five percent of the population carries the CF gene, and one of every 1000 to 2000 infants is born with the disease. As a killer of children, it ranks high on the list, claiming far more lives than some better-known maladies such as rheumatic fever, diabetes, and polio. Only 50 percent of CF patients live past the age of 10; 80 percent do not survive past 20.

The basic defect in CF is not known, but there is general agreement that it is due to an inborn error of metabolism transmitted as a recessive trait. To pass on the disease, both parents, though healthy themselves, must carry a CF gene. Children who receive a combination of two CF genes, one from the mother and one from the father, inherit the disorder. According to the theory of recessive transmission, when both parents carry the gene, one child in four will have CF, two in four will be carriers (inheriting one gene but not exhibiting symptoms of the disease), and one in four will be normal (gene-free). These are average figures; the incidence may be higher or lower in any given family.

The elusive basic defect in CF gives rise to several apparently unrelated abnormalities of the exocrine (outward-secreting) glands of the body, particularly mucus-secreting and sweat glands. This results in three principal complications.

First, and least disabling, is the production of sweat with a high salt content. In almost all CF patients, secretion of salt in sweat is two to five times normal levels. Because of this, many victims are unable to conserve salt, especially in hot weather, and are in constant danger of developing profound dehydration. In extreme circumstances this may be fatal. With widespread use of a sweat test, the unique sweat composition has become the primary diagnostic test for CF.

A second, more serious complication of the disorder stems from abnormal functioning of the body's mucus-secreting glands. Instead of secreting normal, clear, free-flowing fluid, they produce thick and very sticky mucus which clogs the ducts or openings of glands. When ducts of the pancreas are plugged with mucus, digestive enzymes supplied by this gland cannot reach the small intestine to do their work. Food is only partially digested. Depending on the severity of this complication, the child may suffer from malnutrition and its consequence, retarded growth.

The thick mucus which blocks the pancreatic ducts often

results in scarring, or fibrosis, of the pancreas. Thus, when the disease was first discovered, it was called cystic fibrosis of the pancreas. The misnomer persists, despite the fact that we now know that the pancreas is not the only organ affected—in about 15 percent of cases, the pancreas is not affected at all. Many parts of the body may be involved.

The third, and most important, complication of CF involves the lungs. Sooner or later, nearly all CF patients develop chronic lung disease. Sticky, thick mucus clogs the small bronchial tubes in the lungs, causing labored breathing or chronic cough. Then bacteria, which collect in the clogged tubes, multiply and produce infection. In time, the victim may develop chronic bronchitis or pneumonia. CF patients are extremely susceptible to lung disease, which accounts for 90 percent of deaths. Obstructed, damaged lung tissue also may impede local blood circulation, sometimes causing death from chronic heart strain.

Cystic fibrosis is a great simulator of other diseases. Symptoms are diverse and not always clear. The best-trained, best-intentioned physician who is not familiar with the disorder, not alert to the many disguises it may wear, may easily miss it. Familiarity with CF, however, breeds a high index of suspicion in the physician, and he has the means to detect the disease.

Often parents are the first to give doctors a hint that a child has CF. They report that the skin tastes salty when kissed. Or parents may observe that a youngster eats voraciously, yet fails to gain weight and to thrive. Because food passes through the body undigested in the CF child, stools are bulky, fatty, and, at times, foul-smelling. This causes the rectum to protrude. These are all indicative characteristics of CF. They should precipitate an immediate visit to a doctor.

Other symptoms of CF may be a persistent cough that sometimes sounds like whooping cough, wheezing suggestive of asthma, and repeated respiratory infections accompanied by difficulty in breathing and sleeping. In severe cases, additional signs of chronic lung disease—such as acute coughing followed by vomiting, bluish lips, "clubbed" fingers, and a barrel chest—may appear.

About five to 10 percent of CF patients have intestinal obstructions at birth. This form of CF, called meconium ileus, is easy to identify and usually requires surgery. After this condition is corrected, other symptoms of CF usually will develop. The course and outlook of the disease are then about the same as in those who have not had meconium ileus.

Any child with a family history of CF, with intestinal obstruction at birth, or with persistent respiratory or intestinal difficulties at least should be given the sweat test—the simplest and most reliable method of detecting cystic fibrosis.

This test, which is almost always accurate on children of 18 or younger, measures the amount of sodium chloride (salt) in the sweat. A number of methods are used to obtain sweat samples for chemical analysis. Normally a small area of skin is stimulated by local heat or a drug, then the sweat is collected on a gauze pad or filter paper. The finding of an abnormally high salt concentration in the sweat usually confirms the diagnosis of CF when other symptoms of the disease are present.

Additional tests, such as examination of intestinal fluid for pancreatic activity and of chest x-rays to learn whether there have been any lung changes, often are conducted to support the diagnosis. One new and promising diagnostic procedure involves analysis of fingernails, toenails, and hair for elevated concentrations of sodium and potassium. Effective in detecting CF, this technique also may aid in identifying carriers of the gene.

While there is not cure for CF, there are effective methods of treatment, especially when the condition is diagnosed early. Since there are striking variations in the degree and severity from patient to patient, treatment must be individualized.

In general, intestinal problems are managed easily. When there are not enough pancreatic enzymes present for proper digestion, commercially available pancreatic extracts from animals are taken with meals to supply the needed enzymes. Supplementary vitamins and nutrients, plus a diet high in proteins and low in fat content, usually are prescribed. To offset excessive loss of salt in perspiration, extra salt is given, particularly in hot weather.

Respiratory complications usually determine the fate of the patient, accounting for most of the severe disabilities and deaths. Treatment of these disorders is the most important part of therapy. This treatment, often long and expensive, consists of various methods of clearing the lungs of obstruction and combating infection.

Aerosol inhalation therapy is used to help loosen the thick mucus from the lungs and to deposit directly on the bronchial tubes antibiotics, decongestants, and other medications. To further loosen mucus, the CF child frequently sleeps in a mist tent. During periods of low humidity, home humidifiers are helpful in moistening lung secretions.

Used in conjunction with aerosol therapy, postural drainage is one of the most important methods of clearing air passages. Precise poistioning of the child is necessary to achieve efficient drainage of affected lobes of the lungs. A physical therapist, specially trained in the technique, uses chest-clapping and vibration procedures for each position. This therapy, carried out two or three times daily, whether mucus is brought up or not, requires a good deal of time and effort. To be effective, it must be taught to patient and parents, so that it can be practiced at home.

Children with respiratory difficulties develop incorrect breathing habits and tend to have rounded shoulders and barrel chests. To improve respiratory habits, air flow, and posture, the physical therapist may recommend breathing exercises as part of the treatment program. Physical activity often can raise more sputum than other methods; sports and active play should be encouraged.

In general, every effort should be made to permit the youngster to live as normal a life as possible. He should be encouraged to attend school, if his condition permits. His activities should be limited only by his tolerance. He should be given the usual protective immunizations, including measles vaccine. Some parents with CF children have moved their families to avoid extremes of cold, heat, and dampness. But the results of a climate change are not sufficiently striking to justify moving when this entails hardship.

A multiple approach is needed to the many problems presented by the CF patient. Especially important is the role of the physician. He not only must maintain close supervision over a long period of time, but he must establish a strong relationship with patient and family, giving encouragement, support, and guidance. The physician's role should be supplemented by that of the social worker and physical therapist.

Parent counseling plays a significant part in CF treatment. Parents must clearly understand all the therapeutic measures to be carried out at home, so they can cooperate fully. They also should be informed of the genetic aspects of the disease. Knowing that any additional child might inherit cystic fibrosis, they can then decide for themselves whether to risk enlarging their families.

Cystic fibrosis is a social as well as a medical problem. Emotional and financial stresses on the household can be devastating, leading to misunderstanding, tension, and family rifts. Every effort must be made to prevent the CF child from dominating the family emotionally and to allay the guilt feelings of parents, which often develop in connection with inherited severe disease. The support of a social worker familiar with the problems of CF is valuable in dealing with the family's emotional response. She can help parents fully utilize the community's resources for chronically ill patients.

The CF child, who frequently is aware of the demands he makes on the family, should be encouraged to participate in his own care program and to assume some responsibility for himself. His brothers and sisters should be given as much explanation as possible. So they don't develop feelings of rejection, they should understand why attention and care is diverted from them.

Social studies show that the entire family must understand CF and share this knowledge with each other. All the problems of the family must be considered, not just those of the sick child.

Today many research centers throughout the country are engaged in intensive studies to control cystic fibrosis and, perhaps eventually, to prevent it.

Much of the research is conducted and financed by the National Institute of Arthritis and Metabolic Diseases

(NIAMD), a component of the National Institutes of Health. NIAMD scientists in Bethesda, Maryland, and research grant-supported investigators in universities and medical centers across the US. are conducting laboratory and clinical studies in an attempt to uncover the fundamental defect causing abnormal secretions, to further delineate the apparently numerous and varied disease processes of CF, and to develop new and improved methods of diagnosis and treatment.

Recent findings have provided investigators with some dramatic and significant leads.

Evidence has been obtained indicating that excess calcium in the salivary glands of CF patients combines with a certain group of proteins to form an insoluble compound. The possibility that this compound is responsible for widespread obstruction of various organ ducts gives rise to new speculation concerning the evasive nature of the disease. The discovery might help explain many of CF's secrets.

A protein has been found in the blood of CF patients and their parents that makes it possible to identify carriers of the disease. A pediatrician from Duke University in Durham, North Carolina, discovered that when blood samples from parents of CF children are placed on tissues taken from the windpipes of rabbits, the thin hairlike cilia which cover the tissue lose their normal, coordinated wavelike motion and begin to beat erratically. Irregularity of beating also occurs when blood samples from CF children are used.

This ciliary "rabbit test" may lead to useful genetic counseling. But the determination of CF carriers with this method would be difficult to achieve on a mass basis. The precise identity of the blood fraction which disrupts ciliary rhythm, now intensively pursued, might turn up valuable information as to the basic cause of the disease.

Another, and perhaps the most dramatic step in this rapidly changing field is a discovery by a pair of researchers at Cornell University Medical College in New York. They found a genetic marker in the connective tissue cells of skin samples cultured from both CF patients and their parents.

Presumably this is due to the accumulation of a substance in many cells of the body, not just in the cells of exocrine glands. If this observation proves correct, it has far-reaching implications. It may show that cystic fibrosis is not, as long believed, a disease of the exocrine glands alone; dysfunction of other tissues also may be involved.

The existence of cellular abnormality recognizable in skin-tissue cultures from CF patients and carriers offers an opportunity to study the primary defect of the disease at the molecular level. And the technique appears to provide a simple, reliable method of identifying CF carriers. Such a method would greatly facilitate studies on genetic linkage and provide a practical means of genetic counseling on a wider scale.

In an attempt to alleviate the suffering and prolong the lives of CF patients, NIAMD investigators are experimenting with new therapeutic approaches. Other scientists are striving to perfect lung transplantations. So far, such operations on humans have been unsuccessful, due chiefly to the rejection factor.

When this problem is solved, cystic fibrosis patients, because of their youth and pulmonary involvement, will be among the foremost candidates for replacement of lungs or of the affected lobes. Whether or not the disease will continue to destroy the replacement is unknown; at least the life span can be lengthened.

Even today, with improved medical care of a more conservative nature, an increasing number of young cystic fibrosis victims are reaching adolescence and adulthood. In older patients, the disease is similar to that of infants, but differs somewhat in its manifestations.

As a group, older patients do better than younger ones, perhaps because they would not have survived so long unless the respiratory complication had been relatively mild. Digestion and absorption of food seem improved with advancing age; appetite and growth eventually appear to be more normal. Sexual maturation often proceeds normally, but at times it is somewhat delayed. However, the fertility achieved in CF males and females is quite different.

Recent studies show that women with cystic fibrosis can reproduce. In one survey, 10 mothers with the disease reported 11 living, normal children. CF males, on the other hand, while sexually functional, were found to be infertile. Some appeared to lack an unobstructed sperm duct. Others produced nonviable sperm (those not capable of developing). An absence of the sperm needed for fertility has not been proven conclusively in CF males, but the chances against their having children are overwhelming.

In some ways, this might be considered a blessing. What about the impact on the male ego? This can be reduced if the situation is explained to the patient early.

Young CF adults, who look perfectly healthy and who aspire—unrealistically, perhaps—to be doctors, foreign correspondents, astronauts or actresses may have tremendous problems psychological as well as physical. The physician, social worker, and guidance counselor must take these fully into account.

Parents of CF children are not alone. Most communities have services and resources to help these families.

A permanent solution to cystic fibrosis still eludes investigators. But promising findings in basic research, as well as improved methods of diagnosis and treatment, have created a more optimistic outlook for patients.

For Further Information

For details on research in cystic fibrosis, write to the National Institute of Arthritis and Metabolic Diseases, National Institutes of Health, Bethesda, Maryland, 20014.

To receive help for a child who has cystic fibrosis, consult state or county departments of health and welfare. At the community level, contact local rehabilitation services. You also may consult the social service department of a community hospital or a local chapter of the National Cystic Fibrosis Research Foundation.

Visiting nurse and homemaker services, available for chronically ill patients in many communities, can greatly ease the burden of CF patients.

Chapter 14

CHANGING PROSPECTS FOR CHILDREN WITH HEMOPHILIA*

Kenneth M. Brinkhous

~~~~~~

The Disease
Methods of Inheritance
Development of Treatment
Strategy for the Future

~~~~~~

UNTIL RECENTLY THE chances of a child afflicted with a severe case of hemophilia living to adulthood without serious crippling, or having a normal life if he did so, were slim. This hereditary disease of uncontrollable bleeding afflicts mainly males. Made famous by a strain that runs through the royal families of Europe, it has meant for its victims pain, crippling, the necessity of repeated hospitalization for blood plasma transfusions, and constant threat of death from bleeding into the brain, air passages, or other vital organs. It has also brought its victims severe social and psychological problems, stemming from their inability to lead normal lives (Goldy, Katz). Now, however, the prospects for the hemophilic child are much brighter because of a revolutionized method of care made possible by the recent development of blood plasma concentrates.

* Used with permission from *Children*, November-December, 1970.

141

With early diagnosis, prompt treatment, and proper management, life-threatening hemorrhages in hemophiliacs can become a thing of the past. A few boys and young men who have hemophilia are already receiving the plasma concentrates prophylactically for the prevention of hemorrhage, much as the diabetic receives insulin. The concentrates must be given by intravenous injection. This treatment has completely changed the way of life for its recipients. They now can attend school, play, go to work, and live much like normal males of the same age. The life expectancy at birth of a hemophilic child—once estimated at 18 (Sjolin)—may now approach that of normal boys.

But many problems still stand in the way of a normal life for most hemophilic children. A continuous alert for the occurrence of hemorrhages and their prompt treatment must be maintained. Moreover, supplies of plasma concentrates are limited and expensive; it is not unusual for a child with hemophilia to use plasma concentrates costing $12,000 a year.

How many persons there are in this country with hemophilia is unknown. Estimates range from between 10,000 and 15,000 for those with severe forms of the disease up to 100,000, including all who may have a mild form. Many mild bleeders are unaware that they have hemophilia until major surgery or a serious accident reveals deficiency in the clotting of blood. The National Hemophilia Foundation estimates that 40,000 boys and men in the United States have moderate or severe forms of the disease.

THE DISEASE

Hemophilia is a disease of males, inherited through the mother, in whom the blood plasma lacks a specific trace protein that produces clotting. The two main forms, hemophilia A and hemophilia B, cause similar symptoms. However, they differ in the specific types of clotting protein that is missing in the blood. Hemophilia A occurs five or six times as frequently as hemophilia B. The general impression among physicians is that hemophilia B is not as severe as hemophilia A. Patients with hemophilia A seem to require hospitalization and transfusions more frequently than those with hemophilia B.

Both types of hemophilia show up in the same way. The baby boy with hemophilia may bleed excessively when the umbilical cord is cut at birth or after he is circumcised. Parents notice "black and blue" marks and bruises on the infant's body. When the child starts walking and running, troublesome and persistent bleeding into the large joints causes painful swellings, especially of the knees and elbows. Once a joint has been the site of a severe hemorrhage, recurrences of bleeding in the joint are frequent.

Bleeding episodes may occur after mild trauma; many however, may occur unpredictably. The possibility of serious internal bleeding in one form or another haunts the hemophiliac throughout life.

Problems of impaired emotional and social development often arise in the school-age hemophilic child because of his irregular attendance at school and overprotective environment at home. These problems often carry over into adult life. Such problems may later be reflected in the adult hemophiliac's social adjustment and ability to hold a job (Goldy, Katz). With a birth of a hemophilic child, the whole way of life of a family can be greatly affected. This is dramatically demonstrated in Massie's recent best seller, *Nicholas and Alexandra* (Massie), which depicts the effect of the young czarevitch's hemophilia on the course of Russian history.

METHODS OF INHERITANCE

Both A and B types of hemophilia stem from genes that follow a sex-linked pattern of inheritance according to Mendelian law. The male inherits the disease through his mother, who carries the gene for hemophilia but is otherwise normal. There is no father-to-son transmission.

The hemophilic gene is located on the X-chromosome, one of the two chromosomes that determine sex. The other is called Y. A child with two X-chromosomes, XX, is a female; if one of her X-chromosomes carries the hemophilic gene, she is a carrier of the disease. A child with one X-chromosome and one Y-chromosome, XY, is a male; if his X-chromosome carries the hemophilic gene, he will have hemophilia.

A female carrier, with one affected X-chromosome, is protected from the disease by the accompanying normal X-chromosome. Geneticists can predict the average composition of the families of both hemophilic males and carrier females by sex and hemophilic status. For example, a man with hemophilia married to a normal woman will have all carrier daughters and all normal sons. A woman carrier of hemophilia married to a normal man could have four children distributed as follows: a normal daughter, a carrier daughter, a normal son, and a hemophilic son.

In small families the distribution of children by sex is often very different. Hemophilic men may sire only two children, both sons. In this case, there is no transmission of the disease to later generations. Women who are carriers may give birth to three children—all sons, all with hemophilia. Conversely, while a carrier may have three normal sons, such a remarkable event would probably go unrecognized, since the carrier status of the mother would likely not be known. Only if she also has a carrier daughter who eventually gives birth to a hemophilic son would the true situation become apparent.

Some progress has been made in detecting the carrier state in women before the appearance of a hemophilic son. A laboratory test has been developed to measure the amount of the clotting protein or antihemophilic factor in the blood. Women with hemophilic children have been found on the average to have only half as much of the clotting protein in their blood as do their normal sisters.

Laboratory testing, however, involves several problems. The test itself is difficult and expensive to carry out and requires special laboratory equipment. Even with reliable laboratory results, accurate interpretation of the test is not easy. One pitfall lies in the fact that not all carriers have a 50–50 distribution between blood cells that can and cannot produce the clotting protein. For example, if a women has only a few cells that cannot produce the antihemophilic protein, the level of the clotting factor in her blood is in the low normal range although she is a carrier. Also, the use of birth control pills may increase the amount of the hemophilia A clotting protein in the blood of some women, which could further complicate interpretation of the test.

A family history of hemophilia, combined with laboratory testing for low levels of the clotting protein in the blood, provides the most reliable basis for predicting that a woman is a carrier. Many women who have been tentatively identified by laboratory tests as carriers of hemophilia have later confirmed the diagnosis by giving birth to a hemophilic son. At the present time, however, screening the general population of women to find carriers of hemophilia is not feasible.

Some women have given birth to hemophilic children although there was no history of hemophilia in their families. In fact, roughly one-third of the families with hemophilic children are in this category. How did they become carriers? There is no simple explanation. Some of these persons are undoubtedly mutants—that is, their mothers were not carriers, but one of their own X-chromosomes was changed in some unknown manner. On the other hand, with small families the hemophilic gene can be submerged in the genetic pool for long periods of time and a family line may not have a hemophilic son for many generations. Before the potential seriousness of the hemophilia problem is assessed for a woman identified by laboratory tests as a carrier, the findings need to be correlated with her family history.

Many men have a mild form of hemophilia that is not troublesome except at times of operations and accidents. If correctly diagnosed, the mild disease can be readily managed medically. Female carriers of the mild form show low levels of clotting protein in tests, just as do carriers of the severe disease.

Family planning in hemophilic families presents special problems. Limitation in family size is the rule followed by most families once the disease appears. The prediction of carriers can be of real value, by alerting the family early in pregnancy to the possibility of hemophilia.

The liberalized interpretation of abortion laws in many States, combined with application of present knowledge of genetics, offers a means of reducing the hazard of hemophilia in affected families. As a first step the sex of the unborn child must be determined. Early in fetal life this can be done by amniocentesis—the surgical process of tapping the uterus for a small amount of amniotic fluid in which the fetus lives in the pregnant woman. Two methods are used to analyze the fluid: (1) cell culture, which determines whether the sex chromosomes are XX (female) or XY (male); or (2) more simply, the test for the Barr body, a characteristic that is present on the nuclear membrane of female cells.

In families in which the father has hemophilia, if only the males were allowed to come to term, the transmission of the hemophilic gene to a daughter who would be a carrier to later generations would be stopped. If the mother is a carrier, the choices are less clear cut. By having only daughters, she at least avoids the hazard of giving birth to hemophilic sons. In any event where abortion is not prohibited by law, the decision would have to be made on a purely voluntary basis by the parents themselves, after full discussion with their physician.

DEVELOPMENT OF TREATMENT

That blood transfusions have a corrective effect on hemophilic bleeding has been known for over a century. The first transfusion was given in London in 1840 to a hemophilic boy who was bleeding from an operation to correct a squint in one eye. By modern standards the procedure was crude: a few cubic centimeters of blood at a time were withdrawn from the donor and injected directly into the patient. No anticoagulant was used. The bleeding stopped. But with surgery on other hemophilic patients, the bleeding continued in spite of treatment with blood transfusions.

The effectiveness of transfusions in treating hemophilia was a matter of medical controversy for nearly a century. Physicians who found transfusions effective could not agree on what part of the blood was responsible for clotting—the platelets or the plasma.

In 1947, in research laboratories at the University of North Carolina, we were able to show clearly that the active antihemophilic principle resided in the plasma (Brinkhous,

1947). We also demonstrated that the antihemophilic factor was well preserved only as long as the plasma was frozen. We made the first application of this observation in our treatment of hemophilic dogs in 1949 (Graham). Hospital and community blood banks quickly put our findings to use, and fresh frozen plasma became the mainstay in the management of hemophilia for more than 15 years.

Fresh frozen plasma made great improvements possible in the treatment of hemophilia. While it still has a place in treatment today, frozen plasma has serious shortcomings. The main problem is that normal plasma has such a low concentration of the clotting protein that relatively large volumes are needed to control hemophilic bleeding. Bleeding is not always effectively staunched by this treatment. Moreover, injection of such large amounts of plasma often results in an excessive volume of circulating blood and leads to acute congestive heart failure.

The need for a plasma concentrate that would correct clotting has long been recognized. Preparation of antihemophilic material from animal and human blood was first attempted more than 30 years ago—even before the nature of the active principle of hemophilia was known—but with little success. No advances were made until the antihemophilic factor was identified. Then in 1952 the two types of hemophilia were separated; hemophilia A and B were recognized as separate entities that needed distinctly different clotting proteins for treatment. At the same time laboratory studies produced a suitable procedure for identifying and assaying the antihemophilic factor for hemophilia A. A basic procedure known as the partial thromoplastin time test was developed in our laboratory and is now commonly used for assay and diagnosis of both hemophilia A and hemophilia B.

Many concentrates for hemophilia A, the more common type of the disease, have been developed. Their potency is indicated in two ways. One way is the degree of *purification* of the antihemophilic protein, expressed as the ratio of the antihemophilic activity to the total proteins in the concentrate. The other is the *concentration* of the protein in solution as it is ready to be administered to the patient.

We have divided these concentrates into separate generations, similar to the generation classifications used for missiles, to indicate relative stages of development (Brinkhous, 1968).

Generation I consists of the first concentrates to be developed, which had low potency. The generation I materials were often less concentrated than normal plasma.

Generation II concentrates are purified 10 to 100 times. When made into solution ready for administration to the patient, they are five to seven times more potent than the same volume of normal plasma.

The development of generation II concentrates was made possible by two discoveries (Deutsch). One was the finding by Robert H. Wagner at the University of North Carolina in 1962 that glycine could be used to separate the clotting factor from blood plasma by precipitation. Concentrates of the antihemophilic factor precipitated in this way were used to treat hemophiliacs in the period from 1962–68. The superiority of these concentrates to fresh frozen plasma was striking; hemorrhages and bleeding that previously would have been judged to be catastrophic or fatal for hemophilic patients were rapidly brought under effective control.

The second discovery utilized the low solubility of the clotting protein at freezing temperatures, which was first observed in the 1950's. Judith Pool and associates of Stanford University in 1964 found that the precipitate that remains undissolved when frozen plasma is thawed slowly at icebox temperatures can be used to stop bleeding in hemophiliacs. The scientists developed a procedure by which blood banks can collect this material in concentrated form, called cryoprecipitate. This material has largely replaced fresh frozen plasma, and since 1966 has provided the primary mode for treating hemophilia. However, cryoprecipitates as made in blood banks have some disadvantages: their preparation is time consuming and their potency, which varies greatly between units, cannot be determined easily.

The latest developments are generation III or high-potency concentrates made by combining several procedures used in preparing various generation II concentrates. The main advantages of the generation III concentrates are that their potency is high and their exact strength is known. High potency means that only a small volume of fluid is needed for treatment and it can be administered simply by syringe. The known high potency of each vial gives this concentrate a particular advantage over cryoprecipitates. At present, however, the supply of the generation III concentrates is small and the only one generally available is the one we introduced in 1968 (Brinkhous, 1968).

Because exact bio-engineering for the control of hemophilic bleeding has become a reality with the generation III concentrates, a medical team can bring patient's clotting ability to normal in a matter of minutes. With the use of the concentrate, major surgery can be carried out on a hemophiliac without bleeding. In contrast to the preconcentrate days when simple tooth extraction was a major medical and dental procedure for a hemophiliac, today full mouth extractions in a hemophiliac are carried out with no excess bleeding.

Concentrates for hemophilia B became available in this country in 1969. The general problems with bio-assay, isolation of the hemophilia B protein, and translation of scientific findings to a practical therapeutic product paralleled those encountered in developing concentrates for hemophilia A. In certain respects, however, the work with hemophilia B concentrates was somewhat easier because the material is more stable.

A fuller description of the advances in the treatment of hemophilia can be found in the book *Hemophilia and New Hemorrhagic States*, which was written by scientists and physicians who have been significantly involved (Brinkhous, 1970).

It would be a boon indeed if the clotting mechanism of persons with hemophilia could be permanently normalized. One way to accomplish this might be by transplanting from a donor the organ responsible for the manufacture of the antihemophilic protein. But what organ to transplant? Many attempts to identify the organ that produces the antihemophilia A factor have been unsuccessful.

Early studies from our laboratory pointed to the spleen. But in most laboratories in which spleen transplants have been carried out in hemophilic dogs, this procedure did not succeed in correcting the bleeding tendency for more than a few days. This failure may have been due in part to the dogs' rejection of transplanted spleens. However, the experiments suggest that the spleen is a storage depot for the antihemophilic factor rather than the manufacturing site. Our studies then shifted to the kidneys and the liver. Hemophilic dogs seem to have been cured of their disease following liver transplants, but they have lived for only a few weeks or months after the operation. Although research is continuing, transplantation appears to be a long way from becoming an available therapeutic tool for permanently correcting hemophilic defects in humans.

STRATEGY FOR THE FUTURE

With the many advances reported here, it might seem that the problem of hemophilia is well under control. Actually, this is far from the case. Concentrates have improved the lives of hemophiliacs inestimably. But the hemophiliac still requires treatment and close medical attention throughout life.

Use of concentrates in the prevention of hemorrhage appears to be the best approach to the disease, because it eliminates the cost of hospitalization and assures the hemophiliac that he is under hemostatic control. To be most effective, injections with cryoprecipitate are needed daily; injections with high potency concentrates are needed several times a week. Most of the antihemophilic concentrate used today is prepared individually in blood banks. Although 5 to 10 percent of the resources of all blood banks in the country are channeled into the management of this relatively rare condition, the supplies of concentrates—especially those used to treat hemophilia A—currently are inadequate for a preventive program for the entire hemophilic population. Because of the shortage of concentrates, hospitalization will continue to be a common experience for the hemophilic child faced with a severe hemorrhage.

We need to find more effective methods of preparing the antihemophilic factor and to obtain a substitute for the scarce human product. Although animal materials have been produced in the laboratory, they are not in widespread use because they cause hypersensitivity and adverse protein reactions in human recipients.

Prompt transfusion at the first indication of hemorrhage is still vital in treating a hemophilic child. With the increased availability of blood products, transfusions can be done in the doctor's office, the outpatient department of a hospital, or in the patient's home if a member of the family has been trained in the transfusion procedure.

Organization of medical care for the hemophiliac has improved greatly as new discoveries have been made. About 50 specialized hemophilia centers have recently been developed in hospitals in the United States for the care of patients with serious hemorrhages, surgery, management of the complications of hemophilia, and attention to social problems. Multidisciplinary teams—including hematologists, clinical pathologists, orthopedic surgeons, psychiatrists, dentists, social workers, physical therapists, and other specialists—provide diagnosis, continuing comprehensive care, and rehabilitation. The hope for the future is that by prophylaxis and prompt and adequate treatment for each bleeding episode, serious and crippling hemorrhages will occur less and less frequently, and the need for the hemophilic child to travel repeatedly to specialized centers will be greatly reduced.

Hemophiliacs need improved health insurance. Obviously individual families cannot bear the tremendous financial burden brought on by hemophilia, which might well be classed with the "dread diseases." Under a means test based on the costs for treatment of a child with severe hemophilia A, most families in America would be considered medically indigent.

Some State crippled children's services provide treatment for children with hemophilia, but most of them do not have enough money to pay the full cost for families who cannot pay anything or even to make up the difference for families who can pay part of the cost. The same is true of Medicaid. Obviously, attention needs to be given to the special problem of the hemophiliac when methods are revised for the delivery of and payment for medical care of the chronically ill.

Family planning services and information are needed for families with a history of hemophilia. When families become aware of the many social problems related to hemophilia, they are more likely to consider therapeutic abortion as an alternative to the birth of a hemophilic son. Even so, the large number of mutations and the skipping of generations in the appearance of the disease make the elimination of hemophilia in future generations unlikely. Realistically, the goal of the National Hemophilic Foundation, public health and rehabilitation workers, and other persons interested in hemophilia is to reduce the birth rate among affected persons to the greatest extent possible.

While many problems exist for the hemophiliac today, the tremendous advances in the past 20 years should not be over-looked. Crippling has decreased, the need for hospitalization has decreased with modern treatments, and large numbers of hemophiliacs are growing up to become well-adjusted, contributing members of society. These advances are the direct result of laboratory, animal, and clinical research. The struggle of man to uncover Nature's secrets continues. Successes on the research front will be reflected in continued improvement in the treatment of the victims of hemophilia.

REFERENCES

Brinkhous, K.M.: Clotting defect in hemophilia: deficiency in a plasma factor required for platelet utilization. *Proceedings of the Society of Experimental Biology and Medicine,* October 1947.

Brinkhous, K.M.; Shanbrom, E.; Roberts, H.R.; Webster, W.P.; Fekete, L.; Wagner, R.H.: A new high-potency glycine-precipitated antihemophilic factor (AHF) concentrate. *JAMA* Aug. 26, 1968.

Brinkhous, K.M. (Ed.): *Hemophilia and New Hemorrhagic States.* Chapel Hill, N.C., The University of North Carolina Press, 1970.

Deutsch, P.; Deutsch, R.: One man's fight against hemophilia. *Readers' Digest,* August 1967.

Graham, J.B.; Buckwalter, J.A.; Harley, L.J.; Brinkhous, K.M.: Canine hemophilia. *J Exp Med,* Aug. 1, 1949.

Goldy, Florence B.; Katz, Alfred H.: Social adaptation in hemophilia. *Children,* September-October, 1963.

Katz, A.H.: *Hemophilia: A Study in Hope and Reality.* Springfield, Ill. Charles C Thomas, Publisher, 1970.

Massie, Robert K.: *Nicholas and Alexandra: an intimate account of the last of the Romanovs and the fall of Imperial Russia.* Atheneum Publishers, New York, N.Y. 1967.

Sjolin, K.E.: *Haemophilic Diseases in Denmark.* Oxford, England, Blackwell Scientific Publications, 1960.

Chapter 15

AMBULATORY CARE FOR EMPHYSEMA AND CHRONIC BRONCHITIS*

Thomas L. Petty

~~~~~~

Ambulatory Care Program
Effectiveness of Today's Ambulatory Care Program Summary

~~~~~~

THE IMMENSE problem of chronic airway obstruction (CAO) —emphysema and chronic bronchitis—which has now reached epidemic proportions, presents to the practitioner of medicine an increasing number of suffering persons asking for care. These patients are dyspneic, anxious, bewildered by their predicament, sometimes demanding and frightened about prospects for future comfortable life.

Although there has been a tremendous upsurge of interest in the field of respiratory care, and a growing number of nebulizers, humidifiers, physical therapy techniques and drugs, all of the answers on emphysema care are not in. We must admit as physicians that although we are absolutely sure that we save many lives in the organized intensive respiratory care unit in the case of acute respiratory failure (Bigelow; Petty, 1967b), no study has thus far convinced the critics of respiratory care that the natural course of CAO is

* Used with permission from *Chest*, Vol. 58, No. 2, October, 1970.

altered from the standpoint of survival. Nonetheless, today's patients cannot wait for all the answers. They flock to hospitals, clinics and physicians' offices, seeking some relief of their symptoms, some hope for improvement in their status and for prolonged survival. It is therefore mandatory for all physicians interested in chest medicine and interested in their sick patients, to provide some form of service for the growing crowd of puffers and coughers—both pink and blue.

This communication defines a practical clinic and out-patient treatment regimen that is applicable for most individuals suffering severe CAO with disability.

AMBULATORY CARE PROGRAM

Patient Education

The management of any chronic disease must be based upon a high level of patient indoctrination and education. This has been the reason for success in large measures in diabetes mellitus management where for years the sufferer has been instructed in nutrition, activity, insulin dosage, self-management, evaluation of glycosuria and proper clothing, leading to the development of an adjustment to the burdens of disease designed for a maximum of serenity in daily life. It does not take a great deal of talent, although it does take time, to describe the airways, the lungs, the circulation and to explain what is wrong in the emphysema-chronic bronchitis spectrum. The office nurse or clinic nurse, once properly trained herself, is a superb individual to assume the responsibility of this task. Patients receive an in-depth discussion of general care with reinforcement in specific instructions guided by the physician's explicit prescription. These sessions are supplemented by a simple treatment manual (Petty, 1967a) designed to give the patient material for serious reading which will reinforce the personal instruction and probably develop new questions for the nurses on revisits. We not only teach the patients about their disease process, but what physicians, nurses and therapists are trying to do in their therapeutic endeavors. We stress the specific facets in management listed below with details stressed for each individual patient.

Bronchial Hygiene

Much of therapy must be directed at the bronchial element of disease. In many cases we are dealing with the bronchospasm, mucosal edema, retained secretions and impaired mucociliary clearance. Each patient must learn an effective method of bronchial hygiene to be used each day. Fundamental, of course, is the absolute cessation of smoking. This is best handled in a nursing session where the threat of a physician and his authority is less traumatic to the patient.

In specific therapy, individuals are taught to inhale a bronchodilator aerosol followed by moisture, followed by expulsive coughing on a systematic basis at least twice daily. One of the sympathomimetic amines is inhaled for a period of at least ten deep breaths and a duration of, at times, up to ten minutes. Isoetharine with phenylephrine or racemic epinephrine or isoproterenol is used for this purpose. Aerosolized bronchodilators are delivered by a variety of devices, including a simple hand bulb nebulizer which does require some patient coordination and strength, the newly available pump driven nebulizers* or simple hand held IPPB devices which have recently been provided for the practitioner‡ (Fig 2). Ordinarily the drug is diluted with equal amounts of water with individual adjustments based upon side effects and apparent clinical efficacy. Bronchodilators relieve muscular spasm, combat mucosal edema and probably stimulate mucociliary clearance (Miller, 1967; Laurenzi). The use of bronchodilator drugs must become an art with final judgment on the absolute details of therapy, a joint effort between patient and physician, a matter which obviously requires a great trust and orientation on the part of both.

Following the bronchodilator administration, inhaled moisture is the next step. This may be done by simple steaming

---

* Maxi-Myst pump driven nebulizer, Mead Johnson Co., Evansville, Indiana.
† Hand-E-Vent, Ohio Medical Products, Madison, Wisconsin.

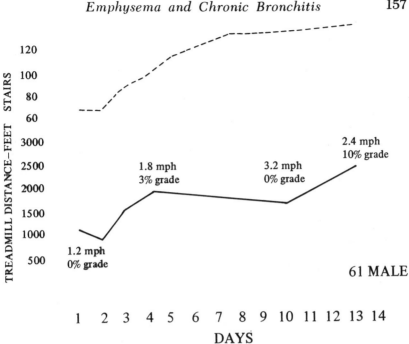

devices, *ie*, nursery humidifier, tea kettle, facial sauna and in some cases a more advanced nebulizer including an ultrasonic nebulizer. The choice of device is a matter of judgment based upon the ability to thin and raise secretions. It should be said and emphasized that general hydration in the form of adequate water intake is fundamental in maintaining adequate mucociliary clearance. The purpose of the moisture, of course, is to help thin secretions, which also facilitates mucociliary clearance. After approximately ten minutes of moisture inhalation, expulsive forceful coughing helps clear retained secretions. If these endeavors are insufficient, simple postural drainage techniques over pillows in bed often help the situation (Nett; Petty, 1969b). At times pummeling, or so-called clapping, is useful in removing secretions. This is usually taught the spouse by the physical therapist.

Breathing retraining stressing abdominal-diaphragmatic control, allowing the abdomen to protrude during inspiration, followed by forceful abdominal contractions during expiration, probably helps empty the lung and improves the efficiency of breathing (Barach, 1955, 1967; Miller, 1958). These maneuvers with exhalation against pursed lips, have been learned by many individuals who suffer dyspnea and who learn that this is a means of relief of symptoms. In a clinical study the pursed-lip maneuver has been shown to reduce the oxygen ventilation equivalent, reduce alveolar arterial oxygen difference and the necessary minute ventilation for a given level of arterial oxygen tension (Mueller). Therefore the pursed-lip breathing maneuver enhances oxygen transport or at least is a more efficient breathing technique. This should be taught to all patients or at least tried in patients who are well indoctrinated in modern methods of emphysema care.

Physical reconditioning in the form of simple daily exercises with increasing goals from the standpoint of more activity has been shown to greatly improve exercise ability (Cherniack, Pierce). Most patients can be taught to participate in comfortable exercise on an increasing basis in spite of the fact that their level of chronic airway obstruction may not change a great deal in response to therapy (Petty, 1969a). Nonetheless, this training is an important activity for it provides increased facility for daily living. Most patients with chronic airway obstruction find dyspnea on exertion their most disabling symptom and any improvement in comfortable mobility can be translated into a better life. Figure 2 demonstrates the measured improved walk tolerance at various rates and grades for an individual trained daily for the first week and every other day for the second week as part of a rehabilitation program. No measurable change in ventilatory function or blood gases (arterial) were observed during this brief training period.‡

Oxygen

The clinical benefit of ambulatory oxygen therapy has been repeatedly demonstrated (Levine; Petty, 1968). In brief, oxygen is valuable for the hypoxemic bronchitic person who is markedly disabled and suffers from heart failure. Oxygen

‡ MVV 31 L: FEV_1 0.91 L.

has been shown to reduce the level of pulmonary hypertension by reducing pulmonary arteriolar resistance and also helps combat the secondary polycythemia of the bronchitic hypoxemic state (Levine). The development of a home based portable oxygen system has made the use of continuous ambulatory oxygen a reality. A lower cannister contains a liquid oxygen supply which usually suffices for three to four days. This cannister is capable of filling a smaller device which provides now, three to six hours of oxygen therapy. The duration is a function of rate of oxygen administration controlled by a flow rate mechanism on the device. Ambulatory oxygen provides for additional mobility. Experience with these devices for over four years has proved the efficacy and safety in over 200 patients with profound hypoxemia who cannot gain mobility by any other means.

Pharmacologic Therapy

The weight of current evidence suggests that the immediate use of antibiotics for specific episodes of bronchitis manifested by increasing cough, leukocytosis, elevated temperature and purulent appearing sputum is effective in reducing the duration of symptoms and fever. Since the most common invading bacterial organisms after the original insult, which may be viral, appear to be *D. pneumonia* and *H. influenza,* the rather empiric use of ampicillin or tetracycline seems advisable. Ampicillin is usually given in doses of 4 gm daily the first two days followed by 2 gm daily for three or four days. Tetracycline is usually given in 2 gm doses daily the first two days followed by 1 gm daily for the duration of therapy, which usually covers five to seven days. Many patients with CAO are provided with a supply of antibiotics for home use to be instituted at first signs of a deep chest infection. It is also wise, however, from the standpoint of communication and further advice to have these individuals contact their physician at the time of institution of these drugs.

Digitalis and diuretic drugs *are* useful in the management of cor pulmonale with heart failure. These drugs, however, are fraught with the difficulty of arrhythmia, but the weight of evidence in recent years indicates that an improved hemodynamic state can be achieved with digitalizing doses of cardiac glycosides along with the use of diuretics if adequate correction of hypoxemia is employed to provide adequate oxygenation of the myocardium and to control the reactive pulmonary hypertension associated with the hypoxemic state (Petty, 1968).

The corticosteroid drugs are definitely useful in some patients with chronic airway obstruction. Indications for their use include the bronchitic patient with marked cough, expectoration and repeated bouts of wheezing or choking spells superimposed upon the chronic symptoms complex. Often these individuals have significant changes in their expiratory flow parameters as they are observed serially. Generally, prednisone 30 mg daily for the first five days followed by a dose of 15 mg daily for the next five days followed by a low maintenance dose of 5 to 10 mg with decisions for further therapy guided by measurements of expiratory flow in the form of forced expiratory volume in one second (FEV_1) or maximum mid-expiratory flow (MMEF). A certain number of patients with apparent chronic irreversible airway obstruction, actually have a reversible component of disease if observed carefully under steroid therapy (Petty, 1970b).

Oral bronchodilators may be useful in an occasional patient. The only harm of the ephedrine-containing drugs aminophylline, amytal, and ephedrine HCl (Amesec), theophylline, phenobarbital, ephedrine HCl (Tedral), etc. is occasional urinary tract obstruction. Although these drugs are not very effective, they are frequently used by patients for reasons good or bad. Soluble xanthines in the form of oxtriphylline (Brondecon) or choline theophyllinate (Choledyl) may also prove useful in some patients.

The expectorants such as saturated solution potassium iodide and guaiacolate have not been proved by critical study to be effective in patients within this spectrum. Nonetheless, they may be used for apparent symptomatic benefit for short periods but should not be an agent of prolonged use.

Polyvalent influenza vaccine should be given each fall for whatever protection is afforded.

Occupational Therapy, Hobbies, and Change of Life Style

If life is to be worthwhile for the emphysema-bronchitis patient, it has to have meaning. The details of therapy enumerated above should not be excessively demanding from the standpoint of time and should be applied in a systematic manner to allow patients to lead a happy and hopefully productive life. A number of patients can be returned to work. Return to work of course has to do with many factors and is basically based upon the energy requirement of the job, the patient's physiologic resources and the patient's personal motivation to maintain a gainful status (Petty, 1970a). Certainly the provision of ambulatory oxygen therapy is a great aid for some patients (Petty, 1968, 1970a). Additional oxygen provides for additional activity and improvement in work capacity while on the job.

For those not so fortunate, occupational therapy in the form of hobbies, is tremendously important. Many patients have a longing or desire to paint, write, garden, golf or simply walk around a bit. This should be encouraged by the total application of the program described above.

EFFECTIVENESS OF TODAY'S AMBULATORY CARE PROGRAM

Although this is difficult to assess with cool scientific certainty, because no clinical care program ever is totally controlled, a number of statements can be made based upon contemporary knowledge about the effectiveness of organized care for CAO.

Symptomatic Improvement

Most patients seek medical care because of adverse symptoms. There is no question that the development of comprehensive care programs have greatly improved the patients' subjective feeling of well being. For example, Table 1 shows the patients' clinical assessment at one and two years following entry into the comprehensive rehabilitation program

TABLE 1

SUBJECTIVE ANALYSIS OF SYMPTOMS

	One Year	%	Two Years	%
Worse	17	13	18	21
Same	36	28	27	32
Better	76	59	39	47

which has been described in this report. The vast majority of patients remain clinically better or at least the same up to two years and in many cases longer.

The application of care principles described above can be assessed by a reduction in hospital needs. A small group of patients requiring hospitalization for respiratory causes were selected and the need for hospitalization following entry into a comprehensive care program were compared to the patients' prior hospital needs. In brief, Table 2 shows the total number of patients requiring hospitalizations was reduced, the total number of hospital days was reduced and the average stay per patient reduced over a one year period compared to the patient's previous performance. It must be admitted that the clinic and outpatient nature of the program emphasized independent existence in order to minimize hospital needs. This makes absolutely no difference, however, and the facts speak for themselves, *ie*, 326 hospital days saved in this small group of patients. One has only to multiply the number of hospital days saved by the average cost of hospitalization today to gain a quick assessment of a tangible economic saving provided by ambulatory care methods.

Return to work in an aging population is not common (Petty, 1970a). Nonetheless certain individuals can return to gainful employment and in some, this may represent a striking improvement over past performance. Most individuals who can return to work or at least maintain their level of gainful employment, are rewarded by a continued sense of pride over their productive state.

Physiologic Changes

One hundred and eighty-two patients were evaluated for CAO and entered into the comprehensive care program which

TABLE 2

REDUCTION IN HOSPITAL DAYS DURING FIRST YEAR OF
PROGRAM COMPARED WITH PREVIOUS YEAR°

	Year Before Entry	*First Year of Program*
Total hospital days	868	542
Number of patients hospitalized (from group)	34	25
Average hospitalized patients	25.5 ± 39.8	21.7 ± 30.2

° Previously reported[14]

is reported here. They were selected on the basis of having irreversible airway obstruction with *expected* pulmonary function deterioration with age (Miller, 1958; Burrows, 1969). The overall physiologic changes in our series suggest that the expected pulmonary function deterioration is retarded. For example, patients at risk for one and two years are the subjects of Tables 3 and 4.* It is apparent that ventilatory function abnormalities do not change significantly. Oxygen tension and saturation are significantly increased at one year. Carbon dioxide rises occur only in the oxygen patients, but not to an important degree since pH remains normal (compensated).

It is probably most noteworthy that in spite of the fact that the patients essentially remain about the same from a physiologic standpoint, they have not deteriorated at the expected rate. Moverover, it may be quite important that increased exercise tolerance is sustained for periods up to two years.

Mortality

Within a 3.5 year period, 56 patients have died (mean survival 1.4 years). This is expressed in life table form by year in Table 5. An analysis of death indicates that at any point in time, early deaths related to the poorest pulmonary function measurements at time of entry into the program. The most common cause of death is combined cardiac and respiratory failure. No claim is currently made that the mortality rate

* Symbols explained in Tables 3 and 4.

TABLE 3

COMPARISONS: PRELIMINARY VERSUS ONE YEAR

	Preliminary			One Year		
	Mean	*SD*	*No.*	*Mean*	*SD*	*P*
VC	2.66	.80	120	2.63	.81	
FEV₁	1.00	.39	120	.95	.49	
MMF	.44	.23	120	.41	.31	
MVV	38.5	51.1	118	37.3	19.4	
All Patients						
pH	7.40	.04	109	7.40	.04	
Pco₂	40.2	8.3	108	43.6	11.7	.0002
Po₂	57.2	8.2	95	60.1	11.5	.025
O₂ sat.	87.5	6.3	109	88.8	5.8	.05
Dist. walked*	609.8	570.0	91	1280.3	862.6	<.0001
Stairs	42.3	23.5	77	68.3	32.4	<.0001
Work on stairs	581.6	304.0	59	874.8	438.6	<.0001
Non O₂ Patients						
pH	7.40	.04	73	7.40	.04	
Pco₂	38.8	7.4	73	39.4	6.0	
Po₂	59.0	7.4	67	61.2	9.1	.05
O₂ sat.	88.8	4.7	73	90.0	4.1	.02
Work	626.0	323.5	44	956.1	457.1	<.0001
Dist. walked*	671.5	616.6	67	1449.1	906.9	<.0001
Stairs	49.7	20.9	52	76.2	28.6	<.0001
O₂ Patients						
pH	7.40	.04	36	7.38	.04	.01
Pco₂	43.0	9.2	35	52.5	15.2	<.0001
Po₂	53.1	8.7	28	57.4	15.7	
O₂ sat.	84.8	8.1	36	86.4	7.9	
Work	451.3	192.3	15	636.1	273.2	.025
Dist. walked*	437.5	370.9	24	809.2	487.1	.01
Stairs	36.7	18.3	16	54.6	28.6	.01

VC	—Vital capacity (liters)
FEV₁	—Forced expiratory volume (liters/sceond)
MMF	—Mid maximal expiratory flow (liters/second)
MVV	—Maximal voluntary ventilation (liters/minute)
pH	—Expression of hydrogen ion concentration (Negative Lung Vol.)
Pco₂	—Carbon dioxide tension in arterial blood
Po₂	—Oxygen tension in arterial blood
O₂ sat.	—Oxygen saturation in arterial blood
Distance walked	—On treadmill (various increasing rates and grades)
Stairs	—Number walked until dyspneic
Work	—Kilogram meters vertical work on stairs

*Various increasing rates and grades.

is decreased except in the case of acute respiratory insufficiency. Nonetheless, our population, averaging 61 years with an FEV₁ of 0.94 liters on entry, represents a most adverse population from the standpoint of age and loss of pulmonary function. Clearly patients with less severe forms of disease will have a better prognosis (Burrows; Petty, in preparation).

TABLE 4

COMPARISONS: PRELIMINARY VERSUS TWO YEAR

	Preliminary			Two Year		
	Mean	SD	No.	Mean	SD	P
VC	2.73	.80	78	2.65	.89	
FEV$_1$	1.04	.42	78	1.00	.58	
MMF	.46	.24	78	.43	.40	
MVV	41.7	15.6	78	38.5	23.2	
All Patients						
pH	7.40	.04	73	7.40	.04	
Pco$_2$	39.0	7.3	73	41.9	9.0	.002
Po$_2$	58.7	8.3	63	61.4	11.1	
O$_2$	88.2	5.9	72	89.3	5.1	
Work	612.8	358.4	29	939.6	608.1	.0001
Dist. walked°	789.7	557.5	41	1276.8	794.3	.001
Stairs	45.1	24.9	34	73.6	38.3	.0001
Non O$_2$ Patients						
pH	7.40	.04	52	7.41	.04	
Pco$_2$	37.4	5.6	52	38.9	5.3	
Po$_2$	60.0	7.8	49	60.2	8.0	
O$_2$ sat.	89.3	4.6	52	89.6	4.0	
Work	663.0	366.8	24	1064.2	593.2	.0001
Dist. walked°	773.5	578.2	31	1429.4	801.8	.0002
Stairs	50.3	24.1	25	79.6	36.8	.0001
O$_2$ Patients						
pH	7.40	.05	21	7.40	.03	
Pco$_2$	43.1	9.2	21	49.2	11.8	.01
Po$_2$	54.5	9.1	14	65.4	18.2	.025
O$_2$ sat.	85.5	7.8	20	88.4	7.3	
Work	371.7	194.8	5	341.7	159.0	
Dist. walked°	839.7	513.1	10	803.6	576.7	
Stairs	39.3	15.7	7	50.0	43.1	

VC —Vital capacity (liters)
FEV$_1$ —Forced expiratory volume (liters/second)
MMF —Mid maximal expiratory flow (liters/second)
MVV —Maximal voluntary ventilation (liters/minute)
pH —Expression of hydrogen ion concentration (Negative Lung Vol.)
Pco$_2$ —Carbon dioxide tension in arterial blood
Po$_2$ —Oxygen tension in arterial blood
O$_2$ sat. —Oxygen saturation in arterial blood
Distance walked —On treadmill (various increasing rates and grades)
Stairs —Number walked until dyspneic
Work —Kilogram meters vertical work
°Various increasing rates and grades.

SUMMARY

An ambulatory care comprehensive program for emphysema and chronic bronchitis has been described. The basic modalities of therapy are patient education, bronchial hygiene using simple home techniques, breathing retraining,

TABLE 5

MORTALITY DATA

Months	At Risk	Dead	Cum Mor %	Surv Rate %
0– 6	179	8	4.5	95.5
6–12	169	9	9.6	90.4
12–18	158	10	15.5	84.5
18–24	139	12	23.2	76.8
24–30	111	12	32.6	67.4
30–36	74	1	33.8	66.2

physical reconditioning, oxygen and ancillary chemotherapeutic agents. The application of these principles in care provides great symptomatic benefit, improved exercise tolerance and a reduction in hospital needs. A reduction in the progressive pulmonary function deterioration which is expected in this disease spectrum has been observed up to two years.

In view of the immense number of patients with CAO, suffering and disabled, the application of outpatient care programs on a nationwide basis will help to reduce the overall social and economic impact of this disease complex.

REFERENCES

Barach A.L.: Diaphragmatic breathing in pulmonary emphysema. *J Chronic Dis, 1:*211, 1955.

Barach A.L.; Chusid E.; Wood L.: Ventilatory effect of decreasing functional residual capacity in pulmonary emphysema. *Ann Allerg, 25:*211, 1967.

Bigelow D.B.; Petty T.L.; Ashbaugh D.G. et al: Acute respiratory failure: experiences of a respiratory care unit. *Med Clin N Amer, 51:*323, 1967.

Boushy S.F.; Coates E.D.: The diagnostic value of pulmonary function tests in emphysema with specific reference to arterial blood studies. *Am Rev Resp Dis 90:*553, 1964.

Burrows B, Earle R.H.: Course and prognosis of chronic olbstructive lung disease. *New Eng J Med, 280:*397, 1969.

Cherniack R.M.: The management of respiratory failure in chronic obstructive lung disease. *Ann NY Acad Sci, 121:*942, 1965.

Howard P.: Evaluation of the ventilatory capacity in chronic bronchitis. *Brit Med J, 3:*392, 1964.

Laurenzi G.: Adverse effect of oxygen on Mucociliary clearance. *New Eng J Med, 279:*333, 1968.

Levine B.E.: Bigelow D.B.; Hamstra R.D., et al: The role of long-term continuous oxygen administration in patients with chronic airway obstruction with hypoxemia. *Ann Intern. Med, 66:*369, 1967.

Miller W.F.: Physical therapeutic measures in the treatment of chronic bronchopulmonary disorders. *Am J Med, 24:*929, 1958.

Miller W.F.: Rehabilitation of patients with chronic obstructive lung disease. *Med Clin N Amer, 51:*349, 1967.

Mueller R.E.; Petty T.L.; Filley G.F.: Ventilation and arterial blood gas changes induced by pursed lip breathing. *J Appl Physiol,* 784, 1970.

Nett L.M.; Petty T.L.: Effective treatment for emphysema and chronic bronchitis. *J Rehab, 33:*10, 1967.

Petty T.L.; Nett L.M.: *For Those Who Live and Breathe With Emphysema and Chronic Bronchitis.* Springfield, Illinois, Charles C Thomas, Publisher, 1967a, p. 108.

Petty T.L.; Bigelow D.B.; Nett L.M.: The intensive respiratory care unit: an approach to the care of acute respiratory failure. *Calif Med, 107:*381, 1967b.

Petty T.L.; Finigan M.M.: The clinical evaluation of prolonged ambulatory oxygen therapy in patients with chronic airway obstruction. *Am J Med, 45:*242, 1968.

Petty T.L.; Nett L.M.; Finigan M.M., et al: A comprehensive care program for chronic airway obstruction: methods and preliminary evaluation of symptomatic and functional improvement. *Ann Intern Med, 70:*1109, 1969a.

Petty T.L.; Nett L.M.: Patient education and emphysema care. *Med Times, 97:*117, 1969b.

Petty T.L.; McIlroy E.; Swigert M.A., et al: Chronic airway obstruction, respiratory insufficiency and gainful employment. *Arch Envir Health, 21:*71, 1970a.

Petty T.L.; Brink G.A.; Corsello P.R.: Objective functional improvement in chronic airway obstruction. *Chest, 57:*216, 1970b.

Petty T.L., Neff T.A.: Prognosis in selected patients with chronic airway obstruction receiving comprehensive respiratory care. In preparation.

Pierce A.K.; Taylor H.F.; Archer R.K., et al: Responses to exercise training in patients with emphysema. *Arch Intern Med, 113:*78, 1964.

CHAPTER 16

TRAINING ACTIVITIES FOR THE MENTALLY RETARDED BLIND*

CHARLES C. CLELAND AND JON D. SWARTZ

~~~~~~

Enhancing the Blind Retardate's Enjoyment of the Sport of Fishing

The Use of Odors in Games for Blind Retardates

Extending the Emotional Experiences of the Blind Retardate

~~~~~~

THE MENTALLY RETARDED and the blind present special problems for classroom teachers and recreation workers. Activities especially designed for the blind often are inappropriate for those of less than normal mental ability, while procedures for training the mentally retarded present difficulties when applied to the blind or the partially sighted. When the child is blind *and* retarded, problems facing teachers and recreation workers seem insurmountable.

The authors have made program suggestions for the blind retardate elsewhere (Cleland and Swartz, 1969; 1970) and the games and activities presented here have been designed especially for the blind mentally retarded of high trainable or educable level (IQs 40–70). They should serve as important additions in the areas of behavior management, boredom relief, and sensory-motor and orientation training, and, by

* Used with permission from *Education of the Visually Handicapped*, October, 1970.

168

extending the range of subjects of emotional significance, should also help foster rapport with sighted individuals.

ENHANCING THE BLIND RETARDATE'S
ENJOYMENT OF THE SPORT OF FISHING

One of the most enjoyable summer activities listed by a group of educable, adult, institutionalized retardates was the occasional outing to a nearby lake to fish. Over a period of two weeks, numerous members of the group spontaneously asked one of the authors, "How about seeing if you can get Mr.——— to take us up to the lake to fish?" During the summer, this group did go to the lake for several fishing trips; but what of those left behind, the sighted trainable retardates and the blind educable and trainable retardates? The sighted educables were vocal and demanding—yet, others more severely handicapped also seem to enjoy this sport. There are certain deterrants, however, to their full enjoyment, and it seems advisable to examine a few of these to see how they can be overcome.

First, although blindness obviously presents a serious sensory problem for the trainable or educable retardate, when one considers fishing, the major problem appears to be the trainable blind retardates' inferior motor skills. For example, it takes a rather well-coordinated and swift motor reaction to catch a fish—to turn a "cork bobble" into a catch. The usual catches for retardates, as for most of us, are the small ones and, yet, these are the elusive bait-stealers. The problem, then, is to develop a fishing pole, line, and hook that will enable a blind, trainable-level retardate (or any person who cannot rely heavily on vision or whose responses are very slow) to land a fish.

If one allows his thinking to proceed from catching a fish to catching a mouse, a more certain way of "hooking" the fish can be developed. The obvious aid would be to add a mechanical device to the usual pole and line, a device that activates almost instantly when the slightest pressure is exerted; and such a device exists in the ordinary mousetrap. Therefore, it could be attached to the pole so that the lightest nibble at the baited hook would snap the spring and hook the fish. By such a method the slow-reacting, blind retardate, even of trainable level, should be able to catch a fish. As any experienced fisherman knows, getting the fish hooked is the most important step in bringing in the catch; and while better ways may be envisioned than the one suggested here, such a method does widen the sport to include those who cannot really enjoy it at present. For the experienced fisherman, the size of catch may be all important, but for many educable and trainable retardates—like young, normal children—just catching a fish can be a great joy. Extending the range of activities in which blind retardates (or other handicapped groups, such as geriatric cases) can meaningfully participate appears important enough to engage staff thinking to its fullest.

THE USE OF ODORS IN GAMES FOR BLIND RETARDATES

Bruner (1951) indicates that ". . . for reasons deep in the nature of man's inhibitions about the excretory functions or perhaps because of their inadequacy as locomotive guides, we utilize smell cues to a very minimum in our Western Society . . ." Nevertheless, Western Society does use smell, and odors constitute the basis for entire industries, i.e., deodorants, mouth washes, and even household sprays to ward off "house-a-tosis"! The point is not to suppress the fact that odors exist, but rather to see if common smells can be employed in teaching or in developing recreational programs for the mentally retarded blind.

Suppose that the blind retardate has smell sensitivity as good as that of the normal, sighted person. If so, then the basis for a game employing smell detection and discrimination exists. Suppose one utilizes 10 players, and stages the game in a room approximately 20 x 20 feet in size. Ten chairs for the players are lined up along one wall, with a chair for the teacher or recreation worker in one of the corners next to the line of players. Diagonally across the room from the teacher's chair is stretched a guide rope at approximately eye level (of players) to which has been attached several "odor bottles" spaced at equal intervals from each other. Each player, in turn, is started from the teacher's position with the instructions, "Smell this? (Teacher holds a bottle up to blind player's nose) Okay? Now I want you to put one hand on the rope here (Teacher places player's hand on rope) and follow it until you come to the first bottle, then the next, and so on until you reach the corner of the room. When you find the bottle that has the same smell as what I have just had you smell, hold up your hand. What I want to see is how good you are at smelling and if you're the best in class, you'll get a prize." To begin a game such as this, based on smell acuity, it might be best to start with only four odors. Also, it might be well to allow each player to experience success on the first trial, since failure experiences probably have been common among the retarded blind. After generating interest, variations could be introduced for didactic purposes. Thus, it might be arranged to send a player out with the instructions, "Find the smell that you think is that of an orange (apple, etc.). When you do, hold up your hand and I will ring a bell once if you are right and twice to signify that you are to keep searching. If you are right the first time, then stop and tell the class where you go to buy oranges, where they are raised . . . all you know about them."

Other smell games could be developed from the basic one suggested here. For example, the first game might use a small number of smells, those that are quite easily distinguished one from another, i.e., garlic, camphor, perfume, and stale cigarette odor. The next game might employ *eight* different odors, and so on. Furthermore, the basic odor game is highly structured, using a guide rope to permit locomotion of subjects. In another variation, cross strings or ropes could be used to hold the bottled odors in the form of an X. This variation would facilitate comprehension of the spatial dimensions of the room. Another might train students in the recognition of electrical fires (distinctive odor). Many other variations will suggest themselves to the creative teacher.

EXTENDING THE EMOTIONAL EXPERIENCES OF THE BLIND RETARDATE

Abelson (1965) poses the question, "Who has not had a sense of awe and grandeur in watching a rising full moon?"

Among those who have *not* experienced this natural phenomenon are the congenitally blind. To what extent is experiencing a rising moon a void in the life of a blind person? Again, Abelson is relevant and writes, "Its (the moon's) special role in emotional matters is evidenced by many popular songs of this era." Indeed, between 1892 and 1964, according to the American Society of Composers, Authors, and Publishers, there appeared 43 hit songs that carried the word *moon* in the title! Thus, viewing a moonrise would appear to be an experience with significant emotional overtones, and relevance in the teaching of the blind and even of educable level blind retardates. Obvious questions are: How can this unique experience be taught? Why should it be attempted? and What department in the academic school should teach it? By simulations, for emotional enrichment and spatial orientation, and through the music department are the logical answers to these three questions.

First, how will simulation accomplish this learning task? Obviously simulation will utilize the remaining intact senses. In approximating the sensation of viewing a full moon, moon songs (ordinarily quiet and contemplative music) will appeal to the sense of hearing. Emotionally, if an accompanying sensation of viewing the moon is one of increasingly becoming awe-struck or transfixed, then volume level of the song might be employed to simulate a rising effect, e.g., from pianissimo to forté—soft to loud. To further implant realism into the simulation, the temperature variable requires attention also. Traditionally, the moon is associated with coolness and the sun with heat. Therefore, an evening or night environment to parallel the actual rise of the moon would complement the sound aspects by the addition of time congruity, and temperature and smell correspondence. Aside from evoking the sensation of awe or grandeur, these simulation aspects should have the further effect of assisting the blind retardate to orient himself in proper day-night sequence. Depending upon the intellectual level of the trainees, it also may be possible to simulate the position of the earth and other planets. This knowledge, plus some very elementary lectures on astronomy, could perhaps change attitudes and increase the outlook of the educable and normal blind toward occupations. More important, and less speculative however, would be the likelihood of a closer rapport with individuals of normal vision and intelligence. Experiencing more of the natural phenomena of our planet, albeit via simulation, should assist the blind to discuss a wider range of subjects of permanent emotional significance.

In summary, although designed primarily to encourage the mentally retarded blind to utilize their intact senses to fullest advantage in game-like atmospheres, these activities also can facilitate discriminations, associations and can even be used to train students in various safety skills.

REFERENCES

Abelson, P.: After the Manned Lunar Landing? *Science,* 1965, 150, No. 3696 (editorial).

Bruner, J.S.: Personality Dynamics and the Process of Perceiving. In Blake, R.R. and Ramsey, G.V. (Eds.): *Perception: An Approach to Personality.* New York; Ronald Press, 1951.

Cleland, C.C., and Swartz, J.D.: *Mental Retardation: Approaches to Institutional Change.* New York: Grune & Stratton, 1969.

Cleland, C.C., and Swartz, J.D.: The Blind Retardate—Three Program Suggestions. *The Training School Bulletin,* 1970, 67, in press.

CHAPTER 17

VISUALLY HANDICAPPED CHILDREN: THEIR ATTITUDES TOWARD BLINDNESS*

LUCIANA VISENTINI STEINZOR

~~~~~~

Two Groups Studied
Elementary School Children
Results
Junior High School Students
Results

~~~~~~

HOW DO VISUALLY handicapped boys and girls adapt to the world of their sighted and blind peers? This is a problem to which a good deal of attention, from impressionistic observations to systematic research, has been given.*

TWO GROUPS STUDIED

While conducting a larger study on visually handicapped boys and girls and their school peers, I investigated some specific aspects of the problem. Do visually-handicapped youngsters think of the sighted and the blind as two opposite and irreconcilable groups with different and exclusive characteristics and functions, groups to which one must relate in

* Used with permission from *The New Outlook*, December, 1966.
** Sommers, 1944; Cutsforth, 1951; Barker, et al., 1953; Norris, et al., 1957; Bertin, 1959; Jervis, 1960; Cowen, et al., 1961.

basically different manners? In what terms do the youngsters define sightedness and blindness? Do they perceive some patterns of behavior as more proper for each group?

Two groups of visually handicapped boys and girls were interviewed, one in an elementary school and one in a junior high school in New York City. I shall report here on the study in each school.

ELEMENTARY SCHOOL CHILDREN

This large elementary school, located in a lower-middle and working class neighborhood, had included classes for multiply handicapped children, for several years. Two classes were for seven grossly "multiply handicapped" blind children; two were for nine "normal" blind children. Only the latter ones were interviewed in the present study. †

During preliminary observations and conversations with teachers and school officials, the impression emerged that the blind children were not isolated from sighted children, although special provisions and schedules were made for them. The fact that five visually handicapped children spent part of their day in regular classes with sighted children made possible not only close classroom contact but also allowed some sighted children to help them to and from classes, and allowed other sighted children to meet them in the corridors.

Subsequent interviews with the blind children were conducted individually. The boys and girls were willing to talk, and they related easily to the interviewer, although some were unable to sustain prolonged contact. ‡

RESULTS

Not Really Blind. It is well known that the definition of "blind" includes a range of ability to see something, to

† Eight interviews were conducted (with five boys and three girls) as the ninth pupil, a girl, was absent because of illness. The age range was seven to eleven years.

‡ Because of this limitation, the interviews could be coded and subjected to statistical analysis only in part. One interview could not be utilized, being too fragmentary. The interview shcedule was structured and open-ended. The interviews were tape recorded and were conducted in January 1964. Non parametric statistics were used.

—

have some light perception, or even perception of shapes. However, the emphasis put by the blind children on how much they could see was so great that the conception of blindness as a world of constant and unrelieved darkness immediately appeared as an unfortunate stereotype. The theme of how much one could see was always spontaneously mentioned by the child himself, and it became evident that it was, for many, one of the hinges on which their self-evaluation and their relation to the "blind" children turned. One girl explained her close relation to another blind schoolmate, "M. can see more than I can, but she trips more and I have to help her a little," and "I like to play with both of them (sighted and blind) but especially with the blind, 'cause blind children I help them . . . 'cause I can see more than the ones I am playing with."

This attitude may have been responsible for an awareness of the blind children of different classes for the visually-handicapped. Five of the seven respondents knew that there were different classes for different groups of visually-handicapped children, and two gave elaborate descriptions of the social structure of these classes: "There are two classes in Room X, and in these classes are those who are smart: in Miss M.'s class are the smartest ones, they get out of school. . . . And then there are other classes; they are dumb, they are not that dumb, but you know they don't know how to talk and they are really, really blind and all that, where we know how to see a little bit."

Being completely blind, for these visually-handicapped children, had the connotation of a most negative stereotype. They saved their self esteem to the extent that they had something that was not "blindness." Being called "blind" was for some children, an offense; being called "blind" was being called names. One boy put it in a most touching way, in an almost poetic lack of common sense logic: "They think that they wanna call me blind, but I am not blind; I can't see."

SEEING AND DOING. The definition of blindness and sightedness was given in terms of what one could not do and what one could do: "To be able to see means that you can walk by yourself, you can get a haircut by yourself, you can go shopping . . .;" "To be blind means you have to ask somebody to help you cross the street;" "Being blind is when you got to do something . . . you can't see . . . like cooking, you don't know where the fire is;" "It's almost like sighted people except that when you go to a new place you may not know where things are and you might bump into them, that's all—the only thing, you have to read braille books." Being able to do becomes equivalent to being less blind. The limitations imposed by blindness, it was felt, can be overcome to the extent that one learns how to do things. This was reflected in aspects of the sighted classes which were attractive to the blind children. Being in a class with sighted children was attractive for one or both or the following reasons: "They help me more," and "We do more work with them." The common element was learning to do, becoming more competent; the notion of "they help me more" did not sound, in this context, as dependency but as "help to learn," being expressed as: "They tell me what is on the blackboard;" "They explain arithmetic, geography, etc." There was only one exception; a girl expressed the notion of being taken care of: "We have more privileges; the [sighted] children read for me."

LEARNING AND PLAYING. There was not a single visually-handicapped child who did not, or would not like being in class with sighted children. However, when it came to playing, none of them expressed preference for playing with the sighted. Four children preferred visually handicapped as playmates. The other three had no preference: "I don't care which is which"; "I play with those who are there." These children felt able to share with the sighted at play only when differences were—realistically or not—obliterated. The children who preferred playing with the visually-handicapped gave clear reasons: "The sighted may suddenly run away and leave you there;" "They can trick you," or "With the blind I can help them." These reasons implied a feeling of being different or inferior in respect to the sighted and finding among the other visually-handicapped children at least avoidance of unpleasant experiences, and a feeling of being able to give and share.

This view of "with the sighted for work, with the blind

for leisure" may have reflected the school environment; contacts between sighted and blind children occurred mostly during classroom activities, rarely during leisure periods. However, the school environment itself may have been an expression of socially accepted attitudes: the blind should be with the sighted to learn more, but with the blind to have feelings of belonging. In this respect it was interesting that the blind children rarely met other blind children outside the school environment except for group meetings on weekends at other social institutions or agencies for the blind.

SIGHTED VS. BLIND. The children were asked to "make up the end" of two sets of stories, each story having as protagonist a child in relation to his parents, siblings and peers. In the first set of stories it was not specified whether the fictional child was sighted or blind; it was left to the respondent to imagine him as handicapped or not. In the second series the child was presented as blind if the respondent had first imagined him as sighted, and vice-versa. Of the seven respondents, five imagined the protagonist of the first set of stories as sighted.

No matter whether they first thought of a sighted or blind child while completing the stories, the respondents did not express any difference in the way sighted and blind children interact with others. The differences between the stories about sighted children and the stories about blind children were small. This finding was consistent with the observations reported above about the refusal on the part of the visually handicapped children to identify themselves with the stereotyped image of "the blind child." When completing stories about the blind, the children were thinking of their immediate experience: themselves or their friends who were not to be considered "really blind;" when completing the stories about sighted children they were also thinking not of the "the sighted child" in general, but of sighted friends or siblings who were probably perceived as quite similar to themselves. In other words, the tendency to think of themselves and their visually-handicapped and sighted schoolmates in terms of degrees of ability to see appeared to prevent a sharp distinction between the extremes of "sighted" and "blind."

WISHES AND ASPIRATIONS. In part of the interview, the children were asked to express three wishes about anything they could think of. Their answers referred almost exclusively to immediate objects and goals, such as having a new drum, a swimming reward, being able to go to high school, etc. There was one exception, a girl who wished "to be a princess or a queen and have eyes." This was one of the girls who attended sighted classes and who appeared to have a good adjustment to her blindness and her school and home environments. This girl was the only child who expressed a wish to have sight, and she put it on the same plane as being a princess, on the plane of phantasy and fairy tales. The other children did not express (at least not directly) the wish to have sight.

A discrepancy was observed in regard to aspirations for the future. The question "How do you imagine your life will be in ten to fifteen years from now?" aroused answers that seemed most "normal"; reference was always made to work position (teacher, mechanic, hairdresser, etc.) and often included being married. One had to realize, however, that no distinction was made by these children between positions that could be held by visually-handicapped people and positions that could not. Consequently, the same boy might wish to be a factory worker or a window cleaner, a teacher or a bus driver. This could be considered as an inconsistency among these children who showed, in other respects, awareness of what they could and could not do. But, of course, this apparent inconsistency was consonant with the fact, mentioned above, thet these children derived their self-concept from what they could and could not do, and defined blindness in terms of abilities to do or not to do. As one girl put it: ". . . I might work in a beauty parlor . . . and everybody tells me I can't do it . . . I say, 'Yes, I can,' but I don't think I can do it, but I wish I could." Or "You know, I would like to do something someone else in my family did, not like M. (a blind friend) would do, like someone would do in my family."

The attempt to find a common ground between the sighted and the blind was evident through the various topics covered by the interviews. The attempt to find a non-opposte position in relation to the sighted world brought into sharp focus the notion of degrees of sightedness, of not being "really blind." The literal meaning of this notion was giving way to the more social meaning of being able to do what the sighted do, of living up to their standards.

JUNIOR HIGH SCHOOL STUDENTS

The junior high school where this part of the study occurred was located in a lower-middle class neighborhood somewhat more homogeneous in ethnic background than neighborhoods where the elementary school study was conducted. In this school there had been a braille class for blind students and a sight conservation class for several years. In the present study only braille students were interviewed (three boys, three girls, twelve to fourteen years in age.)

The school's physical setting suggested equality between sighted and blind. The braille room was simply functional; it looked like the other classrooms except for braille equipment. It was comfortable, not too large, and in the middle of a second-floor corridor with nothing conspicuous about it in terms of special location (in the elementary schools, braille classes were isolated in an effort to offer easy accessibility). The braille classroom was not the center of the blind children's school activities nor a place where they found social satisfaction in relations among themselves at the exclusion of the sighted. The room was very often visited by several sighted children, not only by "guides" who had accompanied blind boys and girls from different classrooms, but also by some who had dropped in for a chat or to try a braille typewriter. The school schedule for sighted and blind children was almost identical and there was no curtailment of the opportunities for getting together.

The six blind students were interviewed individually; the interview schedule was basically similar to that used for the elementary school children.

RESULTS

THE COMMON GROUND. The handicapped boys and girls in this school made a clear distinction between being sighted and being blind; they knew they belonged to a social group. Each of them spontaneously informed me of his degree of sight (usuallylight perception). However, this was not used as a basis for considering themselves and others on a scale of "more" or "less" blind, but rather as a specification of the characteristic of being blind. They were aware that their handicap was only one aspect of their personality. To the question, "What can a blind person do better than a sighted person?" all except one answered to the effect of "it depends on how smart he is."

In the part of the interview wherein respondents had been asked to complete two sets of stories (see above report on elementary school children), to the question about whether the fictional protagonist was sighted or blind, the usual answer was, "I did not think of that; I just thought of a boy in a general way." The recognition and awareness of their handicap was accompanied by the ability to identify with people rather than with one section of humanity, blind people.

EQUALITY AND NEED. The school seemed to provide a setting where being handicapped was taken into account but was not generalized to the whole personality. School peers provided a group with which these youngsters could identify on an equal footing. However, it would be distorting the situation to say that this was achieved effortlessly. The handicapped youngsters still had to live up to sighted standards; they still had to be continuously reminded of their handicap at the moment of being accepted. That the sighted were the majority made living with them and commitment to "their ways" a necessity.

There was the feeling of living in two separate worlds divided by a gap that could not be closed no matter how much good will one might have. The feeling was expressed in simple terms without anger by these youngsters, with a feeling that it was not anybody's fault. They affirmed the fact of irreconcilable modes of perception, of a different core in experiencing, and the ultimate inability to communicate their own experience. One girl said, ". . . there are some questions that they (the sighted) ask that you can't answer, like when somebody asks, 'If you could see, what do you think it would be like?' . . . If I ask them how is it to be able to see they say that it's hard to explain . . . *so I never got anywhere really.*" A boy said to the interviewer, "You are sighted; if you were blind you would probably ask different questions, wouldn't you?" Another boy, ". . . the only thing is that my parents say, 'Just think, if you were only born two months later you would be able to see.' But if you were never able to see, you never know what it is really like, so you can't imagine what you are missing."

There was the feeling that the "encounter" with the sighted, the adjustment of living in a sighted world, was aggravated by attitudes of superiority on the part of the sighted. ". . . With sighted persons, when you first meet them and they find out you are blind, they start acting differently with you than they would with another person. . . . They are afraid of hurting your feelings and when they are afraid of doing that then you just don't talk to them 'cause you both feel pretty bad about it." This boy was revealing a strength which he felt was not respected, and that lack of respect made him wish to withdraw from a belittling relationship: "Then you just don't talk to them." It required a good deal of understanding, self-assurance and an attitude of forgiveness on the part of the blind youngsters to overcome the impulse to "hide" and "not to talk to them." It took the ability to think "I guess they just can't help themselves;" "I don't blame them;" "They probably think that a blind person does not get much. Because of their sight they probably want to do a little extra. . . . It might be that." A boy, a successful student, well liked and respected by his schoolmates had found that the way to live with the sighted was to harden oneself against their comments about the blind: ". . . you learn to adapt more to their ways; you don't get touchy when someone says, 'Did you see him?' or something. You wouldn't fly off the handle as I used to do myself."

The wish for respect and equality by the blind children was accompanied by a recognition that the sighted hold a key to their world—the non-sighted people need the sighted to interpret their world to them (there need not be a contradiction between *needing* the sighted and *feeling equal* to them). The need was justified on the basis of the fact that the sighted were the majority, whose ways the blind wished to learn in order to live with them and make their own contribution as capable persons. "With sighted friends one could do 'most anything . . . you get to learn more; you get to realize what things are like, if you question them about what they see."

WISHES AND ASPIRATIONS. The wishes of the visually handicapped boys and girls in the junior high school presented a most remarkable difference from those of the visually handicapped children in the elementary school. In four of six interviews was mentioned the wish to have sight; in the remaining two interviews, one child could not formulate any wish and one could not mention more than two, and the two mentioned were unusually impersonal (peace in the world, no discrimination). The wish for being sighted seemed to accompany the acceptance of blindness as lack of an ability common to the sighted world to which these youngsters were trying to adjust. It was as if they were thinking, "since the sighted are the group with which we are living and aspire to live, the group that has the power to accept or to reject us, we wish we had as many of their characteristics as possible, and, of course, sightedness is the most essential one." Evidently this could not be the case among the elementary-school children where the group structure was based on being "more blind" or "less blind."

The other wishes expressed referred almost exclusively to some aspect of their family welfare.

To the question, "How do you imagine your life will be in ten to fifteen years from now?" five of the six boys and girls had plans for a career or some specific kind of work; three wished to get married to a sighted person; for the other two, marriage was a possibility, but "too far off to think of." The occupations chosen ranged from typist to teacher of history, from working in a hospital to being an author. Only one boy said, "I can't imagine it; I can't imagine being married and having kids and, you know, working and stuff." But in another part of the interview, he had spoken of becoming a psychologist, like his older brother, ". . . to find out why some people are nice and why some aren't." These occupations seemed to be consonant with restrictions imposed by blindness, yet were varied enough to appear as if they were choices among several possibilities.

The ability to recognize their handicaps and to accept them, their aspirations to find a place in a world based on sight, their ability to identify themselves as persons rather than as blind, and the strength not to gloss over differences between sightedness and blindness seemed to be the main theme expressed by this group of young handicapped people. Their awareness of being blind was paralleled by their recognition of the necessity of adjusting to the sighted, their standards and their ways.

REFERENCES

Barker, R.G.: Wright, Beatrice; Meyerson, L.; Gorrick, Mollie: *Adjustment to Physical Handicap and Illness: A Survey of the Social Psychology of Physique and Disability.* New York: Social Science Research Council, Bull. No. 5s, 1953.

Bertin, A.: A Comparison of Attitudes Toward Blindness. *The International Journal of Education of the Blind,* 9; 1, 1–4, 1959.

Cowen, E.L.; Underberg, Rita; Verrillo, R.T.; Benham, F.: *Adjustment to Visual Disability in Adolescence.* New York: American Foundation for the Blind, 1961.

Cutsforth, T.D.: *The Blind in School and Society.* New York: American Foundation for the Blind, 1951.

Jervis, F.M.: A Comparison of the Self-concepts of Blind and Sighted Children. In *Guidance Programs for Blind Children.* Watertown, Mass.; Perkins School Publication, No. 20, 1960.

Norris, Miriam; Spaulding, Patricia J.; and Brodie, Fern H.: *Blindness in Children.* Chicago: University of Chicago Press, 1957.

CHAPTER 18

RETARDATION AMONG BLIND CHILDREN*

SALLY ROGOW

~~~~~~

Behavior of Young Blind Children
Perceptual Learning

~~~~~~

STUDIES OF BLIND children (Norris, Spaulding and Brodie, 1959) suggest that mental deficiency is no more prevalent among blind children than among sighted. Yet, among blind children for whom additional handicaps are reported, the incidence of retardation sharply increases. It has been estimated that 80.2 percent of multiply impaired blind children are retarded (Moor, 1970). Retardation is the most frequently reported additional handicap among blind children.

The startling incidence of mental retardation among children whose blindness is accompanied by additional handicaps has been a source of confusion about the nature of the retardation among blind children. Is the retardation remediable or preventable? Is it the outcome of understimulation? Are sensory and environmental deprivation sufficient to explain functional retardation? How limiting is blindness to perceptual and cognitive development? These are some of the questions which prompted the writing of this paper.

* Used with permission from *Education for the Visually Handicapped*, *December, 1970.*

185

Whether these same children would have been retarded had they been sighted is pure speculation. The point is that an inordinately large number of blind children function on a retarded level. This paper is an attempt to examine the often subtle ways in which blindness may interfere with perceptual and cognitive learning.

Suppositions based upon comparisons of blind with sighted children can be misleading, and imply that perceptual development of blind children is impaired by the very fact of blindness. The absence of the visual mode is assumed to lead directly to difficulty in perceptual awareness and knowledge about the environment. Vision is an integrating sense: one can scan the environment visually, picking up many useful bits of information, which take the blind child longer to accumulate. Research, however, demonstrates that visual perception is learned. Space perception develops gradually as a part of total perceptual development. (Piaget, 1959)

Burlingham, Sandler and Fraiberg have stressed the devastating effects of blindness upon ego development (Burlingham, 1964; Sandler, 1963; Fraiberg, 1964). Sandler observed that the incidental development of blind infants parallels that of the sighted until about sixteen weeks of age, when "the ego development of the blind child pursues a course which results in his passive self-centeredness and lack of striving toward mastery at later ages" (Sandler, p. 346). Scott notes that "blindness creates increasingly greater difficulties for the young child: and that, as a result, during the early years of life, he drops further behind his sighted peers" (Scott, p. 1935).

On the other hand, Elonen considers parental rejection, overprotection and confusion to be responsible for the distortion in development observed among blind children. Elonen's studies of deviant blind children demonstrate that blindness itself cannot be considered a direct cause of retardation (Elonen, 1964). Her views are consistent with those of Thomas Cutsforth who pointed out long ago that blind children must be assumed to learn differently from the sighted. Cutsforth, who was blind himself, claimed that the insistence that blind children perform as if they were sighted imposes a further handicap among the blind (Cutsforth, 1934).

BEHAVIOR OF YOUNG BLIND CHILDREN

The blind infant is hampered in his exploratory activities. Exploration through touch alone is limited to those objects which are both stationary and can be explored through their haptic features. As the child learns from tactual experience, he develops a schema or touch sequence (Scott, 1969). A schema allows for discrimination between broad classes of objects, but makes it extremely difficult to draw distinctions between objects of the same class. Schematic apprehension can result in a misleading impression. The quality of the very young child's experience is not comparable to that of the sighted (Scott, 1969).

Competence in exploration is learned during the early years. And for those children who are kept in a protected and "safe" environment, competence becomes nearly impossible to acquire. Without encouragement at exploration, the boundaries of the blind child's world are sharply curtailed, and, with them, mastery over objects in the environment. The effect of a barren environment is the impoverishment of motivation to explore (Gibson, 1969). The sameness of surroundings prevents the awareness of differences and contrasts. Auditory clues can seem to come from outer space when they are not supplemented by tactual experience (Scott, 1969). When adults do attempt to verbally interpret the environment to the child, his information is "second-hand". Without the opportunity to touch and taste and smell for himself, the blind child learns no frame of reference for what is explained to him and therefore no way of making the verbal information his own.

Limitations imposed by restrictions of environmental experience have serious consequences for the development of "self-concept" or "self-image". The emergence of a concept of self develops out of the child's recognition of his own impact upon the environment, and the people and objects within it. It is more difficult for the blind baby to realize his impact. The consequences of feeling a loss of control is perhaps one of the most debilitating features of blindness. Once an object is out of reach, it seems to have disappeared.

> "To the blind child, non-self consists of a confusing, ill-defined, diffuse something that comes and goes. It lacks sharpness and contrast and, as such, provides a poor background against which to draw the distinction between it and self. As a result, a conception of self in the blind child is very slow to emerge" (Scott, p. 1032).

While the blind child may be unable to see the impact he has upon others, he does experience the "impact he has upon his own body" (Scott, p. 1932). Naturally then, his interest becomes focused upon himself when nothing beckons from outside. It is at this stage that many mannerisms, such as finger-waving, head-banging, vigorous back-and-forth-rocking, etc., emerge. These mannerisms have been called "blindisms", and the vigor and persistence of the child's activity is frightening to parents. Their presence is often considered a symptom of "brain damage", emotional disturbance and/or mental deficiency. Expectations for the child are accordingly derived. It is to be noted that these very same mannerisms are observed among sighted children, who are more easily understood and therefore not typed as readily by mannerisms alone. There also seems to be a reciprocal relationship between stereotyped behavior among sighted retardates and object manipulation; the more environmental object manipulation observed, the less children develop stereotyped patterns of behavior (Guess, 1967).

The very fact that society considers blindness a seriously debilitating handicap leads to low expectations of the blind child. When blindness is believed to totally incapacitate a child, then anything that child is able to do is considered "amazing". This sort of attitude creates many distortions in the way a child thinks about himself (Scott, 1969).

Visual expressions of emotion and feeling are so much a part of the "sighted" world, that their absence makes it seem that the blind child is not aware of how other people react to him. Yet the most intensive relationships a child has are with his own family. Sensitive to nuance in handling and attitude, the child lives up to the expectations held for him.

Herein lies the dilemma confronting so many blind children. Low expectations are combined with judgments based on the development of sighted children. The blind child is expected to conform to a world which he does not understand. The visual appearance of a world never seen becomes a rather sophisticated concept for which the young child is not ready. Those modes of exploration to which he can readily adapt are denied him for fear he will be hurt and that he is incapable of learning to protect himself.

Basing conclusions about blind children on the observed development of the sighted may be useful for description, but limited in helping to understand the development of the blind. Comparison gives us no clue to why so many blind children are able to compensate so adequately and even achieve brilliance. The answers must be sought in the processes of perceptual and cognitive development, in the search for ways to support compensatory perceptual learning.

PERCEPTUAL LEARNING

Experimental studies suggest that sensory deprivation at critical periods of development prevents the learning of selective control over stimuli. Without selective control, the child is unable to extract information from the range of stimuli presented to him (Gibson, 1969).

Perception is an exploratory activity and should be considered separately from performance. Exploratory perceptual activity "provides information about the environment prior to performance" (Gibson, 1969, p. 447).

Perceptual development proceeds from a general undifferentiation to finer and finer differentiations. "The superordinate structure of language or a melody is recognized before specific differentiations can be made" (Gibson, 1969, p. 447). The differentiation theory of perceptual learning explains perception as the ability to extract distinctive features of the stimulus, the invariant qualities and their respective structures are what is learned. Differentiation begins with gross features and is refined as the child manipulates the objects in space, and move in space.

> Invariants over continuous transformations in time are the basis
> for the perception of an event, a unitary occurrence in time. Percep-
> tual development with regard to events consists in detecting
> invariants of gradually higher order, over a more diverse set of trans-
> formations and a longer time span (Gibson, p. 464).

The capacity to utilize cues is part of the process of perceptual development. Constraints on stimulation may even help
to center attention on the most useful clues. Adaptation to
the environment depends on effective pickup of information
from the environment (Gibson, 1969).

The perception of space is the result of both direct perception and sensory-motor activity. According to Piaget, during
the first year of life the child's own activity leads him,
"through handling objects, turning them over and moving
them about, to grant them physical permanence, together
with constancy of size and shape" (Piaget, pp. 451–452).

> To the extent that sensory-motor activity is already operative at
> the level of perceptual space, it is possible to discern, though in
> a relatively undifferentiated state, the two complementary roles of
> sense perception and motor activity (Piaget, p. 452).

Lauretta Bender has also emphasized the continuous inter-
play between motor and sensory factors in the development
of perception. Normal development arises from "total organic
patterning of behavior based on motor action or motility,
including tonic neck reflex behavior, muscle tone, respiratory
patterns and homeostasis. Sensory or perceptive patterns arise
from these action patterns in response to experienced stimuli
and out of them is developed awareness of the body as the
concept of body image" (Bender, p. 137).

Two independent but parallel developments occur with
increasing control of the environment. One is the ability to
extract useful information and the other is the patterning of
behavior. The latter is where blind children are most likely
to differ from the sighted. Adaptation to the environment is
served best by tactual and auditory modes, and time se-
quences or patterns are more meaningful than spatially
organized concepts. As the child learns from tactual
experience, he develops a schema or touch sequence, which
is temporally organized.

Vision, which for the sighted becomes a "pilot sense," has

an integrating quality. Its absence may have the effect of rendering other systems more efficient, but perceptual unities take longer to develop. Information processing may require more steps in mediating perceptual learning. This is why judgments on the development of perceptual learning should not be made on performance factors alone. Observing how blind children utilize sensory information, how they use their hands and feet in exploration and manipulation can give a more realistic appraisal of their true abilities than conventional tests designed for the sighted.

The blind child may indeed acquire a great deal of information, but he also encounters limiting factors in his performance. The failure to gain sufficient control to manipulate objects on a conceptual level becomes the real barrier to the development of discriminatory ability. Certainly the presence of overprotection and anxious parental attitudes inhibit efforts at exploration and convey the impression that the child is not able to explore.

Blindness accompanied by other physical disabilities, such as a hearing loss, or a crippling condition, intensify the isolation. But multiply impaired children demonstrate ability to learn in suitable educational programs. Awareness of what kinds of experiences help to develop reliance upon a child's own perceptions become crucial. Overwhelming any child with stimulation may result in withdrawal and anxiety.

Fear of abandonment and rejection are also capable of turning potentially bright blind children into non-verbal, passive and stubbornly resistant children, who cling to the routine with curious tenacity. These children claim a desperate dependence which is reinforced by harried, confused, and desperate parents, who unwittingly allow themselves to be controlled. What is not often observed by those who apply the labels of "psychotic", "autistic", or "retarded" to blind children is the very efficient manner in which these children manipulate those around them. Language, which is usually comprehended, is rarely used. There is no need for verbal expression when needs are not only met, but anticipated.

Deprived or discouraged from attempts at exploration, many blind children learn very quickly that safety resides in and with and through their parents. Intolerant of frustration, these children never learn how to cope with conflict; they are motivated in no direction other than insuring that their basic needs are met.

Functional retardation may be prevented with the provision of early parent counseling, early pre-school programs, and the development of educational programs for blind children in schools for the retarded. Retardation for many blind children is the result of impoverishment of experience. Even the most profound forms of retardation are preventable with the provision of early educational programs.

REFERENCES

Bender, L.: In P. Schilder (Ed.): *Contributions To Neuropsychiatry.* New York: International Universities Press, 1964.

Burlingham, D: Some Problems of Ego Development of Blind Children. *The Psychoanalytic Study of the Child,* 1964, *20,* pp. 194–208.

Elonen, A.S. and Zwarenstyn, S.B. : Appraisal of Developmental Lag in Certain Children. *Journal of Pediatrics,* 1964, 65:4, pp. 599–610.

Fraiberg, S. and Freedman, D.A.: Studies in the Ego Development of Congenitally Blind Children, *The Psychoanalytic Study of the Child,* 1964, *19,* pp. 113–169.

Gibson, E.J.: *Principles of Perceptual Learning and Development.* New York: Appleton-Century-Crofts, 1969

Guess, D.: Mental Retardation and Blindness: A Complex and Relatively Unexplored Dyad. *Exceptional Children,* 1967, *33,* pp. 471–480.

Moor, P.: Telling It Like It Is. Address to the British Columbia Mental Retardation Institute, April 11, 1970.

Norris, M.; Spaulding, P.J.; and Brodie, F.H.: *Blindness in Children.* Chicago: University of Chicago Press, 1957.

Piaget, J.: *The Child's Concept of Space.* New York: Basic Books, 1959.

Sandler, A.: Aspects of Passivity and Ego Development in the Blind Infant. *Psychoanalytic Study of the Child,* 1963, *18,* pp. 343–359.

Scott, R.A.: The Socialization of Blind Children. In D.A. Goslin (Ed): *Handbook of Socialization Theory and Research.* New York: Rand McNally, 1969.

CHAPTER 19

DIABETICS IN ORIENTATION
AND MOBILITY*

REX A. WARD

~~~~~~

THE ORIENTATION AND Mobility Specialist's role in the rehabilitation process of the blind diabetic is a very important one. The approach and attitudes toward the student depends greatly upon one's knowledge of diabetes and its effects on the human body. To accomplish a successful rehabilitation experience for the blind diabetic it is essential to have a basic understanding of the following aspects:
  A. WHAT IS DIABETES
  B. SYMPTOMS
  C. EMERGENCY TREATMENT CONCERNING RE-
     ACTIONS
  D. AFTER EFFECTS OF A REACTION
  E. BASIC UNDERSTANDING OF EACH BLIND
     DIABETIC'S PHYSICAL AND MENTAL CAPA-
     BILITIES
Diabetes is a hereditary disease, resulting in the inability of the body to use food properly. This is caused by an insufficient supply of insulin or interference with the action of insulin in the body. Insulin is a hormone, or chemical substance, produced by the pancreas. Insulin is released from the pancreas into the bloodstream to regulate the rate at which the body cells use and store sugar. This sugar, which is derived

* Used with permission from *Education of the Visually Handicapped,* Vol. 4, March, 1972.

from the food we eat, supplies the energy that the body cells need to sustain life and keep the body functioning in a normal manner.

During digestion, much of the food we eat is converted into a form of sugar called "glucose". This sugar is obtained not only from all of the carbohydrates in food but also from approximately 60 per cent of the fat in the diet. Glucose (sugar) is carried to the various parts of the body by the bloodstream; therefore, a certain amount of glucose is present in the blood at all times.

The body cannot use and store glucose without the aid of insulin. Insulin is the "spark" needed by the body cells to "burn" glucose, which in turn produces the "heat" which is the energy required to maintain life.

When the pancreas fails to produce a sufficient supply of insulin, glucose cannot be used or stored properly in the body causing glucose to accumulate in the bloodstream and causing blood sugar levels to rise above normal. When the blood sugar concentration exceeds certain levels, sugar is "spilled over" into the urine. Thus, two chemical signs of diabetes are as follows: (1) excessive amounts of sugar in the blood (hyperglycemia); and (2) excretion of sugar in the urine, known as glycosuria.

Diabetes can develop at any age. The highest incidence occurs between forty and sixty. There exists three million diabetics in the United States today and it is estimated there will be four million in 1973. Approximately 264,000 individuals experience some visual limitations as a result of diabetes.

Treatment of diabetes must be determined on an individual basis. A diet is always included that provides adequate kinds and amounts of food to meet body needs and is the cornerstone in the treatment of all diabetics. Many individuals need daily insulin injections and/or an oral drug in addition to their diabetic diet.

There are two types of reactions that the O & M Specialist should be knowledgeable in—THE DIABETIC COMA and THE INSULIN REACTION:

One may have difficulty determining if the situation is a diabetic coma or insulin reaction; so a good rule of thumb

	DIABETIC COMA	INSULIN SHOCK	
		REGULAR INSULIN	OTHER TYPES OF INSULIN
ONSET	Slow (Days)	Sudden	Gradual (Hours)
CAUSES	Neglect and Ignorance Omission of Insulin and Food, Infections and Other Medical Problems	Overdosage; Delayed, Omitted, or Lost Meals; Excessive Exercise Before Meals.	
SIGNS	Florid Face; Rapid Breathing Dry Skil, Rapid Pulse, Acetone Breath, Comm.	Pallor, Shallow Respiration Sweating, Pulse Normal, Abnormal or Unusual Behavior.	
WHAT TO DO	Call Physician at First Sign or Take Individual to Emergency Room of Hospital.	Administer Sugar, Candy, Orange Juice if Able to Swallow. If Not, Place Sugar Under Tongue or Lip, Take Individual to Emergency Room of Hospital.	

procedure to follow is to administer sugar or some substitute in all cases, and take individual to emergency room of hospital.

The symptoms and after-effects of a reaction are very important for the O & M Specialist to keep in mind. The after-effects of a reaction may last from minutes to permanent depending on severity and duration. Some of the symptomatic after-effects are inward nervousness, fatigue, slow mental response, and general disorientation.

The Specialist should be aware of the personal hygiene of a diabetic, since the condition affects the total bodily functions. Circulation of the blood is most important, particularly in the legs and feet. One can effectively relate to and motivate a blind diabetic by explaining the importance of exercise. In addition to improving physical fitness, exercise causes sugar to be utilized and thus reduces the amount of oral medication or insulin. Exercise also helps to maintain muscle tone. The Specialist should recommend a series of exercises (in conjunction with medical doctor) that the blind diabetic can do every day to maintain proper bodily balance.

Wounds on a diabetic should be carefully watched. Even the most superficial ones at times are slow to heal.

In order to obtain the basic understanding of physical and mental capabilities, the individual's medical record should be read carefully. A discussion of the record with the diabetic is also necessary. The average diabetic will know and understand, or feels that he does, his particular condition almost as well as his own doctor. The factors to be determined in the discussion are:

1. Type of Medication (Oral tablet or Insulin); Amount of dosage will provide some indication of severity of diabetes.
2. Age of Onset—If diabetes is diagnosed in childhood, the incidence of neuropathy increases with duration of diabetes. Diminished vibratory sense, especially of lower extremities, has been reported in many children between ten and twelve. After thirty years of age some juvenile diabetics appear to lose their achilles tendon reflex.
3. Is the individual aware of a reaction developing? The majority of blind diabetics will be able to know, but there are some who cannot tell or may wait to see if the reaction will "pass". Once a reaction has started, it will not "pass" until proper treatment is administered.
4. The blind diabetic should carry sugar, candy, etc.; if he does not already do so, suggest that he does. You, as an instructor, should always have sugar or candy on hand for emergency purposes.
5. Diabetics that have amputations should pay close attention to the stump area—in particular if artificial devices for moving are involved. The stump area should be inspected regularly and cleaned.
6. Discussion of proper footwear and care of feet is very important. Even the smallest blister can create extreme complications for the diabetic. Points to discuss in general care of feet:
   1) General care:
      a. Wash daily with warm, soapy water.
      b. Massage with alcohol or lanolin.
      c. Wear only clean socks or stockings.
      d. Break in new shoes slowly.
      e. Do not use a hot-water bottle or a heating pad in or out of bed.

f. Have someone else cut your nails and examine your feet weekly.

g. Consult your physician or podiatrist regularly.

2) Corns and calluses:

a. Do not cut.

b. Soften in warm, soapy water and rub off.

3) Improve circulation by;

a. Exercise.

b. Massage.

4) Injuries and abrasions:

a. Call physician promptly.

b. Stay off injured foot.

c. Avoid iodine, cresol, and carbolic acid solutions.

It is very important that the Specialist realizes that when a blind diabetic student begins the process of orientation and mobility, the physical demands may be much more than he is previously accustomed to. This will create a period of adjustment not only physically, but also mentally. The student will experience the anxiety of regulation of medications. Usually a proper level of medication amount can be determined, but in some cases, it is a continuing procedure of trial amounts. This often affects the individual's attitude and motivation toward continuing with O & M Specialist.

Another very important aspect relating to the physical capabilities is the degree of tactual awareness existent in the blind diabetic. Many diabetics experience tactual sensation loss. The degree of loss depends upon the individual and his disorder.

For many, it becomes difficult to determine inclines, declines, and type of surfaces they are walking over, and also information gathered from the cane is not always understood properly due to the various degrees of vibratory sensation loss. The majority of blind adult diabetics will have some tactual sensations and the Specialist can assist in establishing tactual awarenesses on the individual's part by continuing to stress concentration on declines and inclines. Pointing out that when one goes down a decline, the cane will feel as if it is moving away from the individual and vice versa when negotiating inclines. Also continued concentration on body position in reference to how one "feels" in the positions of inclines or declines. Also explain that when negotiating a decline one's walking pace will quicken rather suddenly and slow when confronting an incline.

It is important to be able to determine what type of surface one is walking over such as sidewalk, asphalt, dirt, wood, etc., in order to effectively relate to the environmental realities. The blind diabetic needs to develop a very light "touch" with the cane. A light "touch" when coming into contact with surfaces will produce a stronger vibrating conduction throughout the cane and enable one to interpret surface information effectively.

The majority of blind diabetics will be able to relate to their environment to some degree tactually. Some may experience no difficulty in this area. But it is a very important factor to consider in program planning and evaluation.

Reaction reflex is another area to contemplate in regards to the diabetic. Neurological examinations in many cases reveal absence or diminished knee and ankle jerks and vibratory sensation awareness is frequently impaired. When these findings are elicited, motor nerve conduction velocity is reduced in the affected part. Occasionally, the presenting sign is weakness of the extremity thus creating slow reaction time.

Another neurological reflex syndrome which deserves mention is diabetic myopathy. It occurs principally in middle aged or elderly men with mild diabetic conditions and is associated with pain, weakness and wasting in the proximal portions of the lower extremities. This syndrome includes reduction of the patellar tendon reflex. This condition will tend to create difficulty in negotiating stairs and curbs.

If the blind diabetic is experiencing difficulty over-stepping curbs, slow to react to stair-drops and exhibits overall lack of reaction to objects in the environment, several methods can be employed to relieve the situations. One would be development of a kinesthetic awareness of distance negotiated. Practice on determining length of a block and preparing oneself for the approach of a curb. Also have the individual develop, if possible, visual imagery concepts of the environment. For example, have one visually imagine an indoor environment and anticipate such objects as door openings, stairs, and so forth. One last resort would be to lengthen the cane by several inches. This will help to provide a longer reaction time to objects in the environment.

The last area to be discussed is the visual loss and visual fluctuations created by the diabetic condition. Impairment of vision in the diabetic is most commonly caused by (1) retinal hemorrhage, (2) cataract, and (3) refractive errors. Due to these particular visual impairments, fluctuations in vision may occur. This can create a great deal of frustration for the blind diabetic. It has been stated by many diabetics that they have felt like they were losing contact with reality due to the fluctuations of vision. Several have stated that they thought they were "losing their mind".

The O & M Specialist should have factual knowledge of the blind diabetic's eye condition, and the dynamics of blindness. This information is vital for a more complete understanding of the individual's overall emotional reaction to blindness.

Thus the mobility program planned should have a build-in flexibility so that the individual can achieve success and feel the satisfaction of accomplishment and independence.

CHAPTER 20

SIBLINGS OF VISUALLY HANDICAPPED CHILDREN*

Luciana Visentini Steinzor

~~~~~~

Sixteen Siblings Are Interviewed
A Special but Unequal Part of the Family
Blind Siblings Belong to a Different Group
Few Express Resentment Against Blind Siblings
Children Do Not Discuss Blindness with Siblings
Only One Boy Had Read a Book Dealing with the Blind
The Four Who Wished Their Brother or Sister Would Gain Sight
Summary
References

~~~~~~

How is a blind child regarded by his sighted brothers and sisters? What role does he play in the network of relationships with other siblings and parents on one hand, and with peers, relatives and neighbors on the other? Does he serve as the focal point on which all other associations converge? Is he isolated and ignored, or is he involved in many well-differentiated relationships? Is he seen as one of "the blind," with the stereotyped connotations belonging to that phrase?

Few studies on siblings of handicapped children have been

* Used with permission from *The New Outlook*, February, 1967.

conducted (Wood, 1942; Gates, 1946; Prout and White, 1956; Shugart, 1958; Graliker, 1962; Schreiber and Feeley, 1965). None of these deal with visual disability, although there are references to the meaning of sighted children in the same family with a visually handicapped child (Sommers, 1944; Lowenfeld, 1956).

Gaining insight into growing up in close contact with a visually handicapped boy or girl was the aim of the study presented here.

SIXTEEN SIBLINGS ARE INTERVIEWED

This was an exploratory study involving interviews with sixteen siblings of visually handicapped children admitted or seeking admission to a psychiatric clinic connected with an agency for the blind. The severity of the visual handicap was various; in all cases it was complicated by intellectual and emotional disturbances. The age of the siblings ranged from seven to sixteen years; there were seven boys and ten girls in the sample, from nine families. Six of the interviews were conducted in the homes of interviewees, while the remainder were conducted in the researcher's office during the period from June 1963 to March 1964. The interview schedule was structured and open-ended. The analysis of the data consisted almost totally of observations and interpretations of themes common to most or some of the interviews, since the sample's heterogeneity and the study's exploratory nature did not allow more precise statistical investigation.

In one part of the interview respondents were asked to complete two sets of stories. One set had a sighted child as a protagonist; the other, a blind child. Answers to stories about sighted children were compared with those about blind children.

Some trends were very clear. Blind children were presented as needing more help than sighted children. This result can be considered positive since "help" was defined in this study as realistic help, offered without superiority or overprotection. However, attitudes of kindness and attitudes of aggression were expressed more often toward the blind than toward the sighted, pointing to the feeling that special treatment and protection with a tinge of pity characterized relationship with the blind. Attitudes of supervision were expressed with equal frequency toward sighted and blind children indicating that being family members made the siblings more aware that blind children were also supervised, given orders, and expected to live up to common group norms. At least on this ground they were considered part of the group. That this acceptance was limited could be seen by the trend of lower cooperative attitudes toward the blind than toward the sighted, pointing to lack of readiness to share in common activities with equality. The severity of the impairment of the handicapped siblings (all multiply handicapped) may have accounted for this result.

A SPECIAL BUT UNEQUAL PART OF THE FAMILY

The handicapped child was usually considered a special part of the family and was accepted as such. This acceptance took the form, especially among older siblings, of recognizing that the blind child needed particular care and could only partially participate in the usual activities of the family. Emphasis was put by most of the respondents on how easily they could engage in games with their blind siblings. These games could range from outdoors hide-and-seek to just building with blocks or handclapping. In other words, the feeling was expressed that blind children could share in activities, but not in an atmosphere of equality. What was underlined was admiration for the handicapped child's ability to have some part in these games; how well he could hear, how surprising it was he could tell one person from another, how fast he could run, etc. In regard to his participation in family life, it was said that he could, on the whole, take care of his own room; he could put on most of his clothing; he could help with the dishes and a few other housekeeping chores. Again, these statements were made without the matter-of-fact attitude that would have given them a connotation of real acceptance. Anxiety was conveyed about showing the best side of the picture, as if the respondents had, for a long time, put themselves through the process of wanting to see the best in their family situation.

BLIND SIBLINGS BELONG TO A DIFFERENT GROUP

A minority of siblings conveyed a feeling that while their handicapped brother or sister was part of the family, he or she also belonged to a different group with which the sighted children had no relation. The group was one composed of blind children and was usually concretely identified with a special class or summer camp for the blind. "He feels better with other blind children; they understand each other better." "Friends around here are too rough; the blind children in camp are better."

The majority of siblings declared the handicapped boy or girl had sighted friends in the neighborhood; they were the respondent's own friends who came to their home and played games which included the blind child or who alone engaged briefly in play with the blind child. Only one girl, seven years old, thought of her twelve-year-old brother as spending most of his time sitting by himself in the backyard with a transistor radio. She felt he would have been happier with other blind children, and that although her friends and her other siblings' friends at times talked and played with her blind brother, he was in need of friends of his own. This girl was one of four siblings interviewed from the same family; the other three (two boys, ten and fourteen years old, and one fifteen-year-old girl) while saying that their handicapped brother had no friends of his own, stressed the fact that their friends had accepted him and were cordial to him. They did not show concern for his loneliness, as if this were a proper state for him.

FEW EXPRESS RESENTMENT
AGAINST BLIND SIBLINGS

Resentment or jealousy against a handicapped brother or sister was expressed in only a few cases and then by younger siblings. A boy of ten said of his sixteen-year-old sister, "She likes to be blind; she is being taken every place and is treated better than my brother or me." Another ten-year-old boy said that his blind brother aged twelve, "is enjoying it; he is getting practically everything." A seven-year-old girl showed her resentment in a more complex way; she did not feel that her fifteen-year-old brother was better treated in the sense of receiving more from her parents, but she strongly felt a loss of her freedom and resented having to plan her time according to her brother's needs. She would accompany him every day in the playground where he could meet another visually handicapped boy or where she had to keep fetching a ball he would send "five miles away;" her conclusion: "It gets boring."

The prevailing attitude revealed in the study was one of protection and care not to hurt the feelings of the handicapped child. In this context, any feeling of competition was almost totally absent. Only one boy said of his older blind brother, "He is the best eater of all, but now I have got a big appetite and he is the second best." It was interesting that the only competitive note was struck at such a primitive level as eating.

CHILDREN DO NOT DISCUSS
BLINDNESS WITH SIBLINGS

Similarly, there was a lack of openness in discussing the condition of a handicapped boy or girl. None of the respondents had spoken with their handicapped sibling about blindness. They feared hurting the child's feelings, as if blindness and other disturbances were something not to talk about, something that was best to ignore. Questions of friends and neighbors were unwelcome and considered "nosy"; in fact, just one respondent, fifteen-year-old girl, said she did not resent discussing her brother's blindness with friends. Although only one of the siblings recalled a particularly unpleasant episode about a lady offering money to his brother, they all resented people staring at the brother or sister while walking along the street. "I don't like to go out with him because people start looking . . . I'd like then that we would both go away fast." The only persons with whom the respondents seemed to feel free in talking about their siblings and about blindness were their parents, and mainly their mother. They reported talking about what was best for the blind sibling, how to deal with him, what school was desirable, etc. They remembered their mothers helping them, in younger years, in dealing with the handicapped child and telling them how to assist and what to expect.

ONLY ONE BOY HAD READ A BOOK DEALING WITH THE BLIND

In general, being the sibling of a blind child did not seem to make for deeper interest in blindness and in the lot of blind people. The siblings had, as a whole, very little information about blind people in general. Only one boy had read a book dealing with the blind (a book, left by a social worker, on how to help the blind be more self-sufficient). Even the name of Helen Keller was not a familiar one. Contact with other blind people was limited to a few visits to summer camps or very sporadic encounters with schoolmates of the sibling. This scarcity of information was accompanied by a generally stereotyped and negative view of blindness. Blindness was defined as a world of darkness, as the absence of light, as the inability to relate to the outside world through sight. It was defined in negative terms: a blind person was a person who can't relate through sight (a terrible state to be in). The blind person was one who had a definite lack of something essential to normal living, rather than one who relates to the world through other senses, who has his own way of perceiving and imagining objects. Siblings who were blind were categorized on a scale of sightedness-blindness, with great emphasis on how much they could see.

The respondents almost constantly conveyed the wish to know more, to gain a better perspective on blind siblings' comparative abilities, on their own experience of living with a blind person, and on the abilities and possibilities of blind people. Interviewing seemed to provide a setting in which respondents felt their experience with a blind child was exceptional, and that through their unusual experience, they had a contribution to make. They felt that other people might profit from their feelings and thoughts and, especially, might wish to hear these (mainly with themselves, not their handicapped siblings, in mind). The sibling, in this respect, had always received a secondary interest and had not been heard for his own sake.

THE FOUR WHO WISHED THEIR BROTHER
OR SISTER WOULD GAIN SIGHT

Was the handicapped child of great importance in what his siblings wished for and aspired to? Respondents were asked to express their three main wishes and to visualize their life as adults. Only four siblings mentioned the wish for their brother or sister to gain sight. It was of interest that this wish was associated with the denial that the handicapped child belonged to the group of "the blind." It was found exclusively among those respondents who had stressed how relatives and friends already accepted their handicapped sibling. It seemed to accompany the wish to make such acceptance even fuller.

The only disturbing note was found in a small number of interviewees in regard to the view of their future family life. Two girls (ten and thirteen years old) and one boy (ten years old) spoke of a future family as a burden to be avoided as long as possible. One respondent, a boy aged thirteen, spoke of his handicapped brother as having to be part of his future life; he would take care of him when his parents were old and he would get married on the condition that his wife help him with his brother.

SUMMARY

In summary, the siblings of visually handicapped children usually considered their blind brother and sister as a special member of the family, in need of care and kindness, but at the same time capable of participation in common activities, although within limits. Rarely was the handicapped child seen as belonging to "the blind." The siblings had scant information about blindness in general, very little contact with other blind children or adults, and exhibited a stereotyped view of blindness and uncommonly negative opinions of blind people as a group. It was quite evident, however, they wished to know more and to share the experience they were having, and had a need to feel it was valuable and unusual in order to gain a perspective on its meaning. Some disturbances were shown in connection with future family life; these were, however, exhibited by a small minority of respondents.

REFERENCES

Gates, M.F.: A Comparative Study of Some Problems of Social and Emotional Adjustments of Crippled and Non-crippled Girls and Boys. *Journal of Genetic Psychology, 68:*219–244, 1946.

Graliker, Betty: Teenage Reaction to Mentally Retarded Siblings. *American Journal of Mental Deficiency, 66:*838–842, 1962.

Lowenfeld, B.: *Our Blind Children.* Springfield, Illinois: Charles C Thomas, 1956.

Prout, C.T. and White, Mary A.: The Schizophrenic's Siblings. *Journal of Nervous Mental Disease, 123:*162–180, 1965.

Schreiber, M. and Feeley, M.: A Guided Group Experience. In Siblings of the Retarded. *Children,* 12, 6, 221–225, Nov.-Dec., 1965.

Shugart, G.: Anxiety in Siblings Upon Separation. *Social Work,* 3:30–36, 1958.

Sommers, Vita Stein: *The Influence of Parental Attitudes and Social Environments on the Personality and Development of the Adolescent Blind.* New York: American Foundation for the Blind, 1944.

Wood, Mildred L.: Family Relations in Homes Containing Subnormal Child and Sibling. *Smith College Social Studies, 13:* 1942.

PART IV

INFORMATION FOR COUNSELING PURPOSES

The Role of Grief and Fear in the Death of Kidney
  Transplant Patients
The Vocational Counselor and Family Caseworker
  as Joint Leaders in a Group Counseling Program
Counseling the Blind and Severely Visually Impaired

Chapter 21

THE ROLE OF GRIEF AND FEAR
IN THE DEATH OF KIDNEY
TRANSPLANT PATIENTS

By Robert M. Eisendrath

~~~~~~

Abandonment and Anxiety
Case Reports
Discussion
The Role of Affective States
Conclusion

~~~~~~

Eight out of 11 patients who died following renal transplantation were noted to have suffered a sense of abandonment by their families or to have experienced panic and a sense of pessimism about the outcome of the operation, to a degree not observed among patients who survived. The author concludes that preoperative psychotherapy to help mobilize the hopeless patient's will to live may be necessary for his survival.

SPECULATIONS ABOUT the role of emotions, feelings, and object relationships in the outcome of a physical illness have, until fairly recently, been relegated to the family and friends of the patient, who usually do not understand electrolyte balance or organ physiology. Although physicians may

* Used with permission from the *Am J Psychiat, 126*:3, 1969.

often have their private impressions, the translation of emotional states into factors influencing a clinical course is sufficiently mysterious that these observations remain mainly unreported except as anecdotes. This paper presents an observation regarding these factors in patients who died following renal transplantation.

ABANDONMENT AND ANXIETY

These patients who died were distinguished either by a sense of being abandoned during their illness by an important person upon whom they depended and whose esteem and love were integral parts of their lives or by anxiety approaching panic about their ultimate outcome. Not that anxiety, depression, turmoil, and various defensive maneuvers were uncommon—they were the rule with everyone seen. Furthermore, the causes of death were the common complications of renal transplantation: namely, sepsis, hemorrhage, and cardiac failure or arrhythmia. But none of the surviving patients was abandoned and none reached such levels of sustained anxiety as those to be discussed.

During the 21 months of this study, 48 patients received transplants with a kidney donated from a parent, a sibling, or a cadaver. Three patients had two transplants. During this time there were 11 deaths. All but three died within four weeks of their transplants. Most of the patients seen had been sick for some time, had gone into terminal renal failure, and had been referred to the renal service of the Peter Bent Brigham Hospital. They were all hemodialyzed for periods of not less than two months and in some cases as long as 18 months. When the service and the patient were ready, transplants were performed.

Just prior to surgery the patient was put on high dosages of prednisone and azathioprine (Imuran). In some cases a thoracic duct fistula was used to drain off lymphocytes. Rejection crises were treated with increased dosages of drugs or other agents to combat kidney destruction.

Almost all 48 patients had some complications, such as leakage of urine at the ureteral anastomotic junction, infection, leukopenia, rejection, or rupture of an artery. The existence of complications did not seem to correlate with overall outcome, however. A number of the surviving patients lost their kidneys and went back on hemodialysis to await a second or third transplant.

The material for this study was gained through interviews on the wards by the author. The amount of detail obtained varied with the physical and emotional availability of the patients. Additional material was provided by other physicians and by the dialysis and transplant unit nurses. In some cases the family of the patient was interviewed. Almost every patient was seen at least once by the author, although occasionally this was not possible.

Following the observations reported here, which were retrospective in formulation, a further checking was done on the survivors to see whether some important piece of history had been neglected. No further evidence of abandonment or panic was discovered. Interestingly, all those patients whose histories are presented below were brought to the attention of the psychiatric consultant by the nurses because of concern for their emotional state.

CASE REPORTS

The following are brief descriptions of the patients who died after undergoing renal transplants.

CASE 1. A 43-year-old married teacher received the transplant of a kidney donated by her sister; the organ was rejected after one month. While awaiting a second transplant she developed hepatitis and died six months after her initial surgery.

Following the rejection of the transplanted kidney, the donor wrote to the patient, venting her anger at the failure of the kidney to function. The patient's husband's attitude changed from passive interest to disinterest and finally to openly wishing for an end to her illness, her complaining and her depression.

CASE 2. A laconic 42-year-old lawyer received the transplant of a kidney donated by his sister after he had spent one year on home hemodialysis. The patient had been married for the second time three years prior to becoming uremic. With the frank onset of his illness, his wife turned away from him in disgust with his enfeeblement. However, she learned faultless dialysis technique, which became her only contact with him.

He felt helpless and depressed about his marriage but said very little to anyone. He drank and took poor care of himself. The transplant was decided upon as the result of a quarrel between the couple and the wife's refusing to continue dialysis.

The first transplant was acutely rejected. One week after receiving a second transplant with a cadaver kidney, the patient suffered a rupture of the hypogastric artery at the site of the first arterial anastomosis. He complained mildly and in an understated way of discomfort and died without a further word.

CASE 3. A dull 19-year-old high school senior had suffered from crippling neuropathies for two years prior to transplantation. With the onset of his initial kidney failure, his mother abandoned the family because of severe marital discord. During his eight months of hospitalization she visited him once. His kidney never functioned well and his neuropathy and muscular atrophy remained severe. He was uncommunicative, bland, and homesick and spoke of missing his mother and the rest of his family. His prognosis was felt to be poor. No plans were made for a second transplant should the first kidney fail. He was finally discharged with a chronic kidney rejection and died at home of congestive heart failure.

CASE 4. This 26-year-old single school bus driver suffering from simple schizophrenia had a seventh grade education. His parents moved out of the country at about the time he experienced renal failure. Prior to the transplant, with a cadaver kidney, this man expressed bizarre thoughts of death, after which he became comfortably passive and was unable to consider leaving the hospital for "around a year."

He could not manage any of his own care without confusion. He feared leaving the hospital because he might "catch cold," although his medical condition was satisfactory except for some mild leukopenia. He was transferred to a psychiatric hospital for rehabilitation, where he complained about the facilities. His helplessness and lack of responsibility discouraged the staff there. A conference focused about the issue of whether it was worth the effort to treat him. After four weeks there he contracted pneumonia and died of sepsis.

CASE 5. This panicky 37-year-old married clerk had suffered many medical complications while awaiting the transplantation of a cadaver kidney. Afterwards he developed a ureteroanastomotic leak and an arterial rupture with the loss of his kidney. Finally he developed septicemia and died. At times during his illness he had hallucinated, and he was always expecting the worst. He tearfully revealed that from the onset of his illness his parents, with whom he had been very close, seemed to lose interest in him and to avoid him and they never visited him during his long hospitalization.

CASE 6. The patient was a pleasant 17-year-old high school senior. His father had deserted the family five years previously. He became a close companion of patient 5 and felt quite optimistic about the success of the kidney he had received from his mother. Following the death of patient 5, this patient seemed to lose hope. He predicted that he would experience the same complications of leaking, rupture, sepsis, and death, which unfortunately occurred.

CASE 7. This frightened, withdrawn 38-year-old married man clung to and negotiated with the world through his wife. He received his first transplant from his mother, and when the kidney failed after one year he received a cadaver kidney. The second transplant was delayed by an undiagnosed lung lesion, which made a second attempt problematic and left him in an indeterminate state for several months. During the long wait for a decision, he talked little and admitted nothing of his obvious panic. It was, therefore particularly gratifying when the second transplant became possible and went so well that he was discharged eight days postoperatively. He was still inarticulate, however, and talked only to his wife. One week after discharge he developed ventricular fibrillation and died. The chaplain said of him: "Like Hezekiah, he turned his face to the wall."

CASE 8. A 39-year-old prosperous Italian hydraulic engineer received a cadaver kidney transplant, which developed a profuse leak postoperatively. He had been very anxious previously, and with this complication he became frozen with fear at the sight of the urine emerging from his drain. He used his professional training to heighten his panic further as to the dimensions of the defect. The leak continued for several months, and finally exploratory surgery was done in the hope of effecting a repair. Fibrous adhesions occluding the ureter were found and a nephrostomy tube was inserted. Infection set in, and the patient died of septicemia several weeks later.

CASE 9. An extroverted, uneducated 33-year-old married laborer received a transplant with a cadaver kidney. He was euphoric throughout his postoperative course and eluded optimism. He was totally unmanageable in his diet: he lied, hid food, and cheated, seeming to eat all the time. His weight soared. His appetite for life was exceeded only by his appetite for food. He was the friend of all the patients, encouraging them when their spirits lagged. Two and a half months after the transplant operation, he developed acute hepatitis, rapidly became comatose, aspirated, and died.

Patients 10 and 11 died immediately after the transplant operation from septicemia and difficulty in medical management. Neither of these patients was known by the psychiatrist and they were felt to be well adjusted and relatively untroubled. Both had families that supported them and they were not unduly anxious.

DISCUSSION

Of the 11 patients who died following kidney transplantation, eight were either abandoned during their illness by an important figure or manifested palpable anxiety to a degree not noted in survivors. A ninth patient displayed a striking euphoria, which caused him to act as though no problem existed at all. He went into a terminal coma denying that he was ill.

Of course the distinction between those who lived and those who died is not clearly demarcated. There were at least two clear psychotic episodes among the survivors long after toxicity could be a factor. One was an acute, highly regressive, stormy, and short episode in a man who later said, "If you lose hope you die." He is currently awaiting his third transplant. He is also very apprehensive but does not acknowledge it and has tried to turn his disadvantage into something positive. He has contributed money to a new dialysis ward and has identified himself with the service not only as a benefactor but as a medical expert.

Another man lay in his bed for several weeks psychotically depressed without initiating any interaction or taking any responsibility for himself. He seemed without hope. However, after being sent home on a trial basis he brightened remarkably, and after many months of delay went to work. He is still a severe management problem and finds it difficult to follow his diet or to keep records. His kidney is functioning fairly well, however, and he is outwardly happy 20 months after the transplant operation.

Another survivor, a young woman in her 20s, was deserted by her husband just before she came into the hospital. Prior to leaving her, as her condition worsened, he drank more and absented himself from home. During a long program of tests involving calcium metabolism prior to her transplant, she became very upset over her special diet and appeared depressed and unable to stand the program. She talked to a social worker about her marriage and seemed to have come to some resolution about it by the time she was seen in a regular psychiatric interview. At that time she had reestablished her home with her parents (her father was the kidney donor), and spoke with some distance about her unsatisfactory and disappointing husband, as if to say "good riddance." Thus, although she was clearly rejected, she was no longer affectively involved with the lost relationship at the time of the transplant operation.

As in the case of patient 5, several patients reported longstanding rifts with their families, who showed little interest in the patients during their illness. But although they were bitter, these patients seemed accustomed to the situation and had no expectations to be spoiled.

There is a disturbing note in the histories of patient 3 and patient 4. It was as if their despair was infectious. Their withdrawal and blandness made care and identification with them hard, and it seems clear in retrospect that it was not possible for the staff of the service to commit themselves unambivalently to these patients. Thus it evolved that kidney rejection would not be followed with more hemodialysis or a second transplant. To that extent the hopelessness of the patients resulted in the same state of mind on the part of the staff. This mood was so pervasive that when patient 4 was hospitalized in a local psychiatric teaching hospital, there was a considerable sense of futility on the part of the residents, who felt defeated by the man's combined medical-psychological pathology. There, as at the transplant center, the implicit question was whether this man was worth the necessary effort.

In some respects, patient 2's death provided the most dramatic examples of the role of depression and giving up, for a number of our patients have suffered the same complication of rupture of the artery at the site of the renal transplant. This patient complained mildly and died. In contrast, the other patients screamed frantically, drawing attention to themselves, and were rushed to the operating room for a repair.

This man had given evidence in many ways of his loss of interest in living. A year before his transplant he took a fishing trip on at least one occasion, going without dialysis for over a week and arriving home in a state near collapse. His diet, hydration, and physical state had been poor. On the ward he talked to few other people and treated the nurses with distance and withdrawal. He spent much of his time sitting in bed alone reading and denied any feelings or particular interest. He avoided feelings about his wife and the existing state of their marriage. Following his first and ultimately unsuccessful transplant, he waited many weeks without showing affect. When it finally became clear that his kidney would not function, he seemed to shrug it off. When he died it was in the same quiet way that had become his manner on the ward.

Another dramatic change in affect and clinical course occurred with patient 6, who seemed to be doing fairly well until patient 5 died. From that point on this young man failed, reproducing every complication that the other patient had suffered. He identified himself closely with this man. It would seem that the original loss of his own father five years earlier predisposed this patient both to cling and then to feel abandoned by his older friend.

It is unfortunate that so little is known about patients 7 and 8. Their anxiety was striking and unrelieved by what at first seemed to be good recovery with excellent kidney function. Patient 8 had had a great deal of medical indecision to deal with, but others with equally complicated courses (including one man who received a cancer transplant inadvertently along with his kidney) seemed to find more equilibrium. It was striking how patient 8, like patients 5 and 7, clung to his wife, seeming to use her to express his feelings and deal with the world.

Finally, there is the problem characterizing patient 9, who felt "wonderful." The use of denial of the seriousness of the illness at hand is a common mechanism seen among the transplant patients. In fact it is almost the rule. Yet this man displayed denial that approached a delusional state. His dietary recklessness, too, was denied, although his body ballooned almost daily. His wife, along with the staff of the service, felt a sense of helplessness to control his behavior, especially in the face of his proclaimed well-being. One can only speculate as to what depths of terror and depression lay behind this exaggerated sense of health and strength. Clinical experience almost inevitably reveals that behind hypomania of this degree lies a considerable amount of the opposite feelings.

THE ROLE OF AFFECTIVE STATES

The attempt to evaluate psychic states in relation to illness—its onset, course, and outcome—has always been of interest, and lately there have been attempts to formulate some thoughts along these lines. Engel and Schmale (Engel) noted Freud's early attention to this problem:

Persistent affective states of a "depressive" nature (as they are called), such as sorrow, worry, or grief, reduce the state of nourishment of the whole body, cause the hair to turn white, the fat to disappear and the walls of the blood-vessels to undergo morbid changes. . . . The major affects evidently have a large bearing on the capacity to resist infectious illness; a good example of this is to be seen in the medical observation that there is a far greater liability to contract such diseases as typhus and dysentery in defeated armies than in victorious ones. The affects, moreover—this applies almost exclusively to depressive affects—are often sufficient in themselves to bring about both diseases of the nervous system accompanied by manifest anatomical changes and also diseases of other organs. In such cases it must be assumed that the patient already had a predisposition, though hitherto an inoperative one, to the disease in question. . . . There can be no doubt that the duration of life can be appreciably shortened by depressive affects and that a violent shock, or a deep humiliation or disgrace, may put a sudden end to life (Freud).

Engle and Schmale themselves suggested "a giving up—given up" complex based on the observation that the onset or excerbation of disease is commonly "preceded by affective states variously designated as 'despair,' 'depression,' 'giving up,' 'grief,' and others all in some way indicating a sense of irrevocable loss or feelings of depression."

They characterize this complex in several ways that resemble the observations noted here. One is a sense of helplessness and hopelessness about the environment, while another concerns the feeling that relationships and important people are less secure and endangered. The patient's autonomy and ability to get what he needs and wants are also felt to be impaired. The authors note that "object losses constitute the most common provoking situation."

Rees and Lutkins (1967) presented a well-documented and statistically validated report showing the effect of grief on survival. Using a small town in Wales they studied the mortality rate of the 903 close relatives of residents who had died, contrasting it with a control group of 878. They found that the death rate among bereaved relatives was seven times higher than that among the control group within the first year after bereavement. During the second year the comparative figures were almost equal.

They also reported that during the first two years of bereavement the mortality for widowed people in the bereaved group was significantly higher than for those in the control group. During the first year of bereavement 12.2 percent of widowed people in the bereaved group died in contrast to only 1.2 percent of the control group. There was also an increased risk to the bereaved relatives if the original death had occurred in a hospital rather than at home, while those deaths that had occurred away from home or hospital produced an even higher risk of death among the relatives. All of the reported findings were significant statistically; the size of the sample makes this a rather impressive report. Their conclusion that "bereavement carries a considerable increased risk of mortality" appears to be well substantiated.

Visotsky and Hamburg (1961) and Hamburg and associates have discussed what they term "coping behavior" in regard to patients with severe poliomyelitis (1953a) and patients with burns (1967, 1953b). They report that one of the key factors in recovery is the relationship of the patient to his family in reestablishing himself, regaining self-esteem, and adjusting to his illness.

Observations strikingly similar to those reported here were presented at a meeting of the American Psychosomatic Society in March 1968 in Boston, where Kimball (1969) reported the psychological responses to open heart surgery on a group of 54 patients. He found that outcome correlated well with four factors, which he listed as: 1) previous success in coping with life's stress; 2) handling of anxiety regarding surgery; 3) the presence or absence of depression; and 4) the strengths of object relations. He was also able to group his patients into four groups, which he called: 1) adjusted; 2) symbiotic; 3) anxious; and 4) depressed. He then used a subsequent group of 38 patients and assigned to them before surgery one of the above four categories. He found that the most improvements were in the adjusted group, while 80 percent of the mortal.ity occurred in the depressed group. Thirty-three percent of the mortalities and complications occurred in the anxious group, primarily from cardiac arrhythmia.

In a second paper dealing with similar subject matter, Tufo and Ostfeld (1968) reported their study of 100 patients undergoing open heart surgery. They reported that 12 patients showed severe depression, diagnosed and reported before surgery. All 12 of these patients died immediately or in the early post-operative period. there was no correlation with severity of cardiac disease or surgical factors. The authors were struck by the very high mortality risk associated with preoperative depression and felt it had important implications for preoperative psychiatric assessment.

No literature review is needed to remind the clinician that the patient who has lost hope in himself and in his future with his family has a more complicated course of recovery. People do indeed seem to need someone to live for.

CONCLUSION

These observations suggest that one area of concern for the strictly medical recovery of the patient would involve an understanding of the relationship of the patient to his family. Where a dissolution of bonds occurs it may be lifesaving to deal with this specifically. It may also be possible to establish a relationship between the staff and patient that can remind the patient that there are people who care whether he lives or not. In general practice there are many older patients, and perhaps some not so old, who are primarily maintained by a periodic relationship with their physician. This would also suggest that there is an important personal role for the service chiefs in the care of the patients, for they are the ones who are seen to be endowed with power and knowledge and their interest may be the needed love that can rally a tottering patient. So much of the patient care in the research hospital is provided by ever-changing research fellows that the patient may not have a real chance to form a lasting relationship. Contacts and support from them may, if these observations have validity, be lifesaving.

Finally, severe anxiety may be life threatening. Rather than being regarded as something the patient exhibits that is occasionally depreciated as "nervousness," it should be seen as an indication for concern and psychiatric consultation and intervention; forebodings and dreads have all too frequently a tendency to be proven ultimately right.

Thus, it may be that psychiatric preparation for surgery is no less important than any other preparation. The observations made here, and those made by others, suggest that a careful preoperative psychiatric history be taken with special awareness directed toward abandonment and anxiety. Should these factors be present, it may be lifesaving to postpone kidney transplantation while the patient is maintained on hemodialysis and undergoes some form of psychotherapy.

Psychotherapy should focus upon management of some of the issues in the patient's life and upon the formation of a meaningful relationship with the psychiatrist, who can follow him postoperatively. Where the family dynamics are important, it may be essential to mobilize all essential family members until the intricacies of family life are clearly elucidated and manageable. Although such a plan is time-consuming, it may be just as necessary in correction of such well-established dangers as infection, congestive heart failure, uremia, or hyperparathyroidism.

REFERENCES

Engel, G.L., and Schmale, A.H., Jr.: Psychoanalytic Theory of Somatic Disorder Conversion, Specificity, and the Disease Onset Situation. *J Amer Psychoanal Ass, 15*:344–365, 1967.

Freud, S.: "Psychical (or Mental) Treatment (1905). In: *The Complete Psychological Works of Sigmund Freud.* London: Hogarth Press, 1953, vol. 7, pp. 283–302.

Hamburg, D.A., and Adams, J.G.: A Perspective on Coping Behavior. *Arch Gen Phychiat, 17*:227–284, 1967.

Hamburg, D.A., Artz, C.P., Reiss, E., Amspacher, W.H., and Chambers, R.E.: Clinical Importance of Emotional Problems in the Care of Patients with Burns. *New Eng J Med, 248*:355–359, 1953a.

Hamburg, D.A., Hamburg, B., and DeGoza, S.: Adaptive Problems and Mechanisms in Severely Burned Patients. *Psychiatry, 16*:1–20, 1953b.

Kimball, C.P.: Psychological Responses to the Experience of Open Heart Surgery. *Amer J Psychiat, 126*:348–359, 1969.

Rees, W.D., and Lutkins, S.G.: Mortality of Bereavement, *Brit Med J, 4*:13–16, 1967.

Tufo, H.M., and Ostfeld, A.M.: A Prospective Study of Open Heart Surgery. Read at the annual meeting of the American Psychosomatic Society, Boston, Mass., March 29–31, 1968.

Visotsky, H.M., Hamburg, D.A., Goss, M.E., and Lebovits, B.Z.: Coping Behavior Under Extreme Stress. *Arch Gen Psychiat, 5*:423–448, 1961.

CHAPTER 22

THE VOCATIONAL COUNSELOR AND FAMILY CASEWORKER AS JOINT LEADERS IN A GROUP COUNSELING PROGRAM*

BERNARD BERGER AND WILLIAM G. VINE

~~~~~~

~~~~~~

THE JEWISH Community of Metropolitan Toronto numbers approximately 100,000 people. As in so many other communities in North America, a very high proportion of these are youngsters: approximately 40 percent are under 25 years of age.

1965 saw the Jewish community seeking a more sophisticated service for their youth because the old patterns of program did not seem to be meeting their needs or coping

* Used with permission from *Journal of Jewish Communal Service,* XLVI, No. 3, 1970.

with the rising adolescent revolt. The tremendous increase in the number of young people asking for help, and the obvious necessity for immediate attention to these problems demanded an end to lengthy waiting lists at available communal agencies, and a solution not to be discovered within the narrow confines of the services and techniques then available.

Social and vocational counseling groups, conjointly created and conducted by the Jewish Family & Child Service and the Jewish Vocational Service was one of the most effective outgrowths of the earnest attempts to meet this pressing need.

FAMILY AND CHILDREN'S SERVICES

At that time the Jewish Family & Child Service was offering an extensive program, a composite of many services over the previous century, geared to embrace the needs of its clientele from birth to death. This comprehensive plan included services related to the Child, the Family, the Aged and the Indigent, in the form of individual and family interviews, environmental manipulation, financial assistance, and foster care for children and for the aged.

Group techniques had been used for some time, but it was not until 1962 that they became a formal treatment method, along with family therapy and individual casework services.

In January of 1965, the Board of the Jewish Family & Child Service set up a new department with a specific focus on youth, amalgamating heretofore fragmented services available for young people and recommending new programs to fill the gaps. Cases ranged from "normal adolescence problems" to extreme disturbances requiring psychiatric care and in-patient treatment. A significant number, although in their early twenties, were somewhat retarded in their normal emancipation development. One of the sub-groups, for example, could be described as follows:

> eighteen to twenty years of age, attending school, living at home, lacking peer relations, involved in a hostile bind with parents, angry at teachers and principals, under-achieving at school, often involved in anti-social behaviour such as drug abuse or petty thievery, unrealistic vocational goals.

Some of the innovations designed to meet these needs included an extension of a group therapy program, a foster home and co-op placement facility, and a multiple approach whereby the youth would be involved in both family therapy, group therapy and, where appropriate, in individual sessions as well. The casework relationship and family treatment alone had been found to be too often inadequate in making the young client responsible for his own decision-making and helping him to see the consequences if decisions were delayed or averted.

THE JEWISH VOCATIONAL SERVICE VOCATIONAL COUNSELING PROGRAM

The vocational counseling program at Toronto JVS follows closely those provided by most other JVS's in the United States and Canada. The typical client is given an intake interview, a series of paper and pencil tests, group aptitude tests, several individual clinical testing and counseling sessions and an interview with his parents. The average number of interviews per client is seven. In addition, a group counseling program designed to bring career counseling to a wider population through the use of group techniques has been carried out successfully in co-operation with a number of synagogues and group work agencies. Group sessions also serve as a screening mechanism to sort out those clients who should be referred for individual counseling.

The typical group counseling package consists of (a) one or two group meetings at which the career plans and aspirations of the participants are discussed, (b) at least two group test sessions during which time a battery of psychological and aptitude tests of ability, aptitude and personality are administered, (c) individual interviews to discuss testing results and their applications, (d) a group meeting with parents of the counselees to interpret the program and answer questions. Experience has shown that about 25 percent of the adolescents involved in these groups require more intensive individual counseling and so are subsequently referred to a vocational counselor at JVS or to a caseworker at the JF&CS.

NEED FOR CHANGES IN SERVICE

In 1965, the JF&CS was deluged by a flood of young people who as well as being in need of the casework and family therapy services available at that agency, also urgently required vocational assistance. However, because of a shortage of staff the Jewish Vocational Service had, at that time, been forced to build up a waiting list for counseling, and young clients, including referrals from the JF&CS, were having to wait sometimes as long as three months before they were seen.

The JVS had simultaneously become aware of the fact that its counseling program was not meeting all the needs and expectations of its adolescent clients, a number of whom were suffering from emotional problems which were either causing or at least complicating the vocational difficulties they were experiencing. This factor became very apparent after JVS had completed a follow-up study of clients who had passed through the individual counseling program two years previously. A majority of those responding, while expressing satisfaction with the vocational assistance received, deplored the lack of opportunity to discuss personal and social problems with their counselor.

Because of the limited counseling time available to them, JVS counselors, it appeared, had been avoiding any involvement in emotional areas with their adolescent clients. In some cases the difficulties the youngsters were experiencing involved parents and siblings and hence were clearly outside the purview of the JVS.

In addition both agencies felt the need for a group for teenagers whose problems were not so serious or involved as to warrant intensive therapy. Many of these youngsters were already involved in other ways with one or the other agency, and it was felt that what was needed was a group focussing on the common problems of adolescence such as family relationships, school and study difficulties, career goals, dating, relationships with the opposite sex, etc., and taking into account the new and somewhat different attitudes, values and behaviour patterns to which the "Now Generation" subscribe.

It occurred to the writers that groups of adolescents who were clients of either agency and who were experiencing either social or vocational difficulties or both, might greatly benefit from the combined leadership of both a JF&CS caseworker and a JVS counselor. It was often apparent that the client's needs overlapped and could legitimately be dealt with by either agency thus avoiding duplication. More important, this would take care of problems which require skills and services that either agency alone could not supply.

There was another problem for which, it was hoped, the institution of these conjointly operated groups might provide a solution. Although the Jewish Vocational Service had evolved out of a limited placement and guidance service which had functioned as an administrative department within the JF&CS since 1937, the relationship between the two agencies since the founding of a separate vocational facility in 1947 was often less than harmonious.

The dissension centered around a basic difference of approach which in turn had as its source training and ideology stemming from casework on the one hand (JF&CS) and from psychology on the other (JVS). As a result conflicts sprang up between workers of the two agencies who were involved with the same clients. JVS counselors often accused JF&CS caseworkers of being unrealistic, of making unreasonable demands in regard to finding employment for marginal clients. For example, JVS insisted on "selling" a client to an employer on his positive attributes. The absence of such positives would in their opinion make placement on a job impossible. JF&CS caseworkers on the other hand, would insist that since work was necessary and would be highly therapeutic for such a client, an understanding employer should be found who would offer the marginal employee a job out of sympathy.

Moreover, JF&CS workers tended to use JVS for psychological assessment and testing only and in many instances preferred to do the vocational or employment counseling themselves. Needless to say, this caused JVS staff some bitterness. On the other hand, JVS counselors at times tended to be outspokenly critical of the methods that JF&CS workers used in helping their clients cope with their problems. Much of this criticism was due to sheer ignorance on the part of JVS staff of casework methods and family pathology. Some attempt was made to overcome this mutual lack of understanding of each other's roles through one or two joint staff meetings, but these accomplished little except to allow ventilation for both camps. It became obvious that some method which would bring both agencies together to solve their common problems would be much more successful.

THE SOCIAL AND VOCATIONAL GROUP COUNSELING PROGRAM

Groups were set up on the basis of the following criteria:

1. The amount of concern the client displayed with regard to his own problems and the opportunity of solving them.
2. The level of awareness and degree of discomfort the client felt with his present way of coping.
3. The amount of skill or lack of it the client showed in relating to other boys and girls.
4. The client's native intelligence and ability to comprehend his position and its ramifications.
5. The client's behaviour reactions to common problems such as underachievement and projections of difficulties onto others.
6. The client's readiness to contract to attend 10 sessions and his willingness to accept the leadership of a JF&CS caseworker and a JVS counselor conjointly.

Referrals were invited from the general caseload of both agencies and appointments were set up so that both leaders could meet with the proposed individual for three-quarters of an hour. It was decided to limit the group to 10 and by the time it was ready to start ten had been seen and only one rejected.

The primary focus of the group was to assist the individual member in self-assessment and problem-solving. Content was confined to the here and now. Discussion explored individual adaptational problems and the client's role and responsibility in coping with these difficulties. Projections were quickly "knocked down" by the group and pressure was exerted on the individual to change his role and behaviour. Self-pity became a poor excuse for inactivity. Group tests were administered and individual testing was used as required. The results were discussed with the client in private although relevant information was fed back to the group as a whole by members and/or leaders.

Because both leaders felt comfortable with each other they were able to vary their stance—at times supporting, at times disagreeing, and in fact at times competing with each other. Although an arbitrary division was made around content, the family belonging to the caseworker, and school and job belonging to the vocational counselor, some overlapping was inevitable. At times the group interaction became more important than the particular material being discussed. Either group leader was free to intervene at any time and focus on a remark or a piece of behaviour that might have gone unnoticed had he not been present at the meeting. There was no hiding behind the professional role as an excuse for not becoming involved; the leaders were honest and open when questioned by members about their own adolescent life experience. On occasion leadership differences were openly discussed in the group and used as a model to illustrate how certain kinds of conflict could be resolved.

Although the atmosphere was informal and the pace was fast, professional judgement was maintained. Techniques ranged from the development of insight (initiated by the leaders and continued and reinforced by the group), through confrontation with reality, to the sharing of information. Group pressure was found to be highly effective in curtailing acute anti-social behaviour and enhancing long-term planning.

RESULTS

The most dramatic result was the speed with which some of the clients effected change. Several of the young people who had been stalled by anxiety, fear or doubts, were forced into taking action through group pressure. Some who should have left school finally did so. Several others who had difficulty in separating from their parents were helped to make the break and moved out of their homes.

CASE HISTORY #1

Marshall, 18 years old, from an upper middle-class family who were in treatment with the JF&CS was handicapped by his parents' inability to accept the fact that their marital problem was causing disruptions within the family. The father was extremely punitive and hostile, withheld funds from the family, and was using alcohol as a relaxant. The mother was completely subservient and demanded no respect or satisfaction of her own needs from the family.

Marshall withdrew from Grade 13 in order to support himself and live outside of the home. He was depressed, his self-image was impaired and he seriously questioned whether he had any capacity for future education. He had been considering offbeat occupations like film-making, hardly a realistic career goal in Toronto.

The group was helpful in supporting him as he made the break from home, left school and found employment. The group also prevented him from being complaisant about his achievement and encouraged him to seek higher goals.

Since leaving the group Marshall has spent a short time in another JF&CS therapy group, returned home, completed Grade 13 with excellent grades and has now completed his first year at university. He has successfully established a relationship with two or three other students and has in his own words for the first time some real friends because "I now know what it means to be close to people."

CASE HISTORY #2

Nancy was seventeen in grade 12, the eldest of five children. This family had been known to the JF&CS for two years because of the mother's confinement in a mental hospital. At the time she joined the group, Nancy's mother was working and a housekeeper was responsible for the daily care of the children.

Nancy was depressed, took little pride in her appearance and was extremely uncomfortable with other people. On the other hand she was bright and did very well at school, usually in subjects requiring very little class participation. Initially, she was withdrawn and very quiet at group sessions. The group leaders gave her the job of presenting synopses of various parts of the discussions whenever members were unclear as to what was being proposed, communicated, or argued. Gradually she began to participate voluntarily in discussions. Her appearance improved considerably. The group helped her to explore a different role at school and in the community as she became socially more self-assured and active. Ultimately she graduated from high school, and is now attending university.

CASE HISTORY #3

Michael, age 19, came from a middle-class home. He had had several run-ins with the police for petty thievery, after having dropped out of school at grade 11. His mother was hysterical and over-indulgent whereas his father had completely removed himself from the responsibility of disciplining his children and was altogether aloof and seemingly unconcerned about family problems.

Michael was described by the psychiatrist as a "dependent personality with reactive aggressivity." The doctor felt that he was trying hard to stand on his own feet but was continuously being defeated by his dependency needs, covering failure with a facade of aggressiveness. Testing revealed that Michael was of low average intelligence, thus explaining the great difficulty he had had with academic work while in high school. His job pattern before coming to JVS was very unstable.

His involvement in the group forced him to relate to reality, as his bravado and grandiosity were continually challenged by his peers. Gradually his behaviour began to change. He was finally able to complete the bookeeping course in which he had enrolled, and subsequently found a job and achieved financial and emotional independence from his family. He is engaged to be married this summer.

To date there have been seven groups involving six different staff from both agencies. Each year both a senior group and a junior group were set up, based not only on age but upon the level of social skills. A total of 62 youths were served. In general their social adaptability and responsibility were markedly improved following an appropriate selection of vocational goals. For example, three left the academic program, four withdrew but later returned to complete high school requirements in order to enter university, several others improved their performance at school and continued on to university, while three left school for permanent employment.

EVALUATION

Although the group leaders were encouraged by the many positive comments concerning the effectiveness of the social vocational groups from colleagues in both agencies, it was felt that some system of objectifying the results should be found. An attempt to use the Multiple Affect Adjective Check List and the Hildreth Feeling Scale to measure change within the areas of (1) feeling, (2) amount of energy, (3) outlook for the future, (4) mental state, (5) attitudes to work and (6) attitudes to people, proved unsuccessful. This was due chiefly to the fact that client attendance at group meetings was not sufficiently regular to produce significant results.

Another attempt at evaluating the group sessions was more successful. A questionnaire consisting of nineteen questions was drawn up and mailed out to the participants of two groups, some three months after they had disbanded. This questionnaire solicited client opinions about their expectations prior to entering the group, and how these expectations had been fulfilled or not fulfilled. They were asked how they felt the groups were most and least helpful to them and what problems they might have liked discussed which were not. Comments on the dual leadership role were solicited as well as the clients' version of their own participation in the group. Finally they were asked to give their opinions about the effectiveness of the group and its usefulness to others.

The questionnaire was mailed to the 18 participants in groups Two and Three. Thirteen of these were completed and returned. The results are summarized as follows:

The majority (8) indicated they had been eager to join the group because they expected to receive some help with personal and/or school or work problems. The others were somewhat less enthusiastic although no one felt coerced or forced to join. In retrospect they felt that the group experience was very helpful, only two commenting that it was "not too useful." No one felt that it had been a complete waste of time.

Ten of the respondents felt that the area in which the group had proved most helpful was in helping to understand themselves better. It was least helpful in helping to overcome difficulties in school. The majority (8) favoured the closed group and felt that 10 sessions was just about right. The other five felt that there were not enough sessions to suit them.

The dual leadership was "helpful" according to ten partici-

pants, while three felt that having two group leaders was
of no significance. Most were of the opinion that having two
adult leaders provided two points of view. Looking at problems from different vantage points was thought to be
beneficial. According to one client the leaders had often con-
tradicted each other although he did not feel that this was
necessarily bad.

A majority (8) thought that making the groups co-
educational was helpful, four felt that this did not make any
difference, while one (a young man) considered it a hindrance,
(because it inhibited the group he felt, in discussing sex
problems).

There was almost unanimous agreement (12) that they
would recommend this type of group to others. As one young
man wrote, he thought that this type of group would be beneficial to "people who had school, social, family, work, or any
other problem—people who are not afraid to tell others their
difficulties and to discuss them in an adult and mature
manner."

IMPLICATIONS AND CONCLUSIONS

The most welcome and perhaps most tangible result was
an immediate improvement in the relationship between the
two agencies. The direct involvement affected other staff as
well with a concurrently deeper understanding of the point
of view, role and function of each agency. More appropriate
referrals were made to each agency by the other. Regualr
meetings of the supervisors of both agencies were
inaugurated, to iron out conflicts and plan further co-operative
ventures. There was a noticeable decrease in rivalry and an
increase in co-operation.

The new groups also made it possible to cut the waiting
period for adolescents from several months to a few weeks
and provided an answer to JVS's need for a means of helping
adolescent clients who were experiencing social, personal
or family problems.

Because both agencies were represented in the group
through the joint leaders, feedback to case workers and coun-

selors back at the agency was immediate and often reinforced suggestions or provided information that was useful in vocational counseling or casework with the individual.

The venture has had an advantageous effect in yet another direction. Successful methods have a tendency to fossilize; workers continue to use them beyond the time of their greatest effectiveness. This period of interaction between caseworkers and vocational counselors served to teach those involved in the joint effort the possibilities that lie in more flexible and imaginative thinking.

This joint undertaking proves beyond a doubt that any program which has as one of its goals the improvement of relationships between two agencies must involve purposeful and meaningful common activities. The consequence of this, as we have seen, would be to engender an attitude of mutual trust and understanding within the staffs of both agencies, greatly facilitating the realization of their goals.

This single initiative, although unable to provide a comprehensive solution to developing community needs has, in the opinion of the writers, more than demonstrated the feasibility and effectiveness of combining the talents and resources of two or more agencies and disciplines. The complexity and diversity of the problems now arising in many communities throughout the United States and Canada demand just such dynamic and co-operative methods, if they are to be successfully resolved.

Chapter 23

COUNSELING THE BLIND &
SEVERELY VISUALLY IMPAIRED

Richard E. Hardy and John G. Cull

~~~~~~~~~~~~~~~~~~~~~~~~~~~~~~~~~~~~~

~~~~~~~~~~~~~~~~~~~~~~~~~~~~~~~~~~~~~

WHAT IS COUNSELING?

COUNSELING HAS BEEN defined in various terms and by many experts. Gustad (1953) has written that "counseling is a learning oriented process, carried on in a simple, one-to-one social environment in which a counselor, professionally competent in relative psychological skills and knowledge, seeks to assist the client to learn more about himself, to know how to put understanding into effect in relation to clearly perceived, realistically defined goals to the end that the client may become a happier and more productive member of his society."

While definitions vary according to the orientation of the counselor, certain truisms have resulted from the enormous amount of research concerning the effectiveness of counseling. These will be explained in the following paragraphs.

No matter what particular school or theory of counseling is accepted by the practitioner, the most important factor determining the outcome of counseling effectiveness is the "personality" of the counselor himself. In other words, whether he counts himself as Rogerian, Ellisonian, or eclectic, the personality of the counselor will come through in counseling sessions and affect the outcome to a degree which will determine whether or not the counseling session is effective. Just as teachers can bring about enormous growth and changes in students by modifying their attitudes toward various subject matter, the counselor can bring about substantial changes in his client for better or worse.

Effective counseling requires certain basic ingredients. As the strength or weakness of these ingredients vary so does the ability of the counselor to help the client. There are three basic prerequisites to effective counseling. First, the counselor must accept the client without imposing conditions for this acceptance. He must be willing to work with the client and become actively involved with him as an individual no matter what the counselee's race, attitudes, or mode of life may be. This is necessary in order for the counselee to gain the knowledge that the counselor as a person wishes to help him with his problems and is not prejudging.

The counselor must be "genuine" in that he must function in a way which indicates to the client that he is being true to his own feelings and to himself. To be otherwise is to present a facade to the client—a false image which will act as a deterrant to a successful relationship. Counselors must avoid artificiality in their relationships. If the counselor hides behind a professional mystique, he may find that the counselee is better at "fooling" him than he is at deceiving the client. The professional worker cannot expect his client to be open, sincere, and genuine if he himself does not represent these characteristics well.

In addition, the counselor must have an empathetic understanding and feeling vis-à-vis the client. He must make a sincere effort to see the client's problem through the "client's eyes" and he must be able to communicate the depth of his understanding.

Counseling can be considered a relationship between two persons which is conducive to good mental health. Inherent in an effective counseling relationship is the absence of threat. The counselor must remove threat if the client is to grow and be able to solve his problems in an uninhibited manner. Counseling as a relationship is also typified by the types of feelings that many of us have for our closest friends. True close friendships are characterized by honest caring, genuine interest, and a high level of concern about helping in a time of need. Real friendships often require one person to put aside his own selfish needs in order to listen long enough and with enough empathy so that a friend's problem may begin to work itself out in a natural and constructive manner.

There are a number of adjectives which apply to various types of counseling (religious, marital, rehabilitation, educational, personal, vocational, and others). Counseling services vary according to the needs of the client, not the counselor. A counselee who comes to the counselor for help will often at first outline a concern which is not the real problem. The counselor must have considerable flexibility and insight to know what is required in each individual situation.

REHABILITATION COUNSELING

Rehabilitation counselors are concerned mainly with individuals who have vocational handicaps. These handicaps may result from physical disability, emotional or mental illness, social or cultural deprivation. In each individual case, the counselor must be able to decide what remedy is required in order to move the counselee toward successful personal adjustment in his family, community, and on the job.

Rehabilitation counseling requires the ingredients mentioned earlier for effective counselor-client relationships; however, much of rehabilitation counseling consists of advice-giving and coordination of services to the client. In a sense, "rehabilitation counseling" can be considered a misnomer when the term is applied across the board. A substantial number of clients need considerable advice and information which the counselor has to offer concerning social and rehabilitation services from which they can profit. When the counselee needs advice and information, the rehabilitation counselor must be able to recognize this need and provide what is required. There also will be many instances in which the client and counselor must enter into a number of counseling sessions in depth. The counselor must make the judgment concerning what type of help is needed for the client to solve his particular problems. Rehabilitation counselors need appropriate training that will enable them to decide whether or not they are qualified to do the kind of counseling which is necessary.

Many counselors fall into the trap of wanting to play the role of "junior therapist" and involve high percentages of their clients in in-depth counseling sessions. This is particularly true of the graduates of many rehabilitation counselor training programs. Some workers hide behind "counseling" (as synonomous with quality) in terms of their justifying low numbers of rehabilitated clients. There is much talk of quality services and in-depth counseling which require considerable time. The rehabilitation counselor who is an effective manager of his caseload can "rehabilitate" the number of persons required by his agency administrator and while doing so can provide counseling services as needed to his clients.

Rehabilitation work requires a broad definition of counseling which includes the offering of some, and coordination of other professional services to clients. Generally, agency administrators—especially those trained in counseling—do not accept the explanation of "the time required and quality services" for a low client rehabilitation rate. Any agency administrator or supervisor knows that some cases require much involved counseling, and that these cases in many instances are the most difficult ones. They are time-consuming, and they can test the fiber of the rehabilitation counselor. Untrained counselors generally cannot handle such cases without help from someone who has had some advanced orientation in counseling. However, counselors who play the role of "junior therapist" in trying to become deeply involved with all of their clients—whether or not this type of service is called for—will be ineffective and probably will not remain long in rehabilitation work.

The rehabilitation counselor will find his coordinating and

facilitating role highly rewarding when it is done well and gets needed services. One of the greatest satisfactions that the counselor can have is the assurance that he knows when certain types of services are required and whether these should be more therapeutically oriented or more oriented toward advice, information, and coordination of community resources and professional services.

Rehabilitation counselors should not rank-order their clients in a psychological need hierarchy which places the individual with severe psychological problems at the top of the counselor's list for services. Certainly, these persons should be served immediately upon the counselor's realization that severe psychological problems exist. They should be referred to the appropriate psychologist or psychiatrist if problems are so severe that the counselor cannot handle them alone, or they should be served by rehabilitation counselors who are competent in the type of service required. The point to be made here is that the rehabilitation process is a complicated procedure; the client who may be adjusting normally to a loss and who does not need substantial in-depth therapeutic involvement is as good a case for services as one requiring more therapeutic work. Coordination of services of supportive personnel and professional personnel is a substantial part of the work of the rehabilitation counselor. In many cases, he will have to bring this team together in order that the client can continue to receive effective and necessary rehabilitation services.

The rehabilitation counselor must actively involve himself within the community in order to be fully aware of the many resources which exist that can be of substantial benefit to his clients. Generally, counselors have indicated that so much of their time is taken with counseling and coordination of services that they are unable to put forward enough effort to learn all that the community has to offer. Counselors who utilize community resources effectively are very familiar with the offerings of various agencies and through coordination and cooperation find that their work load is lessened by the support of other social service programs.

The counselor will wish to offer his services to various

types of community agencies. For instance, most counselors can give a great deal of useful advice to such programs as the community action and model cities efforts sponsored by the Federal Government. Agencies and organizations such as family service programs and welfare agencies can be of considerable help in getting needed services for the rehabilitation client. The counselor should take a major responsibility in coordinating efforts of agencies and programs that can help in the rehabilitation of clients, and he should volunteer his time and energies to help strengthen other social service programs.

The rehabilitation counselor must keep in mind that he should be moving the client toward end objectives of independence and successful adjustment on the job. Rehabilitation differs from some other social service professions in the regard that a substantial test of the counselor's work is made at the end of the rehabilitation process. That test consists of the appropriateness of the client's behavior in work situation (Hardy, 1972).

REHABILITATION COUNSELING WITH THE BLIND AND SEVERELY VISUALLY IMPAIRED

No special counseling theory need be constructed in order for the rehabilitation counselor to serve blind persons. There is, however, a substantial body of knowledge with which the counselor should be thoroughly familiar. Topics include the etiology of diseases related to blindness, problems in adjustment to visual loss including mobility, social adjustment, occupational advice and job placement. The counselor serving blind persons has a real responsibility to undertake considerable study in order to acquaint himself with what Father Carroll (1961) has called in the title of his book, *Blindness: What It Is, What It Does, and How to Live with It.*

The rehabilitation counselor serving blind persons has as much or more of a coordinating function as does the counselor in a general agency setting. A counselor concerned with the blind will work closely with the educational services specialist, the social worker, the ophthalmologist, the placement specialist, the rehabilitation teacher, and the mobility instructor who help in the team effort of moving the blind individual toward adjustment to his visual problem and later to adjustment on the job.

Rehabilitation counselors serving the blind, just as counselors working with any other rehabilitation clients, must be certain that their clients are without need of further medical or psychological treatment. In this regard, the counselor helping the partially sighted should make certain that no visual aid or professional service can offer additional help to the client. He should be fully aware of the various problems which go hand in hand with a loss of sight. Persons who are experiencing a severe physical inadequacy lose some ability to be independent. They feel socially inadequate and in some cases may have additional problems which at first might not be apparent to the counselor. Advanced age or other physical incapabilities may add to the blind person's adjustment problems.

The client will be very much interested in the prognosis for his future, and the rehabilitation counselor should make sure that valid information is provided. An effective counselor must be ready to help the blind person understand what his opportunities are for education, employment, social activities. He should also talk with those persons who give information to the blind client, especially professional individuals such as ophthalmologists, to make certain that they have useful information concerning blindness and the services of the state rehabilitation agency.

Bauman and Yoder (1966) have suggested that the rehabilitation counselor must offer

> a combination of several qualities: (1) his own emotional acceptance of blindness (he must be the first person to whom the client has spoken who did not immediately show great pity and anxiety—a helping new experience for the client); (2) formal or informal instruction in procedures which make it easier to live as a blind person (the home teacher and also some adjustment on pre-vocational training can help here); (3) realistic planning for the future, including vocational planning if the age and general health of the client make this appropriate. It is true that all of these may be rejected for a time, in which case the counselor must offer (4) understanding,

patients, and a gentle persistence which keeps him available until the client and his family are able to reorient themselves to the future instead of clinging to the past.

In counseling with blind persons, the rehabilitation counselor must remember that he is working with individuals who cannot see or whose sight is impaired. The client will differ from fellow blind persons as much as he will differ from sighted persons. Some blind persons are very healthy; others are sickly. Some are well adjusted psychologically; others are poorly adjusted. In many cases blindness will have caused severe psychological stress which has not been overcome, just as an accident or some other type of traumatic experience may have caused either a sighted or a blind person severe psychological difficulty.

Often, reaction to partial vision causes as much or more frustration and anxiety than reaction to total blindness. One reason for this seems to be that partially sighted persons are unable to function normally and do not want to accept their loss of sight as a reality. They live in a no-man's-world between blindness and sight.

The rehabilitation counselor serving blind and severely visually impaired persons must be even more planful and thoughtful than the counselor who is concerned with individuals who are sighted. Often it will be necessary to anticipate problems which may arise for the blind client. For instance, simply getting to and from the counselor's office may become a very troublesome and embarrassing task. The blind client may be traveling over unfamiliar terrain with or without the help of relatives or friends. The counselor, in many cases, may want to visit initially in the home and later during the relationship invite the client to the rehabilitation agency.

The counselor must be very much aware that this blind client is "tuned in" to auditory clues (yes's and unhum's may be helpful), since the usual eye contact and other nonverbal communications are not effective with blind persons. For instances, silence over a considerable period of time often takes place in counseling sessions, but when the counselor is working with a blind client, silence may be interpreted at times as disinterest or rejection.

It is respectful and appropriate for the counselor to look directly into the face and eyes of the client just as if the counselee were fully sighted. Blind persons are often aware that sighted persons are not looking at them and they get the impression, which may be true, that the counselor is not listening.

Counselors should be particularly careful about shuffling papers, tapping a pencil on the desk, or making other sounds that are distracting. They should also be aware that many blind persons, especially the congenitally blind, give the counselor little to go by in terms of facial expression. The counselor who is used to reading emotionality in various facial responses may be at a considerable loss with some persons who have been blind for a number of years and who are not nearly as responsive in this respect as sighted people (Jordan, 1962).

A rehabilitation counselor providing professional services to blind persons must avoid fostering unnecessary dependence. Often counselors, unknowingly as well as knowingly, build their own self-esteem by continually allowing clients to rely on them for personal advice and other services. On the other hand, many rehabilitation counselors are afraid to show sufficient interest in the problems of the client because they are concerned about being forced to give a great deal of time and attention to the client. Neither of these extremes will allow the counselor to be effective.

SUMMARY

It has been said that the most important variable for helping people which the counselor brings to the counseling relationship is "himself." The rehabilitation counselor, whether he is working with blind or sighted clients, must make a substantial effort to maintain genuineness, openness, sincerity, honesty, and respect for the client. While techniques and procedures are important in accomplishing goals in counseling sessions, the real key to successful counseling is whether the counselor genuinely cares for the individual. A rehabilitation counselor provides substantial professional and coordinated services from which the client benefits enormously. Most rehabilitation counselors will have certain quotas to meet and the effective counselor, through proper caseload management, will be able to provide quality and quantity services. He will also realize that his coordinative and facilitative function is as important as his counseling function. He must serve clients according to *their needs* and not his own; when this is done, counselees will not claim that his work lacks quality because he will have been much more concerned with them as individuals than with whether or not his services were "professional" in nature.

REFERENCES

Bauman, Mary K. and Yoder, Norman M.: *Adjustment to Blindness—Re-Viewed.* Springfield, Thomas, 1966.

Carroll, Thomas J.: *Blindness: What It Is, What It Does, and How to Live with It.* Boston, Little, 1961.

Gustad, J.W.: The definition of counseling. In Berdie, R.F.: *Roles and Relationship in Counseling.* Minneapolis, U. of Minn., 1953.

Hardy, Richard E.: Vocational placement. In Cull, John G. and Hardy, Richard E.: *Vocational Rehabilitation: Profession and Process.* Springfield, Thomas, 1972.

Jordan, John E.: Counseling the blind. *Personnel and Guidance Journal,* 39:3:10–214, 1962.

Morgan, Clayton A.: Personality of counseling. *Blindness,* AAWB Annual, American Association of Workers for the Blind, Inc., Washington, D.C., 1969.

Truax, Charles B. and Cartkuff, Robert R.: *Toward Effective Counseling and Psychotherapy: Training and Practice.* Chicago, Aldine, 1967.

INDEX